THE THEORY OF
THE RELATIVITY OF
MOTION

RICHARD C. TOLMAN

Published by

Hawk Press
4836/24, Ansari Road, Daryaganj
New Delhi – 110 002
Phones: +91-11-23278618, +91-11-43667199
E-mail: thehawkpress@gmail.com
www.thehawkpress.com

TO
H. E.

THE THEORY OF THE RELATIVITY OF MOTION.

BY
RICHARD C. TOLMAN, PH.D.
TABLE OF CONTENTS.

PREFACE.

Thirty or forty years ago, in the field of physical science, there was a widespread feeling that the days of adventurous discovery had passed forever, and the conservative physicist was only too happy to devote his life to the measurement to the sixth decimal place of quantities whose significance for physical theory was already an old story. The passage of time, however, has completely upset such bourgeois ideas as to the state of physical science, through the discovery of some most extraordinary experimental facts and the development of very fundamental theories for their explanation.

On the experimental side, the intervening years have seen the discovery of radioactivity, the exhaustive study of the conduction of electricity through gases, the accompanying discoveries of cathode, canal and X-rays, the isolation of the electron, the study of the distribution of energy in the hohlraum, and the final failure of all attempts to detect the earth's motion through the supposititious ether. During this same time, the theoretical physicist has been working hand in hand with the experimenter endeavoring to correlate the facts already discovered and to point the way to further research. The theoretical achievements, which have been found particularly helpful in performing these functions of explanation and prediction, have been the development of the modern theory of electrons, the application of thermodynamic and statistical reasoning to the phenomena of radiation, and the development of Einstein's brilliant theory of the relativity of motion.

It has been the endeavor of the following book to present an introduction to this theory of relativity, which in the decade since the publication of Einstein's first paper in 1905 (*Annalen der Physik*) has become a necessary part of the theoretical equipment of every physicist. Even if we regard the Einstein theory of relativity merely as a convenient tool for the prediction of electromagnetic and optical phenomena, its importance to the physicist is very great, not only because its introduction greatly simplifies the deduction of many theorems which were already familiar in the older theories based on a stationary ether, but also because it leads simply and directly to correct conclusions in the case of such experiments as those of Michelson and Morley, Trouton and Noble, and Kaufman and Bucherer, which can be made to agree with the idea of a stationary ether only by the introduction of complicated and *ad hoc* assumptions. Regarded from a more philosophical point of view, an acceptance of the Einstein theory of relativity shows us the advisability of completely remodelling some of our most fundamental ideas. In particular we shall now do well to change our concepts of space and time in such a way as to give up the old idea of their complete independence, a notion which we have received as the inheritance of a long ancestral experience with bodies moving with slow velocities, but which no longer proves pragmatic when we deal with velocities approaching that of light.

The method of treatment adopted in the following chapters is to a considerable extent original, partly appearing here for the first time and partly already published elsewhere.* Chapter III follows a method which was first developed by Lewis and Tolman,[†] and the last chapter a method developed by Wilson and Lewis.[‡] The writer must also express his special obligations to the works of Einstein, Planck, Poincaré, Laue, Ishiwara and Laub.

It is hoped that the mode of presentation is one that will be found well adapted not only to introduce the study of relativity theory to those previously unfamiliar with the subject but also to provide the necessary methodological equipment for those who wish to pursue the theory into its more complicated applications.

** Philosophical Magazine*, vol. 18, p. 510 (1909); *Physical Review*, vol. 31, p. 26 (1910); *Phil. Mag.*, vol. 21, p. 296 (1911); *ibid.*, vol. 22, p. 458 (1911); *ibid.*, vol. 23, p. 375 (1912); *Phys. Rev.*, vol. 35, p. 136 (1912); *Phil. Mag.*, vol. 25, p. 150 (1913); *ibid.*, vol. 28, p. 572 (1914); *ibid.*, vol. 28, p. 583 (1914).

[†] *Phil. Mag.*, vol. 18, p. 510 (1909).

[‡] *Proceedings of the American Academy of Arts and Sciences*, vol. 48, p. 389 (1912).

After presenting, in the first chapter, a brief outline of the historical development of ideas as to the nature of the space and time of science, we consider, in Chapter II, the two main postulates upon which the theory of relativity rests and discuss the direct experimental evidence for their truth. The third chapter then presents an elementary and non-mathematical deduction of a number of the most important consequences of the postulates of relativity, and it is hoped that this chapter will prove especially valuable to readers without unusual mathematical equipment, since they will there be able to obtain a real grasp of such important new ideas as the change of mass with velocity, the non-additivity of velocities, and the relation of mass and energy, without encountering any mathematics beyond the elements of analysis and geometry.

In Chapter IV we commence the more analytical treatment of the theory of relativity by obtaining from the two postulates of relativity Einstein's transformation equations for space and time as well as transformation equations for velocities, accelerations, and for an important function of the velocity. Chapter V presents various kinematical applications of the theory of relativity following quite closely Einstein's original method of development. In particular we may call attention to the ease with which we may handle the optics of moving media by the methods of the theory of relativity as compared with the difficulty of treatment on the basis of the ether theory.

In Chapters VI, VII and VIII we develop and apply a theory of the dynamics of a particle which is based on the Einstein transformation equations for space and time, Newton's three laws of motion, and the principle of the conservation of mass.

We then examine, in Chapter IX, the relation between the theory of relativity and the principle of least action, and find it possible to introduce the requirements of relativity theory at the very start into this basic principle for physical science. We point out that we might indeed have used this adapted form of the principle of least action, for developing the dynamics of a particle, and then proceed in Chapters

X, XI and XII to develop the dynamics of an elastic body, the dynamics of a thermodynamic system, and the dynamics of an electromagnetic system, all on the basis of our adapted form of the principle of least action.

Finally, in Chapter XIII, we consider a four-dimensional method of expressing and treating the results of relativity theory. This chapter contains, in Part I, an epitome of some of the more important methods in four-dimensional vector analysis and it is hoped that it can also be used in connection with the earlier parts of the book as a convenient reference for those who are not familiar with ordinary three-dimensional vector analysis.

In the present book, the writer has confined his considerations to cases in which there is a *uniform* relative velocity between systems of coördinates. In the future it may be possible greatly to extend the applications of the theory of relativity by considering accelerated systems of coördinates, and in this connection Einstein's latest work on the relation between gravity and acceleration is of great interest. It does not seem wise, however, at the present time to include such considerations in a book which intends to present a survey of accepted theory.

The author will feel amply repaid for the work involved in the preparation of the book if, through his efforts, some of the younger American physicists can be helped to obtain a real knowledge of the important work of Einstein. He is also glad to have this opportunity to add his testimony to the growing conviction that the conceptual space and time of science are not God-given and unalterable, but are rather in the nature of human constructs devised for use in the description and correlation of scientific phenomena, and that these spatial and temporal concepts should be altered whenever the discovery of new facts makes such a change pragmatic.

The writer wishes to express his indebtedness to Mr. William H. Williams for assisting in the preparation of Chapter I.

CHAPTER I.

HISTORICAL DEVELOPMENT OF IDEAS AS TO THE NATURE OF SPACE AND TIME.

1. Since the year 1905, which marked the publication of Einstein's momentous article on the theory of relativity, the development of scientific thought has led to a complete revolution in accepted ideas as to the nature of space and time, and this revolution has in turn profoundly modified those dependent sciences, in particular mechanics and electromagnetics, which make use of these two fundamental concepts in their considerations.

In the following pages it will be our endeavor to present a description of these new notions as to the nature of space and time,* and to give a partial account of the consequent modifications which have been introduced into various fields of science. Before proceeding to this task, however, we may well review those older ideas as to space and time which until now appeared quite sufficient for the correlation of scientific phenomena. We shall first consider the space and time of Galileo and Newton which were employed in the development of the classical mechanics, and then the space and time of the ether theory of light.

PART I. THE SPACE AND TIME OF GALILEO AND NEWTON.

2. The publication in 1687 of Newton's *Principia* laid down so satisfactory a foundation for further dynamical considerations, that it seemed as though the ideas of Galileo and Newton as to the nature of space and time, which were there employed, would certainly remain forever suitable for the interpretation of natural phenomena. And indeed upon this basis has been built the whole structure of classical mechanics which, until our recent familiarity with very high velocities,

---

*Throughout this work by "space" and "time" we shall mean the *conceptual* space and time of science.

has been found completely satisfactory for an extremely large number of very diverse dynamical considerations.

An examination of the fundamental laws of mechanics will show how the concepts of space and time entered into the Newtonian system of mechanics. Newton's laws of motion, from which the whole of the classical mechanics could be derived, can best be stated with the help of the equation

$$\mathbf{F} = \frac{d}{dt}(m\mathbf{u}). \tag{1}$$

This equation defines the force $\mathbf{F}$ acting on a particle as equal to the rate of change in its momentum (*i.e.*, the product of its mass m and its velocity $\mathbf{u}$), and the whole of Newton's laws of motion may be summed up in the statement that in the case of two interacting particles the forces which they mutually exert on each other are equal in magnitude and opposite in direction.

Since in Newtonian mechanics the mass of a particle is assumed constant, equation (1) may be more conveniently written

$$\mathbf{F} = m\frac{d\mathbf{u}}{dt} = m\frac{d}{dt}\left(\frac{d\mathbf{r}}{dt}\right),$$

or

$$F_x = m\frac{d}{dt}\left(\frac{dx}{dt}\right),$$

$$F_y = m\frac{d}{dt}\left(\frac{dy}{dt}\right), \tag{2}$$

$$F_z = m\frac{d}{dt}\left(\frac{dz}{dt}\right),$$

and this definition of force, together with the above-stated principle of the equality of action and reaction, forms the starting-point for the whole of classical mechanics.

The necessary dependence of this mechanics upon the concepts of space and time becomes quite evident on an examination of this fundamental equation (2), in which the expression for the force acting on a particle is seen to contain both the variables x, y, and z, which specify the position of the particle in *space*, and the variable t, which specifies the *time*.

3. Newtonian Time. To attempt a definite statement as to the meaning of so fundamental and underlying a notion as that of time is a task from which even philosophy may shrink. In a general way, conceptual time may be thought of as a *one-dimensional, unidirectional, one-valued* continuum. This continuum is a sort of framework in which the instants at which actual occurrences take place find an ordered position. Distances from point to point in the continuum, that is intervals of time, are measured by the periods of certain continually recurring cyclic processes such as the daily rotation of the earth. A unidirectional nature is imposed upon the time continuum among other things by an acceptance of the second law of thermodynamics, which requires that actual progression in time shall be accompanied by an increase in the entropy of the material world, and this same law requires that the continuum shall be one-valued since it excludes the possibility that time ever returns upon itself, either to commence a new cycle or to intersect its former path even at a single point.

In addition to these characteristics of the time continuum, which have been in no way modified by the theory of relativity, the *Newtonian mechanics always assumed a complete independence of time and the three-dimensional space continuum* which exists along with it. In dynamical equations time entered as an *entirely independent* variable in no way connected with the variables whose specification determines position in space. In the following pages, however, we shall find that the theory of relativity requires a very definite interrelation between time and space, and in the Einstein transformation equations we shall see the exact way in which measurements of time depend upon the choice of a set of variables for measuring position in space.

4. Newtonian Space. An exact description of the concept of space is perhaps just as difficult as a description of the concept of time. In a general way we think of space as a *three-dimensional, homogeneous,* *isotropic* continuum, and these ideas are common to the conceptual spaces of Newton, Einstein, and the ether theory of light. The space of Newton, however, differs on the one hand from that of Einstein because of a tacit assumption of the complete independence of space and time measurements; and differs on the other hand from that of the ether theory of light by the fact that "free" space was assumed completely empty instead of filled with an all-pervading quasi-material medium— the ether. A more definite idea of the particularly important characteristics of the Newtonian concept of space may be obtained by considering somewhat in detail the actual methods of space measurement.

Positions in space are in general measured with respect to some arbitrarily fixed system of reference which must be threefold in character corresponding to the three dimensions of space. In particular we may make use of a set of Cartesian axes and determine, for example, the position of a particle by specifying its three Cartesian coördinates x, y and z.

In Newtonian mechanics the particular set of axes chosen for specifying position in space has in general been determined in the first instance by considerations of convenience. For example, it is found by experience that, if we take as a reference system lines drawn upon the surface of the earth, the equations of motion based on Newton's laws give us a simple description of nearly all dynamical phenomena which are merely terrestrial. When, however, we try to interpret with these same axes the motion of the heavenly bodies, we meet difficulties, and the problem is simplified, so far as planetary motions are concerned, by taking a new reference system determined by the sun and the fixed stars. But this system, in its turn, becomes somewhat unsatisfactory when we take account of the observed motions of the stars themselves, and it is finally convenient to take a reference system relative to which the sun is moving with a velocity of twelve miles per second in the direction of the constellation Hercules. This system of axes is so chosen that the great majority of stars have on the average no motion with respect to it, and the actual motion of any particular star with respect to these coördinates is called the peculiar motion of the star.

Suppose, now, we have a number of such systems of axes in uniform relative motion; we are confronted by the problem of finding some method of transposing the description of a given kinematical occurrence from the variables of one of these sets of axes to those of another. For example, if we have chosen a system of axes S and have found an equation in x, y, z, and t which accurately describes the motion of a given point, what substitutions for the quantities involved can be made so that the new equation thereby obtained will again correctly describe the same phenomena when we measure the displacements of the point relative to a new system of reference S' which is in uniform motion with respect to S? The assumption of Galileo and Newton that "free" space is entirely empty, and the further tacit assumption of the complete independence of space and time, led them to propose a very simple solution of the problem, and the transformation equations which they used are generally called the Galileo Transformation Equations to distinguish them from the Einstein Transformation Equations which we shall later consider.

5. The Galileo Transformation Equations. Consider two systems of right-angled coördinates, S and S', which are in relative motion in the X direction with the velocity V; for convenience let the X axes, OX and $O'X'$, of the two systems coincide in direction, and for further simplification let us take as our zero point for time measurements the instant when the two origins O and O' coincide. Consider now a point which at the time t has the coördinates x, y and z measured in system S. Then, according to the space and time considerations of Galileo and Newton, the coördinates of the point with reference to system S' are given by the following transformation equations:

$$x' = x - Vt, \tag{3}$$

$$y' = y, \tag{4}$$

$$z' = z, \tag{5}$$

$$t' = t. \tag{6}$$

These equations are fundamental for Newtonian mechanics, and may appear to the casual observer to be self-evident and bound up with necessary ideas as to the nature of space and time. Nevertheless, the truth of the first and the last of these equations is absolutely dependent on the unsupported assumption of the complete independence of space and time measurements, and since in the Einstein theory we shall find a very definite relation between space and time measurements we shall be led to quite a different set of transformation equations. Relations (3), (4), (5) and (6) will be found, however, to be the limiting form which the correct transformation equations assume when the velocity between the systems V becomes small compared with that of light. Since until very recent times the human race in its entire past history has been familiar only with velocities that are small compared with that of light, it need not cause surprise that the above equations, which are true merely at the limit, should appear so self-evident.

6. Before leaving the discussion of the space and time system of Newton and Galileo we must call attention to an important characteristic which it has in common with the system of Einstein but which is not a feature of that assumed by the ether theory. If we have two systems of axes such as those we have just been considering, we may with equal right consider either one of them at rest and the other moving past it. All we can say is that the two systems are in relative motion; it is meaningless to speak of either one as in any sense "*absolutely*" at rest. The equation $x' = x - Vt$ which we use in transforming the description of a kinematical event from the variables of system S to those of system S' is perfectly symmetrical with the equation $x = x' + Vt'$ which we should use for a transformation in the reverse direction. Of all possible systems no particular set of axes holds a unique position among the others. We shall later find that this important principle of the relativity of motion is permanently incorporated into our system of physical science as the *first postulate of relativity*. This principle, common both to the space of Newton and to that of Einstein, is not characteristic of the space assumed by the classical theory of light. The space of this theory was supposed to be filled with a stationary medium, the luminiferous ether, and a system of axes stationary with respect to this ether would hold a unique position among the other systems and be the one peculiarly adapted for use as the ultimate system of reference for the measurement of motions.

We may now briefly sketch the rise of the ether theory of light and point out the permanent contribution which it has made to physical science, a contribution which is now codified as the second postulate of relativity.

PART II. THE SPACE AND TIME OF THE ETHER THEORY.

7. Rise of the Ether Theory. Twelve years before the appearance of the *Principia*, Römer, a Danish astronomer, observed that an eclipse of one of the satellites of Jupiter occurred some ten minutes later than the time predicted for the event from the known period of the satellite and the time of the preceding eclipse. He explained this delay by the hypothesis that it took light twenty-two minutes to travel across the earth's orbit. Previous to Römer's discovery, light was generally supposed to travel with infinite velocity. Indeed Galileo had endeavored to find the speed of light by direct experiments over distances of a few miles and had failed to detect any lapse of time between the emission of a light flash from a source and its observation by a distant observer. Römer's hypothesis has been repeatedly verified and the speed of light measured by different methods with considerable exactness. The mean of the later determinations is 2.9986×10^{10} cm. per second.

8. At the time of Römer's discovery there was much discussion as to the nature of light. Newton's theory that it consisted of particles or corpuscles thrown out by a luminous body was attacked by Hooke and later by Huygens, who advanced the view that it was something in the nature of wave motions in a supposed space-filling medium or ether. By this theory Huygens was able to explain reflection and refraction and the phenomena of color, but assuming *longitudinal* vibrations he was unable to account for polarization. Diffraction had not yet been observed and Newton contested the Hooke-Huygens theory chiefly on the grounds that it was contradicted by the fact of rectilinear propagation and the formation of shadows. The scientific prestige of Newton was so great that the emission or corpuscular theory continued to hold its ground for a hundred and fifty years. Even the masterly researches of Thomas Young at the beginning of the nineteenth century were unable to dislodge the old theory, and it was not until the French physicist, Fresnel, about 1815, was independently led to an undulatory theory and added to Young's arguments the weight of his more searching mathematical analysis, that the balance began to turn. From this time on the wave theory grew in power and for a period of eighty years was not seriously questioned. This theory has for its essential postulate the existence of an all-pervading medium, the ether, in which wave disturbances can be set up and propagated. And the physical properties of this medium became an enticing field of inquiry and speculation.

9. Idea of a Stationary Ether. Of all the various properties with which the physicist found it necessary to endow the ether, for us the most important is the fact that it must apparently remain stationary, unaffected by the motion of matter through it. This conclusion was finally reached through several lines of investigation. We may first consider whether the ether would be dragged along by the motion of nearby masses of matter, and, second, whether the ether enclosed in a moving medium such as water or glass would partake in the latter's motion.

10. Ether in the Neighborhood of Moving Bodies. About the year 1725 the astronomer Bradley, in his efforts to measure the parallax of certain fixed stars, discovered that the apparent position of a star continually changes in such a way as to trace annually a small ellipse in the sky, the apparent position always lying in the plane determined by the line from the earth to the center of the ellipse and by the direction of the earth's motion. On the corpuscular theory of light this admits of ready explanation as Bradley himself discovered, since we should expect the earth's motion to produce an apparent change in the direction of the oncoming light, in just the same way that the motion of a railway train makes the falling drops of rain take a slanting path across the window pane. If c be the velocity of a light particle and v the earth's velocity, the apparent or relative velocity would be $c-v$ and the tangent of the angle of aberration would be $\frac{v}{c}$.

Upon the wave theory, it is obvious that we should *also* expect a similar aberration of light, provided only that the ether shall be quite stationary and unaffected by the motion of the earth through it, and this is one of the important reasons that most ether theories have assumed a *stationary ether unaffected by the motion of neighboring matter.**

In more recent years further experimental evidence for assuming that the ether is not dragged along by the neighboring motion of large masses of matter was found by Sir Oliver Lodge. His final experiments were performed with a large rotating spheroid of iron with a narrow groove around its equator, which was made the path for two rays of light, one travelling in the direction of rotation and the other in the opposite direction. Since by interference methods no difference could be detected in the velocities of the two rays, here also the conclusion was reached that *the ether was not appreciably dragged along by the rotating metal.*

11. Ether Entrained in Dielectrics. With regard to the action of a moving medium on the ether which might be entrained within it, experimental evidence and theoretical consideration here too finally led to the supposition that the ether itself must remain perfectly stationary. The earlier view first expressed by Fresnel, in a letter written to Arago in 1818, was that the entrained ether did receive a fraction of the total velocity of the moving medium. Fresnel gave to this fraction

---

*The most notable exception is the theory of Stokes, which did assume that the ether moved along with the earth and then tried to account for aberration with the help of a velocity potential, but this led to difficulties, as was shown by Lorentz.

the value $\dfrac{\mu^2 - 1}{\mu^2}$, where μ is the index of refraction of the substance forming the medium. On this supposition, Fresnel was able to account for the fact that Arago's experiments upon the reflection and refraction of stellar rays show no influence whatever of the earth's motion, and for the fact that Airy found the same angle of aberration with a telescope filled with water as with air. Moreover, the later work of Fizeau and the accurate determinations of Michelson and Morley on the velocity of light in a moving stream of water did show that the speed was changed by an amount corresponding to Fresnel's fraction. The fuller theoretical investigations of Lorentz, however, did not lead scientists to look upon this increased velocity of light in a moving medium as an evidence that the ether is pulled along by the stream of water, and we may now briefly sketch the developments which culminated in the Lorentz theory of a completely stationary ether.

12. The Lorentz Theory of a Stationary Ether. The considerations of Lorentz as to the velocity of light in moving media became possible only after it was evident that optics itself is a branch of the wider science of electromagnetics, and it became possible to treat transparent media as a special case of dielectrics in general. In 1873, in his *Treatise on Electricity and Magnetism*, Maxwell first advanced the theory that electromagnetic phenomena also have their seat in the luminiferous ether and further that light itself is merely an electromagnetic disturbance in that medium, and Maxwell's theory was confirmed by the actual discovery of electromagnetic waves in 1888 by Hertz.

The attack upon the problem of the relative motion of matter and ether was now renewed with great vigor both theoretically and experimentally from the electromagnetic side. Maxwell in his treatise had confined himself to phenomena in stationary media. Hertz, however, extended Maxwell's considerations to moving matter on the assumption that the entrained ether is carried bodily along by it. It is evident, however, that in the field of optical theory such an assumption could not be expected to account for the Fizeau experiment, which had already been explained on the assumption that the ether receives only a fraction of the velocity of the moving medium; while in the field of electromagnetic theory it was found that Hertz's assumptions would lead us to expect *no* production of a magnetic field in the neighborhood of a rotating electric condenser providing the plates of the condenser and the dielectric move together with the same speed and this was decisively disproved by the experiment of Eichenwald. The conclusions of the Hertz theory were also out of agreement with the important experiments of H. A. Wilson on moving dielectrics. It remained for Lorentz to develop a general theory for moving dielectrics which was consistent with the facts.

The theory of Lorentz developed from that of Maxwell by the addition of the idea of the *electron*, as the atom of electricity, and his treatment is often called the "electron theory." This atomistic conception of electricity was foreshadowed by Faraday's discovery of the quantitative relations between the amount of electricity associated with chemical reactions in electrolytes and the weight of substance involved, a relation which indicates that the atoms act as carriers of electricity and that the quantity of electricity carried by a single particle, whatever its nature, is always some small multiple of a definite quantum of electricity, the electron. Since Faraday's time, the study of the phenomena accompanying the conduction of electricity through gases, the study of radioactivity, and finally indeed the isolation and exact measurement of these atoms of electrical charge, have led us to a very definite knowledge of many of the properties of the electron.

While the experimental physicists were at work obtaining this more or less first-hand acquaintance with the electron, the theoretical physicists and in particular Lorentz were increasingly successful in explaining the electrical and optical properties of matter in general on the basis of the behavior of the electrons which it contains, the properties of conductors being accounted for by the presence of movable electrons, either free as in the case of metals or combined with atoms to form ions as in electrolytes, while the electrical and optical properties of dielectrics were ascribed to the presence of electrons more or less bound by quasi-elastic forces to positions of equilibrium. This Lorentz electron theory of matter has been developed in great mathematical detail by Lorentz and has been substantiated by numerous quantitative experiments. Perhaps the greatest significance of the Lorentz theory is that such properties of matter as electrical conductivity, magnetic permeability and dielectric inductivity, which occupied the position of rather accidental experimental constants in Maxwell's original theory, are now explainable as the statistical result of the behavior of the individual electrons.

With regard now to our original question as to the behavior of *moving* optical and dielectric media, the Lorentz theory was found capable of accounting quantitatively for all known phenomena, including Airy's experiment on aberration, Arago's experiments on the reflection and refraction of stellar rays, Fresnel's coefficient for the velocity of light in moving media, and the electromagnetic experiments upon moving dielectrics made by Röntgen, Eichenwald, H. A. Wilson, and others. For us the particular significance of the Lorentz method of explaining these phenomena is that he does *not* assume, as did Fresnel, that the ether is partially dragged along by moving matter. His investigations show rather that the ether must remain perfectly stationary, and that such phenomena as the changed velocity of light in moving media are to be accounted for by the modifying influence which the electrons in the moving matter have upon the propagation of electromagnetic disturbances, rather than by a dragging along of the ether itself.

Although it would not be proper in this place to present the mathematical details of Lorentz's treatment of moving media, we may obtain a clearer idea of what is meant in the Lorentz theory by a stationary ether if we look for a moment at the five fundamental equations upon which the theory rests. These familiar equations, of which the first four are merely Maxwell's four field equations, modified by the introduction of the idea of the electron, may be written

$$\operatorname{curl} \mathbf{h} = \frac{1}{c}\frac{\partial \mathbf{e}}{\partial t} + \rho \frac{\mathbf{u}}{c},$$

$$\operatorname{curl} \mathbf{e} = -\frac{1}{c}\frac{\partial \mathbf{h}}{\partial t},$$

$$\operatorname{div} \mathbf{e} = \rho,$$

$$\operatorname{div} \mathbf{h} = 0,$$

$$\mathbf{f} = \rho\left\{\mathbf{e} + \left[\frac{\mathbf{u}}{c} \times \mathbf{h}\right]^{*}\right\}$$

in which the letters have their usual significance. (See Chapter XII.) Now the whole of the Lorentz theory, including of course his treatment of moving media, is derivable from these five equations, and the fact that the idea of a stationary ether does lie at the basis of his theory is most clearly shown by the first and last of these equations, which contain the velocity $\mathbf{u}$ with which the charge in question is moving, and *for Lorentz this velocity is to be measured with respect to the assumed stationary ether.*

We have devoted this space to the Lorentz theory, since his work marks the culmination of the ether theory of light and electromagnetism, and for us the particularly significant fact is that by this line of attack science was *inevitably led to the idea of an absolutely immovable and stationary ether.*

13. We have thus briefly traced the development of the ether theory of light and electromagnetism. We have seen that the space continuum assumed by this theory is not empty as was the space of Newton and Galileo but is assumed filled with a stationary medium, the ether, and in conclusion should further point out that the *time continuum* assumed by the ether theory was apparently the same as that of Newton and Galileo, and in particular that the *old ideas as to the absolute independence of space and time were all retained.*

PART III. RISE OF THE EINSTEIN THEORY OF RELATIVITY.

14. The Michelson-Morley Experiment. In spite of all the brilliant achievements of the theory of a stationary ether, we must now call attention to an experiment, performed at the very time when the success of the ether theory seemed most complete, whose result was in direct contradiction to its predictions. This is the celebrated Michelson-Morley experiment, and to the masterful interpretation of its consequences at the hands of Einstein we owe the whole theory of relativity, a theory which will nevermore permit us to assume that space and time are independent.

If the theory of a stationary ether were true we should find, contrary to the expectations of Newton, that systems of coördinates in relative motion are not symmetrical, a system of axes fixed relatively to the ether would hold a unique position among all other systems moving relative to it and would be peculiarly adapted for the measurement of displacements and velocities. Bodies at rest with respect to this system of axes fixed in the ether would be spoken of as "absolutely" at rest and bodies in motion through the ether would be said to have "absolute" motion. From the point of view of the ether theory one of the most important physical problems would be to determine the velocity of various bodies, for example that of the earth, through the ether.

Now the Michelson-Morley experiment was devised for the very purpose of determining the relative motion of the earth and the ether. The experiment consists essentially in a comparison of the velocities of light parallel and perpendicular to the earth's motion in its orbit. A ray of light from the source S falls on the half silvered mirror A, where it is divided into two rays, one of which travels to the mirror B and the other to the mirror C, where they are totally reflected. The rays are recombined and produce a set of interference fringes at O. (See Fig. 1.)

We may now think of the apparatus as set so that one of the divided paths is parallel to the earth's motion and the other perpendicular to it. On the basis of the stationary ether theory, the velocity of the light with reference to the apparatus would evidently be different over the two paths, and hence on rotating the apparatus through an angle of ninety degrees we should expect a shift in the position of the fringes. Knowing the magnitude of the earth's velocity in its orbit and the dimensions of the apparatus, it is quite possible to calculate the magnitude of the expected shift, a quantity entirely susceptible of experimental determi-

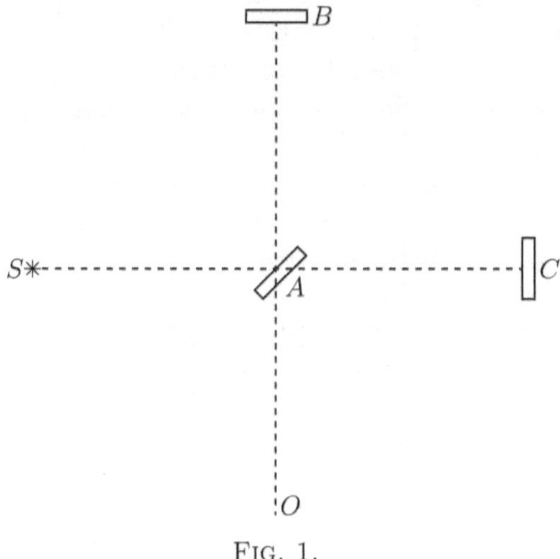

Fig. 1.

nation. Nevertheless the most careful experiments made at different times of day and at different seasons of the year entirely failed to show any such shift at all.

This result is in direct contradiction to the theory of a stationary ether and could be reconciled with that theory only by very arbitrary assumptions. Instead of making such assumptions, the Einstein theory of relativity finds it preferable to return in part to the older ideas of Newton and Galileo.

15. The Postulates of Einstein. In fact, in accordance with the results of this work of Michelson-Morley and other confirmatory experiments, the Einstein theory takes as its *first postulate* the idea familiar to Newton of the relativity of all motion. It states that there is nothing out in space in the nature of an ether or of a fixed set of coördinates with regard to which motion can be measured, that there is no such thing as absolute motion, and that all we can speak of is the relative motion of one body with respect to another.

Although we thus see that the Einstein theory of relativity has returned in part to the ideas of Newton and Galileo as to the nature of space, it is not to be supposed that the ether theory of light and electromagnetism has made no lasting contribution to physical science. Quite on the contrary, not only must the ideas as to the periodic and polarizable nature of the light disturbance, which were first appreciated and understood with the help of the ether theory, always remain incorporated in every optical theory, but in particular the Einstein theory of relativity takes as the basis for its *second postulate* a principle that has long been familiar to the ether theory, namely that the velocity of light is independent of the velocity of the source. We shall see in following chapters that it is the combination of this principle with the first postulate of relativity that leads to the whole theory of relativity and to our new ideas as to the nature and interrelation of space and time.

CHAPTER II.

THE TWO POSTULATES OF THE EINSTEIN THEORY OF RELATIVITY.

16. There are two general methods of evaluating the theoretical development of any branch of science. One of these methods is to test by direct experiment the fundamental postulates upon which the theory rests. If these postulates are found to agree with the facts, we may feel justified in assuming that the whole theoretical structure is a valid one, providing false logic or unsuspected and incorrect assumptions have not later crept in to vitiate the conclusions. The other method of testing a theory is to develop its interlacing chain of propositions and theorems and examine the results both for their internal coherence and for their objective validity. If we find that the conclusions drawn from the theory are neither self-contradictory nor contradictory of each other, and furthermore that they agree with the facts of the external world, we may again feel that our theory has achieved a measure of success. In the present chapter we shall present the two main postulates of the theory of relativity, and indicate the direct experimental evidence in favor of their truth. In following chapters we shall develop the consequences of these postulates, show that the system of consequences stands the test of internal coherence, and wherever possible compare the predictions of the theory with experimental facts.

The First Postulate of Relativity.

17. The first postulate of relativity as originally stated by Newton was that it is impossible to measure or detect absolute translatory motion through space. No objections have ever been made to this statement of the postulate in its original form. In the development of the theory of relativity, the postulate has been modified to include the impossibility of detecting translatory motion through any medium or ether which might be assumed to pervade space.

In support of the principle is the general fact that no effects due to the motion of the earth or other body through the supposed ether have ever been observed. Of the many unsuccessful attempts to detect the earth's motion through the ether we may call attention to the experiments on the refraction of light made by Arago, Respighi, Hoek, Ketteler and Mascart, the interference experiments of Ketteler and Mascart, the work of Klinkerfuess and Haga on the position of the absorption bands of sodium, the experiment of Nordmeyer on the intensity of radiation, the experiments of Fizeau, Brace and Strasser on the rotation of the plane of polarized light by transmission through glass plates, the experiments of Mascart and of Rayleigh on the rotation of the plane of polarized light in naturally active substances, the electromagnetic experiments of Röntgen, Des Coudres, J. Koenigsberger, Trouton, Trouton and Noble, and Trouton and Rankine, and finally the Michelson and Morley experiment, with the further work of Morley and Miller. For details as to the nature of these experiments the reader may refer to the original articles or to an excellent discussion by Laub of the experimental basis of the theory of relativity.*

In none of the above investigations was it possible to detect any effect attributable to the earth's motion through the ether. Nevertheless a number of these experiments *are* in accord with the final form given to the ether theory by Lorentz, especially since his work satisfactorily accounts for the Fresnel coefficient for the changed velocity of light in moving media. Others of the experiments mentioned, however, could be made to accord with the Lorentz theory only by very arbitrary assumptions, in particular those of Michelson and Morley, Mascart and Rayleigh, and Trouton and Noble. For the purposes of our discussion we shall accept the principle of the relativity of motion as an experimental fact.

---

* *Jahrbuch der Radioaktivität*, vol. 7, p. 405 (1910).

The Second Postulate of the Einstein Theory of Relativity.

18. The second postulate of relativity states that *the velocity of light in free space appears the same to all observers regardless of the relative motion of the source of light and the observer.* This postulate may be obtained by combining the first postulate of relativity with a principle which has long been familiar to the ether theory of light. This principle states that the velocity of light is unaffected by a motion of the emitting source, in other words, that the velocity with which light travels past any observer is not increased by a motion of the source of light towards the observer. The first postulate of relativity adds the idea that a motion of the source of light towards the observer is identical with a motion of the observer towards the source. The second postulate of relativity is seen to be merely a combination of these two principles, since it states that the velocity of light in free space appears the same to all observers regardless *both* of the motion of the source of light and of the observer.

19. It should be pointed out that the two principles whose combination thus leads to the second postulate of Einstein have come from very different sources. The first postulate of relativity practically denies the existence of any stationary ether through which the earth, for instance, might be moving. On the other hand, the principle that the velocity of light is unaffected by a motion of the source was originally derived from the idea that light is transmitted by a stationary medium which does not partake in the motion of the source. This combination of two principles, which from a historical point of view seem somewhat contradictory in nature, has given to the second postulate of relativity a very extraordinary content. Indeed it should be particularly emphasized that the remarkable conclusions as to the nature of space and time forced upon science by the theory of relativity are the special product of the second postulate of relativity.

A simple example of the conclusions which can be drawn from this postulate will make its extraordinary nature evident.

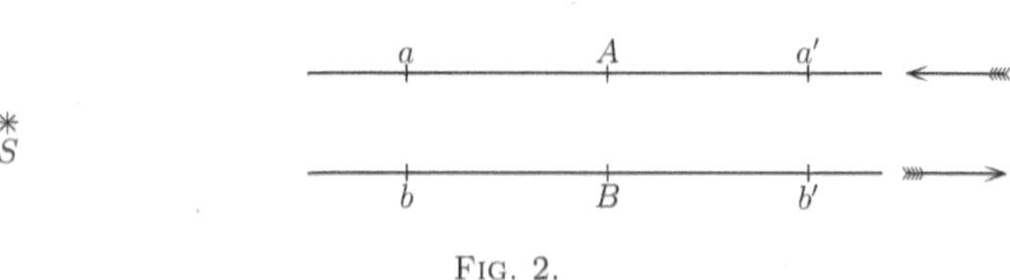

Fig. 2.

S is a source of light and A and B two moving systems. A is moving *towards* the source S, and B *away* from it. Observers on the systems mark off equal distances aa' and bb' along the path of the light and determine the time taken for light to pass from a to a' and b to b' respectively. Contrary to what seem the simple conclusions of common sense, the second postulate requires that the time taken for the light to pass from a to a' shall measure the same as the time for the light to go from b to b'. Hence if the second postulate of relativity is correct it is not surprising that science is forced in general to new ideas as to the nature of space and time, ideas which are in direct opposition to the requirements of so-called common sense.

Suggested Alternative to the Postulate of the Independence of the Velocity of Light and the Velocity of the Source.

20. Because of the extraordinary conclusions derived by combining the principle of the relativity of motion with the postulate that the velocity of light is independent of the velocity of its source, a number of attempts have been made to develop so-called *emission* theories of relativity based on the principle of the relativity of motion and the further postulate that the velocity of light and the velocity of its source are additive.

Before examining the available evidence for deciding between the rival principles as to the velocity of light, we may point out that this proposed postulate, of the additivity of the velocity of source and light, would as a matter of fact lead to a very simple kind of relativity theory without requiring any changes in our notions of space and time. For if light or other electromagnetic disturbance which is being emitted from a source did partake in the motion of that source in such a way that the velocity of the source is added to the velocity of emission, it is evident that a system consisting of the source and its surrounding disturbances would act as a whole and suffer no *permanent* change in configuration if the velocity of the source were changed. This result would of course be in direct agreement with the idea of the relativity of motion which merely requires that the physical properties of a system shall be independent of its velocity through space.

As a particular example of the simplicity of emission theories we may show, for instance, how easily they would account for the negative result of the Michelson-Morley experiment. If O, Fig. 3, is a source of light and A and B are mirrors placed a meter away from O, the Michelson-Morley experiment shows that the time taken for light to travel to A and back is the same as for the light to travel to B and back, in spite of the fact that the whole apparatus is moving through space in the direction $O - B$, due to the earth's motion around the sun. The basic assumption of emission theories, however, would require exactly this result, since it says that light travels out from O with a constant velocity in all directions with respect to O, and not with respect to some ether through which O is supposed to be moving.

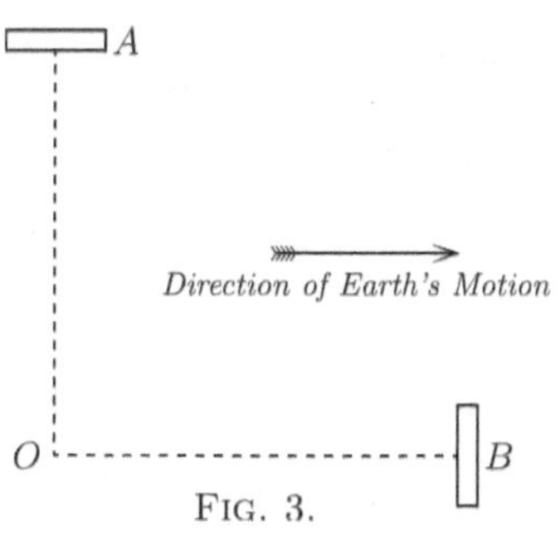

FIG. 3.

The problem now before us is to decide between the two rival principles as to the velocity of light, and we shall find that the bulk of the evidence is all in favor of the principle which has led to the Einstein theory of relativity with its complete revolution in our ideas as to space and time, and against the principle which has led to the superficially simple emission theories of relativity.

21. Evidence Against Emission Theories of Light. All emission theories agree in assuming that light from a moving source has a velocity equal to the vector sum of the velocity of light from a stationary source and the velocity of the source itself at the instant of emission. And without first considering the special assumptions which distinguish one emission theory from another we may first present certain astronomical evidence which apparently stands in contradiction to this basic assumption of all forms of emission theory. This evidence was pointed out by Comstock[*] and later by de Sitter.[†]

Consider the rotation of a binary star as it would appear to an observer situated at a considerable distance from the star and in its plane of rotation. (See Fig. 4.) If an emission theory of light be true, the velocity of light from the star in position A will be $c + u$, where u is the velocity of the star in its orbit, while in the position B the velocity will be $c - u$. Hence the star will be observed to arrive in position A, $\dfrac{l}{c + u}$ seconds after the event has actually occurred, and in position B, $\dfrac{l}{c - u}$ seconds after the event has occurred. This will make the period of half rotation from A to B appear to be

$$\Delta t - \frac{l}{c + u} + \frac{l}{c - u} = \Delta t + \frac{2ul}{c^2},$$

where Δt is the actual time of a half rotation in the orbit, which for simplicity may be taken as circular. On the other hand, the period of the next half rotation from B back to A would appear to be

$$\Delta t - \frac{2ul}{c^2}.$$

Now in the case of most spectroscopic binaries the quantity $\dfrac{2ul}{c^2}$ is not only of the same order of magnitude as Δt but oftentimes probably

---

[*] *Phys. Rev.*, vol. 30, p. 291 (1910).
[†] *Phys. Zeitschr.*, vol. 14, pp. 429, 1267 (1913).

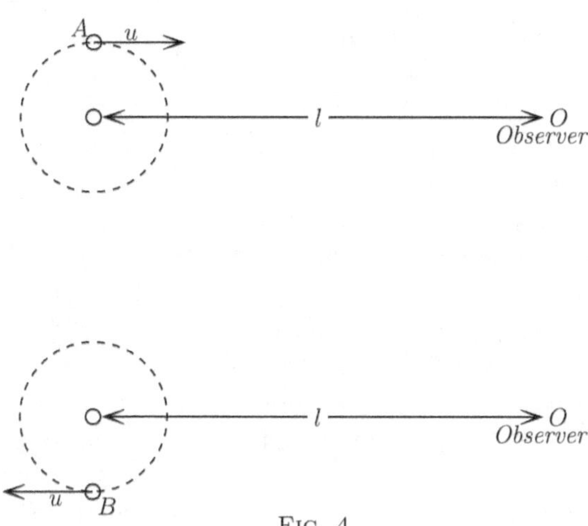

Fig. 4.

even larger. Hence, if an emission theory of light were true, we could hardly expect without correcting for the variable velocity of light to find that these orbits obey Kepler's laws, as is actually the case. This is certainly very strong evidence against any form of emission theory. It may not be out of place, however, to state briefly the different forms of emission theory which have been tried.

22. Different Forms of Emission Theory. As we have seen, emission theories all agree in assuming that light from a moving source has a velocity equal to the vector sum of the velocity of light from a stationary source and the velocity of the source itself at the instant of emission. Emission theories differ, however, in their assumptions as to the velocity of light after its reflection from a mirror. The three assumptions which up to this time have been particularly considered are (1) that the excited portion of the reflecting mirror acts as a new source of light and that the reflected light has the same velocity c with respect to the mirror as has original light with respect to its source;

(2) that light reflected from a mirror acquires a component of velocity equal to the velocity of the mirror image of the original source, and hence has the velocity c with respect to this mirror image; and (3) that light retains throughout its whole path the component of velocity which it obtained from its original moving source, and hence after reflection spreads out with velocity c in a spherical form around a center which moves with the same speed as the original source.

Of these possible assumptions as to the velocity of reflected light, the first seems to be the most natural and was early considered by the author but shown to be incompatible, not only with an experiment which he performed on the velocity of light from the two limbs of the sun,[*] but also with measurements of the Stark effect in canal rays.[†] The second assumption as to the velocity of light was made by Stewart,[‡] but has also been shown[†] to be incompatible with measurements of the Stark effect in canal rays. Making use of the third assumption as to the velocity of reflected light, a somewhat complete emission theory has been developed by Ritz,[§] and unfortunately optical experiments for deciding between the Einstein and Ritz relativity theories have never been performed, although such experiments are entirely possible of performance.[†] Against the Ritz theory, however, we have of course the general astronomical evidence of Comstock and de Sitter which we have already described above.

For the present, the observations described above, comprise the whole of the direct experimental evidence against emission theories of light and in favor of the principle which has led to the second postulate of the Einstein theory. One of the consequences of the Einstein theory, however, has been the deduction of an expression for the mass of a moving body which has been closely verified by the Kaufmann-

---

[*] *Phys. Rev.*, vol. 31, p. 26 (1910).

[†] *Phys. Rev.*, vol. 35, p. 136 (1912).

[‡] *Phys. Rev.*, vol. 32, p. 418 (1911).

[§] *Ann. de chim. et phys.*, vol. 13, p. 145 (1908); *Arch. de Génève* vol. 26, p. 232 (1908); *Scientia*, vol. 5 (1909).

Bucherer experiment. Now it is very interesting to note, that starting with what has thus become an *experimental* expression for the mass of a moving body, it is possible to work backwards to a derivation of the second postulate of relativity. For the details of the proof we must refer the reader to the original article.*

Further Postulates of the Theory of Relativity.

23. In the development of the theory of relativity to which we shall now proceed we shall of course make use of many postulates. The two which we have just considered, however, are the only ones, so far as we are aware, which are essentially different from those common to the usual theoretical developments of physical science. In particular in our further work we shall assume without examination all such general principles as the homogeneity and isotropism of the space continuum, and the unidirectional, one-valued, one-dimensional character of the time continuum. In our treatment of the dynamics of a particle we shall also assume Newton's laws of motion, and the principle of the conservation of mass, although we shall find, of course, that the Einstein ideas as to the connection between space and time will lead us to a non-Newtonian mechanics. We shall also make extensive use of the principle of least action, which we shall find a powerful principle in all the fields of dynamics.

** Phys. Rev.*, vol. 31, p. 26 (1910).

CHAPTER III.

SOME ELEMENTARY DEDUCTIONS.

24. In order gradually to familiarize the reader with the consequences of the theory of relativity we shall now develop by very elementary methods a few of the more important relations. In this preliminary consideration we shall lay no stress on mathematical elegance or logical exactness. It is believed, however, that the chapter will present a substantially correct account of some of the more important conclusions of the theory of relativity, in a form which can be understood even by readers without mathematical equipment.

Measurements of Time in a Moving System.

25. We may first derive from the postulates of relativity a relation connecting measurements of time intervals as made by observers in systems moving with different velocities. Consider a system S (Fig. 5) provided with a plane mirror $a\,a$, and an observer A, who has a clock

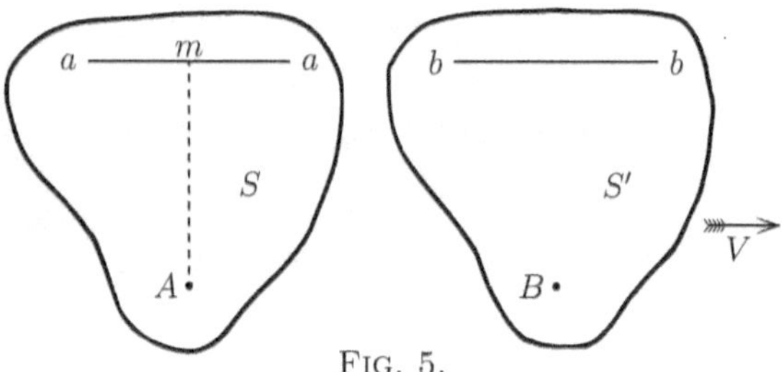

FIG. 5.

so that he can determine the time taken for a beam of light to travel up to the mirror and back along the path $A\,m\,A$. Consider also another similar system S', provided with a mirror $b\,b$, and an observer B, who also has a clock for measuring the time it takes for light to go up to his mirror and back. System S' is moving past S with the velocity V, the direction of motion being parallel to the mirrors $a\,a$ and $b\,b$, the two systems being arranged, moreover, so that when they pass one another the two mirrors $a\,a$ and $b\,b$ will coincide, and the two observers A and B will also come into coincidence.

A, considering his system at rest and the other in motion, measures the time taken for a beam of light to pass to his mirror and return, over the path $A\,m\,A$, and compares the time interval thus obtained with that necessary for the performance of a similar experiment by B, in which the light has to pass over a longer path such as $B\,n\,B'$, shown in Fig. 6, where $B\,B'$ is the distance through which the observer B has moved

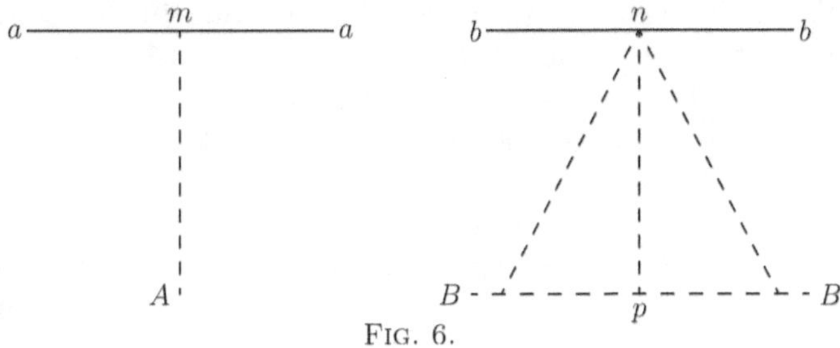

Fig. 6.

during the time taken for the passage of the light up to the mirror and back.

Since, in accordance with the second postulate of relativity, the velocity of light is independent of the velocity of its source, it is evident that the ratio of these two time intervals will be proportional to the ratio of the two paths $A\,m\,A$ and $B\,n\,B'$, and this can easily be calculated in terms of the velocity of light c and the velocity V of the system S'.

From Fig. 6 we have

$$(A\,m)^2 = (p\,n)^2 = (B\,n)^2 - (B\,p)^2.$$

Dividing by $(B\,n)^2$,

$$\frac{(A\,m)^2}{(B\,n)^2} = 1 - \frac{(B\,p)^2}{(B\,n)^2}.$$

But the distance $B\,p$ is to $B\,n$ as V is to c, giving us

$$\frac{A\,m}{B\,n} = \sqrt{1 - \frac{V^2}{c^2}}\,,$$

and hence A will find, either by calculation or by direct measurement if he has arranged clocks at B and B', that it takes a longer time for the performance of B's experiment than for the performance of his own in the ratio $1 : \sqrt{1 - \dfrac{V^2}{c^2}}$.

It is evident from the first postulate of relativity, however, that B himself must find exactly the same length of time for the light to pass up to his mirror and come back as did A in his experiment, because the two systems are, as a matter of fact, entirely symmetrical and we could with equal right consider B's system to be the one at rest and A's the one in motion.

We thus find that two observers, A and B, who are in relative motion will not in general agree in their measurements of the time interval necessary for a given event to take place, the event in this particular case, for example, having been the performance of B's experiment; indeed, making use of the ratio obtained in a preceding paragraph, we may go further and make the quantitative statement that measurements of *time intervals made with a moving clock must be multiplied by the quantity* $\dfrac{1}{\sqrt{1 - \dfrac{V^2}{c^2}}}$ *in order to agree with measurements made with a stationary system of clocks.*

It is sometimes more convenient to state this principle in the form: A stationary observer using a set of stationary clocks will obtain a greater measurement in the ratio $1 : \sqrt{1 - \dfrac{V^2}{c^2}}$ for a given time interval than an observer who uses a clock moving with the velocity V.

Measurements of Length in a Moving System.

26. We may now extend our considerations, to obtain a relation between measurements of *length* made in stationary and moving systems.

As to measurements of length *perpendicular* to the line of motion of the two systems S and S', a little consideration will make it at once evident that both A and B must obtain identical results. This is true because the possibility is always present of making a direct comparison of the meter sticks which A and B use for such measurements by holding them perpendicular to the line of motion. When the relative motion of the two systems brings such meter sticks into juxtaposition, it is evident from the first postulate of relativity that A's meter and B's meter must coincide in length. Any difference in length could be due only to the different velocity of the two systems through space, and such an occurrence is ruled out by our first postulate. *Hence measurements made with a moving meter stick held perpendicular to its line of motion will agree with those made with stationary meter sticks.*

27. With regard to measurements of length *parallel* to the line of motion of the systems, the affair is much more complicated. Any direct comparison of the lengths of meter sticks in the two systems would be very difficult to carry out; the consideration, however, of a simple experiment on the velocity of light parallel to the motion of the systems will lead to the desired relation.

Let us again consider two systems S and S' (Fig. 7), S' moving past S with the velocity V.

A and B are observers on these systems provided with clocks and meter sticks. The two observers lay off, each on his own system, paths for measuring the velocity of light. A lays off a distance of one meter, $A\,m$, so that he can measure the time for light to travel to the mirror m and return, and B, using a meter stick which has the same length as A's when they are both at rest, lays off the distance $B\,n$.

Each observer measures the length of time it takes for light to travel

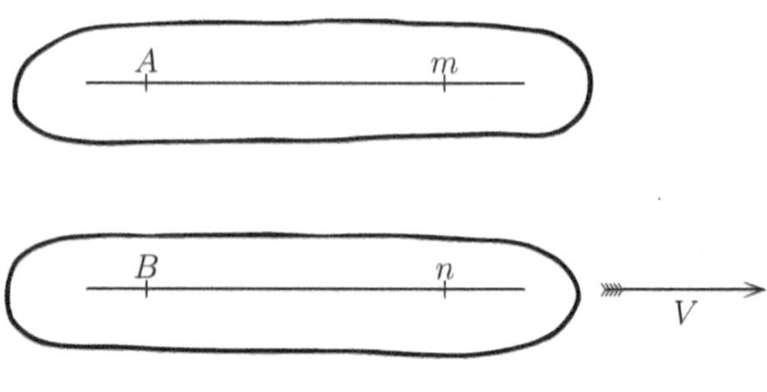

FIG. 7.

to his mirror and return, and will evidently have to find the same length of time, since the postulates of relativity require that the velocity of light shall be the same for all observers.

Now the observer A, taking himself as at rest, finds that B's light travels over a path $B\,n'\,B'$ (Fig. 8), where $n\,n'$ is the distance through

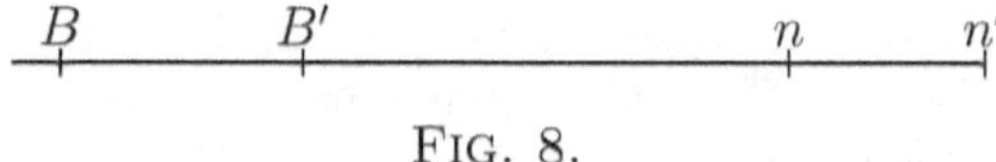

FIG. 8.

which the mirror n moves while the light is travelling up to it, and $B\,B'$ is the distance through which the source travels before the light gets back. It is easy to calculate the length of this path.

We have

$$\frac{n\,n'}{B\,n'} = \frac{V}{c}$$

and

$$\frac{B\,B'}{B\,n'\,B'} = \frac{V}{c}.$$

Also, from the figure,

$$B\,n' = B\,n + n\,n',$$
$$B\,n'\,B' = B\,n\,B + 2\,n\,n' - B\,B'.$$

Combining, we obtain

$$\frac{B\,n'\,B'}{B\,n\,B} = \frac{1}{1 - \dfrac{V^2}{c^2}} \, .$$

Thus A finds that the path traversed by B's light, instead of being exactly two meters as was his own, will be longer in the ratio of $1 : \left(1 - \dfrac{V^2}{c^2}\right)$. For this reason A is rather surprised that B does not report a longer time interval for the passage of the light than he himself found. He remembers, however, that he has already found that measurements of time made with a moving clock must be multiplied by the quantity $\dfrac{1}{\sqrt{1 - \dfrac{V^2}{c^2}}}$ in order to agree with his own, and sees that this will account for part of the discrepancy between the expected and observed results. To account for the remaining discrepancy the further conclusion is now obtained *that measurements of length made with a moving meter stick, parallel to its motion, must be multiplied by the quantity* $\sqrt{1 - \dfrac{V^2}{c^2}}$ *in order to agree with those made in a stationary system.*

In accordance with this principle, a stationary observer will obtain a smaller measurement for the length of a moving body than will an observer moving along with the object. This has been called the Lorentz shortening, the shortening occurring in the ratio

$$\sqrt{1 - \frac{V^2}{c^2}} : 1$$

in the line of motion.

The Setting of Clocks in a Moving System.

28. It will be noticed that in our considerations up to this point we have considered cases where only a *single* moving clock was needed in performing the desired experiment, and this was done purposely, since we shall find, not only that a given time interval measures shorter on a moving clock than on a system of stationary clocks, but that a system of moving clocks which have been set in synchronism by an observer moving along with them will not be set in synchronism for a stationary observer.

Consider again two systems S and S' in relative motion with the velocity V. An observer A on system S places two carefully compared clocks, unit distance apart, in the line of motion, and has the time on each clock read when a given point on the other system passes it. An observer B on system S' performs a similar experiment. The time interval obtained in the two sets of readings must be the same, since the first postulate of relativity obviously requires that the relative velocity of the two systems V shall have the same value for both observers.

The observer A, however, taking himself as at rest, and familiar with the change in the measurements of length and time in the moving system which have already been deduced, expects that the velocity as measured by B will be greater than the value that he himself obtains in the ratio $\dfrac{1}{1 - \dfrac{V^2}{c^2}}$, since any particular one of B's clocks gives a shorter value for a given time interval than his own, while B's measurements of the length of a moving object are greater than his own, each by the factor $\sqrt{1 - \dfrac{V^2}{c^2}}$. In order to explain the actual result of B's experiment he now has to conclude that the clocks which for B are set synchronously are not set in synchronism for himself.

From what has preceded it is easy to see that in the moving system, from the point of view of the stationary observer, clocks must be set further and further ahead as we proceed towards the rear of the system, since otherwise B would not obtain a great enough difference in the readings of the clocks as they come opposite the given point on the other system. Indeed, if two clocks are situated in the moving system, S', one in front of the other by the distance l', as measured by B, then for A it will appear as though B had set his rear clock ahead by the amount $\dfrac{l'V}{c^2}$.

29. We have now obtained all the information which we shall need in this chapter as to measurements of time and length in systems moving with different velocities. We may point out, however, before proceeding to the application of these considerations, that our choice of A's system as the one which we should call stationary was of course entirely arbitrary and immaterial. We can at any time equally well take B's system as the one to which we shall ultimately refer all our measurements, and indeed all that we shall mean when we call one of our systems stationary is that for reasons of convenience we have picked out that particular system as the one with reference to which we particularly wish to make our measurements. We may also point out that of course B has to subject A's measurements of time and length to just the same multiplications by the factor $\dfrac{1}{\sqrt{1 - \dfrac{V^2}{c^2}}}$ as did A in order to make them agree with his own.

These conclusions as to measurements of space and time are of course very startling when first encountered. The mere fact, however, that they appear strange to so-called "common sense" need cause us no difficulty, since the older ideas of space and time were obtained from an ancestral experience which never included experiments with high relative velocities, and it is only when the ratio $\dfrac{V^2}{c^2}$ becomes appreciable that we obtain unexpected results. To those scientists who do not wish to give up their "common sense" ideas of space and time we can merely say that if they accept the two postulates of relativity then they will also have to accept the consequences which can be deduced therefrom. The remarkable nature of these consequences merely indicates the very imperfect nature of our older conceptions of space and time.

The Composition of Velocities.

30. Our conclusions as to the setting of clocks make it possible to obtain an important expression for the composition of velocities. Suppose we have a system S, which we shall take as stationary, and on the system an observer A. Moving past S with the velocity V is another system S' with an observer B, and finally moving past S' in the same direction is a body whose velocity is u' as measured by observer B. What will be the velocity u of this body as measured by A?

Our older ideas led us to believe in the simple additivity of velocities and we should have calculated u in accordance with the simple expression

$$u = V + u'.$$

We must now allow, however, for the fact that u' is measured with clocks which to A appear to be set in a peculiar fashion and running at a different rate from his own, and with meter sticks which give longer measurements than those used in the stationary system.

The determination of u' by observer B would be obtained by measuring the time interval necessary for the body in question to move a given distance l' along the system S'. If t' is the difference in the respective clock readings when the body reaches the ends of the line l', we have

$$u' = \frac{l'}{t'}.$$

We have already seen, however, that the two clocks are for A set $\frac{l'V}{c^2}$ units apart and hence for clocks set together the time interval would have measured $t' + \frac{l'V}{c^2}$. Furthermore these moving clocks give time measurements which are shorter in the ratio $\sqrt{1 - \frac{V^2}{c^2}} : 1$ than those obtained by A, so that for A the time interval for the body to move from one end of l' to the other would measure

$$\frac{t' + \dfrac{l'V}{c^2}}{\sqrt{1 - \dfrac{V^2}{c^2}}};$$

furthermore, owing to the difference in measurements of length, this line l' has for A the length $l'\sqrt{1 - \dfrac{V^2}{c^2}}$. Hence A finds that the body is moving past S' with the velocity,

$$\frac{l'\sqrt{1 - \dfrac{V^2}{c^2}}}{\dfrac{t' + \dfrac{l'V}{c^2}}{\sqrt{1 - \dfrac{V^2}{c^2}}}} = \frac{\dfrac{l'}{t'}\left(1 - \dfrac{V^2}{c^2}\right)}{1 + \dfrac{l'}{t'}\dfrac{V}{c^2}} = \frac{u'\left(1 - \dfrac{V^2}{c^2}\right)}{1 + \dfrac{u'V}{c^2}}.$$

This makes the total velocity of the body past S equal to the sum

$$u = V + \frac{u'\left(1 - \dfrac{V^2}{c^2}\right)}{1 + \dfrac{u'V}{c^2}},$$

or

$$u = \frac{V + u'}{1 + \dfrac{u'V}{c^2}}.$$

This new expression for the composition of velocities is extremely important. When the velocities u' and V are small compared with the velocity of light c, we observe that the formula reduces to the simple additivity principle which we know by common experience to be true for all ordinary velocities. Until very recently the human race has had practically no experience with high velocities and we now see that for velocities in the neighborhood of that of light, the simple additivity principle is nowhere near true.

In particular it should be noticed that by the composition of velocities which are themselves less than that of light we can never obtain any velocity greater than that of light. As an extreme case, suppose for example that the system S' were moving past S itself with the velocity of light (*i.e.*, $V = c$) and that in the system S' a particle should itself be given the velocity of light in the same direction (*i.e.*, $u' = c$); we find on substitution that the particle still has only the velocity of light with respect to S. We have

$$u = \frac{c + c}{1 + \dfrac{c^2}{c^2}} = \frac{2c}{2} = c.$$

By the consideration of such conclusions as these the reader will appreciate more and more the necessity of abandoning his older naïve ideas of space and time which are the inheritance of a long human experience with physical systems in which only slow velocities were encountered.

The Mass of a Moving Body.

31. We may now obtain an important relation for the mass of a moving body. Consider again two similar systems, S at rest and S' moving past with the velocity V. The observer A on system S has a sphere made from some rigid elastic material, having a mass of m grams, and the observer B on system S' is also provided with a similar sphere. The two spheres are made so that they are exactly alike when both are at rest; thus B's sphere, since it is at rest with respect to him, looks to him just the same as the other sphere does to A. As the two systems pass each other (Fig. 9) each of these clever experimenters rolls his sphere towards the other system with a velocity of u cm. per second, so that they will just collide and rebound in a line perpendicular to the direction of motion. Now, from the first postulate of relativity, system S' appears to B just the same as system S appears to A, and B's ball appears to him to go through the same evolutions that A finds for his ball. A finds that his ball on collision undergoes the algebraic change of velocity $2u$, B finds the same change in velocity $2u$ for his ball. B reports this fact to A, and A knowing that B's measurements of length agree with his own in this transverse direction, but that his

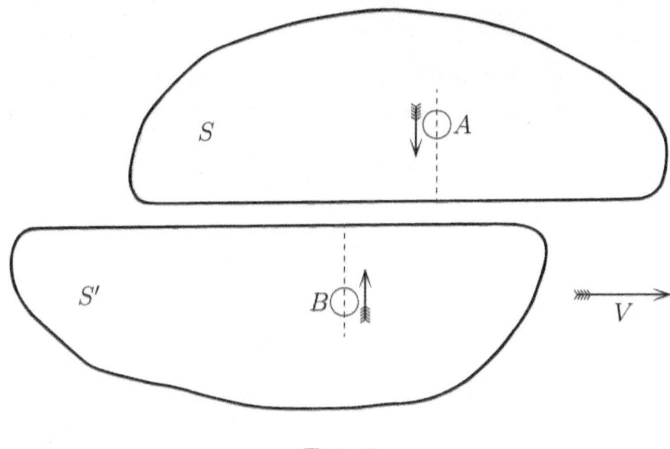

F $_\text{IG}$. 9.

clock gives time intervals that are shorter than his own in the ratio $\sqrt{1 - \dfrac{V^2}{c^2}} : 1$, calculates that the change in velocity of B's ball must be $2u\sqrt{1 - \dfrac{V^2}{c^2}}$.

From the principle of the conservation of momentum, however, A knows that the change in momentum of B's ball must be the same as that of his own and hence can write the equation

$$m_a u = m_b u \sqrt{1 - \frac{V^2}{c^2}},$$

where m_a is the mass of A's ball and m_b is the mass of B's ball. Solving we have

$$m_b = \frac{m_a}{\sqrt{1 - \dfrac{V^2}{c^2}}}.$$

In other words, B's ball, which had the same mass m_a as A's when both were at rest, is found to have the larger mass $\dfrac{m_a}{\sqrt{1 - \dfrac{v^2}{c^2}}}$ when placed in a system that is moving with the velocity V.*

The theory of relativity thus leads to the general expression

$$m = \frac{m_0}{\sqrt{1 - \dfrac{v^2}{c^2}}}$$

for the mass of a body moving with the velocity u and having the mass m_0 when at rest.

Since we have very few velocities comparable with that of light it is obvious that the quantity $\sqrt{1 - \dfrac{v^2}{c^2}}$ seldom differs much from unity, which makes the experimental verification of this expression difficult. In the case of electrons, however, which are shot off from radioactive substances, or indeed in the case of cathode rays produced with high potentials, we do have particles moving with velocities comparable to that of light, and the experimental work of Kaufmann, Bucherer, Hupka and others in this field provides one of the most striking triumphs of the theory of relativity.

The Relation Between Mass and Energy.

32. The theory of relativity has led to very important conclusions as to the nature of mass and energy. In fact, we shall see that matter

---

*In carrying out this experiment the transverse velocities of the balls should be made negligibly small in comparison with the relative velocity of the systems V.

and energy are apparently different names for the same fundamental entity.

When we set a body in motion it is evident from the previous section that we increase both its mass as well as its energy. Now we can show that there is a definite ratio between the amount of energy that we give to the body and the amount of mass that we give to it.

If the force f acts on a particle which is free to move, its increase in kinetic energy is evidently

$$\Delta E = \int f \, dl.$$

But the force acting is, by definition, equal to the rate of increase in the momentum of the particle

$$f = \frac{d}{dt}(mu).$$

Substituting we have

$$\Delta E = \int \frac{d(mu)}{dt} \, dl = \int \frac{dl}{dt} \, d(mu) = \int u \, d(mu).$$

We have, however, from the previous section,

$$m = \frac{m_0}{\sqrt{1 - \dfrac{u^2}{c^2}}},$$

which, solved for u, gives us

$$u = c\sqrt{1 - \frac{m_0{}^2}{m^2}}.$$

Substituting this value of u in our equation for ΔE we obtain, after simplification,

$$\Delta E = \int c^2 \, dm = c^2 \, \Delta m.$$

This says that the increase of the kinetic energy of the particle, in ergs, is equal to the increase in mass, in grams, multiplied by the square of the velocity of light. If now we bring the particle to rest it will give up both its kinetic energy and its excess mass. Accepting the principles of the conservation of mass and energy, we know, however, that neither this energy nor the mass has been destroyed; they have merely been passed on to other bodies. There is, moreover, every reason to believe that this mass and energy, which were associated together when the body was in motion and left the body when it was brought to rest, still remain always associated together. For example, if the body should be brought to rest by setting another body into motion, it is of course a necessary consequence of our considerations that the kinetic energy and the excess mass both pass on together to the new body which is set in motion. A similar conclusion would be true if the body is brought to rest by frictional forces, since the heat produced by the friction means an increase in the kinetic energies of ultimate particles.

In general we shall find it pragmatic to consider that matter and energy are merely different names for the same fundamental entity. One gram of matter is equal to 10^{21} ergs of energy.

$$c^2 = (2.9986 \times 10^{10})^2 = \text{approx. } 10^{21}.$$

This apparently extraordinary conclusion is in reality one which produces the greatest simplification in science. Not to mention numerous special applications where this principle is useful, we may call attention to the fact that the great laws of the conservation of mass and of energy have now become identical. We may also point out that those opposing camps of philosophic materialists who defend matter on the one hand or energy on the other as the fundamental entity of the universe may now forever cease their unimportant bickerings.

CHAPTER IV.

THE EINSTEIN TRANSFORMATION EQUATIONS FOR SPACE AND TIME.

The Lorentz Transformation.

33. We may now proceed to a systematic study of the consequences of the theory of relativity.

The fundamental problem that first arises in considering spatial and temporal measurements is that of transforming the description of a given kinematical occurrence from the variables of one system of coördinates to those of another system which is in motion relative to the first.

Consider two systems of right-angled Cartesian coördinates S and S' (Fig. 10) in relative motion in the X direction with the velocity V. The

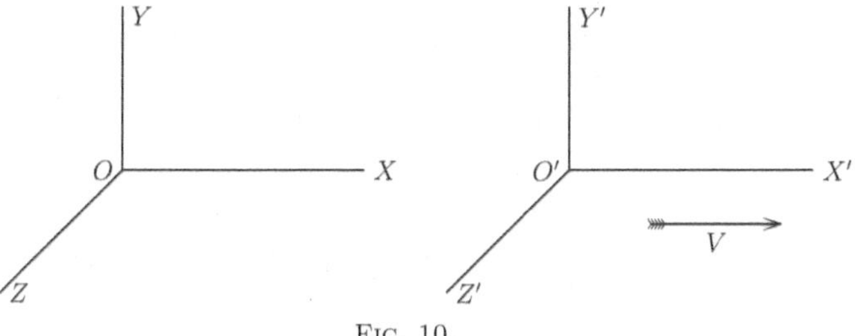

Fig. 10.

position of any given point in space can be determined by specifying its coördinates x, y, and z with respect to system S or its coördinates x', y' and z' with respect to system S'. Furthermore, for the purpose of determining the *time* at which any event takes place, we may think of each system of coördinates as provided with a whole series of clocks placed at convenient intervals throughout the system, the clocks of each series being set and regulated* by observers in the corresponding system. The time at which the event in question takes place may be denoted by t if determined by the clocks belonging to system S and by t' if determined by the clocks of system S'.

For convenience the two systems S and S' are chosen so that the axes OX and $O'X'$ lie in the same line, and for further simplification we choose, as our starting-point for time measurements, t and t' both equal to zero when the two origins come into coincidence.

The specific problem now before us is as follows: If a given kinematical occurrence has been observed and described in terms of the variables x', y', z' and t', what substitutions must we make for the values of these variables in order to obtain a correct description of the *same* kinematical event in terms of the variables x, y, z and t? In other words, we want to obtain a set of transformation equations from the variables of system S' to those of system S. The equations which we shall present were first obtained by Lorentz, and the process of changing from one set of variables to the other has generally been called the Lorentz transformation. The significance of these equations from the point of view of the theory of relativity was first appreciated by Einstein.

Deduction of the Fundamental Transformation Equations.

34. It is evident that these transformation equations are going to depend on the relative velocity V of the two systems, so that we may write for them the expressions

$$x' = F_1(V, x, y, z, t),$$

---

*We may think of the clocks as being set in any of the ways that are usual in practice. Perhaps the simplest is to consider the clocks as mechanisms which have been found to "keep time" when they are all together where they can be examined by one individual observer. The assumption can then be made, in accordance with our ideas of the homogeneity of space, that they will continue to "keep time" after they have been distributed throughout the system.

$$y' = F_2(V, x, y, z, t),$$
$$z' = F_3(V, x, y, z, t),$$
$$t' = F_4(V, x, y, z, t),$$

where F_1, F_2, etc., are the unknown functions whose form we wish to determine.

It is possible at the outset, however, greatly to simplify these relations. If we accept the idea of the homogeneity of space it is evident that any other line parallel to OXX' might just as well have been chosen as our line of X-axes, and hence our two equations for x' and t' must be independent of y and z. Moreover, as to the equations for y' and z' it is at once evident that the only possible solutions are $y' = y$ and $z' = z$. This is obvious because a meter stick held in the system S' perpendicular to the line of relative motion, OX', of the system can be directly compared with meter sticks held similarly in system S, and in accordance with the first postulate of relativity they must agree in length in order that the systems may be entirely symmetrical. We may now rewrite our transformation equations in the simplified form

$$x' = F_1(V, t, x),$$
$$y' = y,$$
$$z' = z,$$
$$t' = F_2(V, t, x),$$

and have only two functions, F_1 and F_2, whose form has to be determined.

To complete the solution of the problem we may make use of three further conditions which must govern the transformation equations.

35. Three Conditions to be Fulfilled. In the first place, when the velocity V between the systems is small, it is evident that the transformation equations must reduce to the form that they had in Newtonian mechanics, since we know both from measurements and from everyday experience that the Newtonian concepts of space and time are correct as long as we deal with slow velocities. Hence the limiting form of the equations as V approaches zero will be (cf. Chapter I, equations (3), (4), (5), (6))

$$x' = x - Vt,$$
$$y' = y,$$
$$z' = z,$$
$$t' = t.$$

36. A second condition is imposed upon the form of the functions F_1 and F_2 by the first postulate of relativity, which requires that the two systems S and S' shall be entirely symmetrical. Hence the transformation equations for changing from the variables of system S to those of system S' must be of exactly the same form as those used in the reverse transformation, containing, however, $-V$ wherever $+V$ occurs in the latter equations. Expressing this requirement in mathematical form, we may write as true equations

$$x = F_1(-V, t', x'),$$
$$t = F_2(-V, t', x'),$$

where F_1 and F_2 must have the same form as above.

37. A final condition is imposed upon the form of F_1 and F_2 by the second postulate of relativity, which states that the velocity of a beam of light appears the same to all observers regardless of the motion of the source of light or of the observer. Hence our transformation equations must be of such a form that a given beam of light has the same velocity, c, when measured in the variables of either system. Let us suppose, for example, that at the instant $t = t' = 0$, when the two origins come into coincidence, a light impulse is started from the common point occupied by O and O'. Then, measured in the coördinates of either system, the optical disturbance which is generated must spread out from the origin in a spherical form with the velocity c. Hence, using the variables of system S, the coördinates of any point on the surface of the disturbance will be given by the expression

$$x^2 + y^2 + z^2 = c^2 t^2, \tag{7}$$

while using the variables of system S' we should have the similar expression

$$x'^2 + y'^2 + z'^2 = c^2 t'^2. \tag{8}$$

Thus we have a particular kinematical occurrence, the spreading out of a light disturbance, whose description is known in the variables of either system, and our transformation equations must be of such a form that their substitution will change equation (8) to equation (7). In other words, the expression $x^2 + y^2 + z^2 - c^2 t^2$ is to be an invariant for the Lorentz transformation.

38. The Transformation Equations. The three sets of conditions which, as we have seen in the last three paragraphs, are imposed upon the form of F_1 and F_2 are sufficient to determine the solution of the problem. The natural method of solution is obviously that of trial, and we may suggest the solution:

$$x' = \frac{1}{\sqrt{1 - \dfrac{V^2}{c^2}}} (x - Vt) = \kappa(x - Vt), \tag{9}$$

$$y' = y, \tag{10}$$

$$z' = z, \tag{11}$$

$$t' = \frac{1}{\sqrt{1 - \dfrac{V^2}{c^2}}} \left(t - \frac{V}{c^2} x \right) = \kappa \left(t - \frac{V}{c^2} x \right), \tag{12}$$

where we have placed κ to represent the important and continually recurring quantity $\dfrac{1}{\sqrt{1 - \dfrac{V^2}{c^2}}}$.

It will be found as a matter of fact by examination that these solutions do fit all three requirements which we have stated. Thus, when V becomes small compared with the velocity of light, c, the equations do reduce to those of Galileo and Newton. Secondly, if the equations are solved for the unprimed quantities in terms of the primed, the resulting expressions have an unchanged form except for the introduction of $-V$ in place of $+V$, thus fulfilling the requirements of symmetry imposed by the first postulate of relativity. And finally, if we substitute the expressions for x', y', z' and t' in the polynomial $x'^2 + y'^2 + z'^2 = c^2 t'^2$, we shall obtain the expression $x^2 + y^2 + z^2 - c^2 t^2$ and have thus secured the invariance of $x^2 + y^2 + z^2 - c^2 t^2$ which is required by the second postulate of relativity.

We may further point out that the whole series of possible Lorentz transformations form a group such that the result of two successive transformations could itself be represented by a single transformation provided we picked out suitable magnitudes and directions for the velocities between the various systems.

It is also to be noted that the transformation becomes imaginary for cases where $V > c$, and we shall find that this agrees with ideas obtained in other ways as to the speed of light being an upper limit for the magnitude of all velocities.

Further Transformation Equations.

39. Before making any applications of our equations we shall find it desirable to obtain by simple substitutions and differentiations a series of further transformation equations which will be of great value in our future work.

By the simple differentiation of equation (12) we can obtain

$$\frac{dt'}{dt} = \kappa \left(1 - \frac{\dot{x}V}{c^2} \right), \qquad (13)$$

where we have put $\dot{x}$ for $\dfrac{dx}{dt}$.

40. Transformation Equations for Velocity. By differentiation of the equations for x', y' and z', nos. (9), (10) and (11), and substitution of the value just found for $\dfrac{dt'}{dt}$ we may obtain the following transformation equations for velocity:

$$\dot{x}' = \frac{\dot{x} - V}{1 - \dfrac{\dot{x}V}{c^2}} \qquad \text{or} \qquad u'_x = \frac{u_x - V}{1 - \dfrac{u_x V}{c^2}}, \tag{14}$$

$$\dot{y}' = \frac{\dot{y}\kappa^{-1}}{1 - \dfrac{\dot{y}V}{c^2}} \qquad\qquad u'_y = \frac{u_y \kappa^{-1}}{1 - \dfrac{u_x V}{c^2}}, \tag{15}$$

$$\dot{z}' = \frac{\dot{z}\kappa^{-1}}{1 - \dfrac{\dot{z}V}{c^2}} \qquad\qquad u'_z = \frac{u_z \kappa^{-1}}{1 - \dfrac{u_x V}{c^2}}, \tag{16}$$

where the placing of a dot has the familiar significance of differentiation with respect to time, $\dfrac{dx}{dt}$ being represented by $\dot{x}$ and $\dfrac{dx'}{dt'}$ by $\dot{x}'$.

The significance of these equations for the transformation of velocities is as follows: If for an observer in system S a point appears to be moving with the uniform velocity $(\dot{x}, \dot{y}, \dot{z})$ its velocity $(\dot{x}', \dot{y}', \dot{z}')$, as measured by an observer in system S', is given by these expressions (14), (15) and (16).

41. Transformation Equations for the Function $\dfrac{1}{\sqrt{1 - \dfrac{u^2}{c^2}}}$.

These three transformation equations for the velocity components of a point permit us to obtain a further transformation equation for an important function of the velocity which we shall find continually recurring in our later work. This is the function $\dfrac{1}{\sqrt{1 - \dfrac{u^2}{c^2}}}$, where we have

indicated the total velocity of the point by u, according to the expression $u^2 = \dot{x}^2 + \dot{y}^2 + \dot{z}^2$. By the substitution of equations (14), (15) and (16) we obtain the transformation equation

$$\frac{1}{\sqrt{1 - \dfrac{u^2}{c^2}}} = \frac{\left(1 - \dfrac{u_x V}{c^2}\right)\kappa}{\sqrt{1 - \dfrac{u^2}{c^2}}}. \tag{17}$$

42. Transformation Equations for Acceleration. By further differentiating equations (14), (15) and (16) and simplifying, we easily obtain three new equations for transforming measurements of *acceleration* from system S' to S, viz.:

$$\ddot{x}' = \left(1 - \frac{\dot{x} V}{c^2}\right)^{-3} \kappa^{-3} \ddot{x}, \tag{18}$$

$$\ddot{y}' = \left(1 - \frac{\dot{x} V}{c^2}\right)^{-2} \kappa^{-2} \ddot{y} + \dot{y}\,\frac{V}{c^2}\left(1 - \frac{\dot{x} V}{c^2}\right)^{-3} \kappa^{-2} \ddot{x}, \tag{19}$$

$$\ddot{z}' = \left(1 - \frac{\dot{x} V}{c^2}\right)^{-2} \kappa^{-2} \ddot{z} + \dot{z}\,\frac{V}{c^2}\left(1 - \frac{\dot{x} V}{c^2}\right)^{-3} \kappa^{-2} \ddot{x}, \tag{20}$$

or

$$\dot{u}'_x = \left(1 - \frac{u_x V}{c^2}\right)^{-3} \kappa^{-3} \ddot{u}_x, \tag{18}$$

$$\dot{u}'_y = \left(1 - \frac{u_x V}{c^2}\right)^{-2} \kappa^{-2} \ddot{u}_y + u_y\,\frac{V}{c^2}\left(1 - \frac{u_x V}{c^2}\right)^{-3} \kappa^{-2} \dot{u}_x, \tag{19}$$

$$\dot{u}'_z = \left(1 - \frac{u_x V}{c^2}\right)^{-2} \kappa^{-2} \ddot{u}_z + u_z\,\frac{V}{c^2}\left(1 - \frac{u_x V}{c^2}\right)^{-3} \kappa^{-2} \dot{u}_x. \tag{20}$$

CHAPTER V.

KINEMATICAL APPLICATIONS.

43. The various transformation equations for spatial and temporal measurements which were derived in the previous chapter may now be used for the treatment of a number of kinematical problems. In particular it will be shown in the latter part of the chapter that a number of optical problems can be handled with extraordinary facility by the methods now at our disposal.

The Kinematical Shape of a Rigid Body.

44. We may first point out that the conclusions of relativity theory lead us to quite new ideas as to what is meant by the shape of a rigid body. We shall find that the shape of a rigid body will depend entirely upon the relative motion of the body and the observer who is making measurements on it.

Consider a rigid body which is at rest with respect to system S'. Let x_1', y_1', z_1' and x_2', y_2', z_2' be the coördinates in system S' of two points in the body. The coördinates of the same points as measured in system S can be found from transformation equations (9), (10) and (11), and by subtraction we can obtain the following expressions

$$(x_2 - x_1) = \sqrt{1 - \frac{V^2}{c^2}}\,(x_2' - x_1'), \tag{21}$$

$$(y_2 - y_1) = (y_2' - y_1'), \tag{22}$$

$$(z_2 - z_1) = (z_2' - z_1'), \tag{23}$$

connecting the distances between the pair of points as viewed in the two systems. In making this subtraction terms containing t have been cancelled out since we are interested in the *simultaneous* positions of the points. In accordance with these equations we may distinguish then between the *geometrical shape* of a body, which is the shape that it has when measured on a system of axes which are at rest relative to it, and its *kinematical shape*, which is given by the coördinates which express the *simultaneous* positions of its various points when it is in motion with respect to the axes of reference. We see that the kinematical shape of a rigid body differs from its geometrical shape by a shortening of all its dimensions in the line of motion in the ratio $\sqrt{1 - \dfrac{V^2}{c^2}} : 1;$ thus a sphere, for example, becomes a Heaviside ellipsoid.

In order to avoid incorrectness of speech we must be very careful not to give the idea that the kinematical shape of a body is in any sense either more or less real than its geometrical shape. We must merely learn to realize that the shape of a body is entirely dependent on the particular set of coördinates chosen for the making of space measurements.

The Kinematical Rate of a Clock.

45. Just as we have seen that the shape of a body depends upon our choice of a system of coördinates, so we shall find that the rate of a given clock depends upon the relative motion of the clock and its observer. Consider a clock or any mechanism which is performing a periodic action. Let the clock be at rest with respect to system S' and let a given period commence at t_1' and end at t_2', the length of the interval thus being $\Delta t' = t_2' - t_1'$.

From transformation equation (12) we may obtain

$$t_1' = \frac{1}{\sqrt{1 - \dfrac{V^2}{c^2}}} \left(t_1 - \frac{V}{c^2}\, x_1 \right),$$

$$t_2' = \frac{1}{\sqrt{1 - \dfrac{V^2}{c^2}}} \left(t_2 - \frac{V}{c^2}\, x_2 \right),$$

and by subtraction, since $x_2 - x_1$ is obviously equal to Vt, we have

$$t_2 - t_1 = \frac{1}{\sqrt{1 - \dfrac{V^2}{c^2}}} (t_2' - t_1'),$$

$$\Delta t = \frac{1}{\sqrt{1 - \dfrac{V^2}{c^2}}} \Delta t'.$$

Thus an observer who is moving past a clock finds a longer period for the clock in the ratio $1 : \sqrt{1 - \dfrac{V^2}{c^2}}$ than an observer who is stationary with respect to it. Suppose, for example, we have a particle which is turning alternately red and blue. For an observer who is moving past the particle the periods for which it remains a given color measure longer in the ratio $1 : \sqrt{1 - \dfrac{V^2}{c^2}}$ than they do to an observer who is stationary with respect to the particle.

46. A possible opportunity for testing this interesting conclusion of the theory of relativity is presented by the phenomena of canal rays. We may regard the atoms which are moving in these rays as little clocks, the frequency of the light which they emit corresponding to the period of the clock. If now we should make spectroscopic observations on canal rays of high velocity, the frequency of the emitted light ought to be less than that of light from stationary atoms of the same kind if our considerations are correct. It would of course be necessary to view the canal rays at right angles to their direction of motion, to prevent a confusion of the expected shift in the spectrum with that produced by the ordinary Doppler effect (see Section 54).

The Idea of Simultaneity.

47. We may now also point out that the idea of the *absolute* simultaneity of two events must henceforth be given up. Suppose, for example, an observer in the system S is interested in two events which take place simultaneously at the time t. Suppose one of these events occurs at a point having the X coördinate x_1 and the other at a point having the coördinate x_2; then by transformation equation (12) it is evident that to an observer in system S', which is moving relative to S with the velocity V, the two events would take place respectively at the times

$$t_1' = \frac{1}{\sqrt{1 - \dfrac{V^2}{c^2}}} \left(t - \frac{V}{c^2} x_1 \right)$$

and

$$t_2' = \frac{1}{\sqrt{1 - \dfrac{V^2}{c^2}}} \left(t - \frac{V}{c^2} x_2 \right)$$

or the difference in time between the occurrence of the events would appear to this other observer to be

$$t_2' - t_1' = \frac{V}{c^2 \sqrt{1 - \dfrac{V^2}{c^2}}} (x_1 - x_2). \tag{25}$$

The Composition of Velocities.

48. The Case of Parallel Velocities. We may now present one of the most important characteristics of Einstein's space and time, which can be best appreciated by considering transformation equation (14), or more simply its analogue for the transformation in the reverse direction

$$u_x = \frac{u_x' + V}{1 + \dfrac{u_x'V}{c^2}}. \tag{26}$$

Consider now the significance of the above equation. If we have a particle which is moving in the X direction with the velocity u'_x as measured in system S', its velocity u_x with respect to system S is to be obtained by adding the relative velocity of the two systems V *and dividing the sum of the two velocities by* $1 + \dfrac{u_x'V}{c^2}$. Thus we see that we must completely throw overboard our old naïve ideas of the direct additivity of velocities. Of course, in the case of very slow velocities, when u'_x and V are both small compared with the velocity of light, the quantity $\dfrac{u_x'V}{c^2}$ is very nearly zero and the direct addition of velocities is a close approximation to the truth. In the case of velocities, however, which are in the neighborhood of the speed of light, the direct addition of velocities would lead to extremely erroneous results.

49. In particular it should be noticed that by the composition of velocities which are themselves less than that of light we can never obtain any velocity greater than that of light. Suppose, for example, that the system S' were moving past S with the velocity of light (*i.e.*, $V = c$), and that in the system S' a particle should itself be given the velocity of light in the X direction (*i.e.*, $u'_x = c$); we find on substitution that the particle still has only the velocity of light with respect to S. We have

$$u_x = \frac{c + c}{1 + \dfrac{c^2}{c^2}} = \frac{2c}{2} = c.$$

If the relative velocity between the systems should be one half the velocity of light, $\dfrac{c}{2}$, and an experimenter on S' should shoot off a particle in the X direction with half the velocity of light, the total velocity with respect to S would be

$$u_x = \frac{\tfrac{1}{2}c + \tfrac{1}{2}c}{1 + \dfrac{\tfrac{1}{4}c^2}{c^2}} = \frac{4}{5}c.$$

50. Composition of Velocities in General. In the case of particles which have components of velocity in other than the X direction it is obvious that our transformation equations will here also provide methods of calculation to supersede the simple addition of velocities. If we place

$$u^2 = u_x{}^2 + u_y{}^2 + u_z{}^2,$$
$$u'^2 = u_x{}'^2 + u_y{}'^2 + u_z{}'^2,$$

we may obtain by the substitution of equations (14), (15) and (16)

$$u = \frac{\left(u'^2 + V^2 + 2u'V\cos\alpha - \dfrac{u'^2 V^2 \sin^2\alpha}{c^2}\right)^{1/2}}{1 + \dfrac{u'V\cos\alpha}{c^2}}, \tag{27}$$

where α is the angle in the system S' between the X' axis and the velocity of the particle u'. For the particular case that V and u' are in the same direction, the equation obviously reduces to the simpler form

$$u = \frac{u' + V}{1 + \dfrac{u'V}{c^2}},$$

which we have already considered.

51. We may also call attention at this point to an interesting characteristic of the equations for the transformation of velocities. It will be noted from an examination of these equations that if to any observer a particle appears to have a constant velocity, *i.e.*, to be unacted on by any force, it will also appear to have a *uniform* although of course different velocity to any observer who is himself in uniform motion with respect to the first. An examination, however, of the transformation equations for acceleration (18), (19), (20) will show that here a different state of affairs is true, since it will be seen that a point which has *uniform acceleration* $(\ddot{x}, \ddot{y}, \ddot{z})$ with respect to an observer in system S

will not in general have a uniform acceleration in another system S', since the acceleration in system S' depends not only on the constant acceleration but also on the velocity in system S, which is necessarily varying.

Velocities Greater than that of Light.

52. In the preceding section we have called attention to the fact that the mere composition of velocities which are not themselves greater than that of light will never lead to a speed that is greater than that of light. The question naturally arises whether velocities which are greater than that of light could ever possibly be obtained in any way.

This problem can be attacked in an extremely interesting manner. Consider two points A and B on the X axis of the system S, and suppose that some impulse originates at A, travels to B with the velocity u and at B produces some observable phenomenon, the starting of the impulse at A and the resulting phenomenon at B thus being connected by the relation of *cause and effect*.

The time elapsing between the cause and its effect as measured in the units of system S will evidently be

$$\Delta t = t_B - t_A = \frac{x_B - x_A}{u}, \tag{28}$$

where x_A and x_B are the coördinates of the two points A and B.

Now in another system S', which has the velocity V with respect to S, the time elapsing between cause and effect would evidently be

$$\Delta t' = t'_B - t'_A = \frac{1}{\sqrt{1 - \frac{V^2}{c^2}}} \left(t_B - \frac{V}{c^2} x_B \right) - \frac{1}{\sqrt{1 - \frac{V^2}{c^2}}} \left(t_A - \frac{V}{c^2} x_A \right),$$

where we have substituted for t'_B and t'_A in accordance with equation (12). Simplifying and introducing equation (28) we obtain

$$\Delta t' = \frac{1 - \dfrac{uV}{c^2}}{\sqrt{1 - \dfrac{V^2}{c^2}}} \, \Delta t. \tag{29}$$

Let us suppose now that there are no limits to the possible magnitude of the velocities u and V, and in particular that the causal impulse can travel from A to B with a velocity u greater than that of light. It is evident that we could then take a velocity u great enough so that $\dfrac{uV}{c^2}$ would be greater than unity and $\Delta t'$ would become negative. In other words, for an observer in system S' the effect which occurs at B would *precede* in time its cause which originates at A. Such a condition of affairs might not be a logical impossibility; nevertheless its extraordinary nature might incline us to believe that no causal impulse can travel with a velocity greater than that of light.

We may point out in passing, however, that in the case of kinematic occurrences in which there is no causal connection there is no reason for supposing that the velocity must be less than that of light. Consider, for example, a set of blocks arranged side by side in a long row. For each block there could be an *independent* time mechanism like an alarm clock which would go off at just the right instant so that the blocks would fall down one after another along the line. The velocity with which the phenomenon would travel along the line of blocks could be arranged to have any value. In fact, the blocks could evidently all be fixed to fall just at the same instant, which would correspond to an infinite velocity. It is to be noticed here, however, that there is no causal connection between the falling of one block and that of the next, and no transfer of energy.

Application of the Principles of Kinematics to Certain Optical Problems.

53. Let us now apply our kinematical considerations to some problems in the field of optics. We may consider a beam of light as a periodic electromagnetic disturbance which is propagated through a vacuum with the velocity c. At any point in the path of a beam of light the intensity of the electric and magnetic fields will be undergoing periodic changes in magnitude. Since the intensities of both the electric and the magnetic fields vary together, the statement of a single vector is sufficient to determine the instantaneous condition at any point in the path of a beam of light. It is customary to call this vector (which might be either the strength of the electric or of the magnetic field) the light vector.

For the case of a simple plane wave (*i.e.*, a beam of monochromatic light from a distant source) the light vector at any point in the path of the light may be put proportional to

$$\sin \omega \left(t - \frac{lx + my + nz}{c} \right), \tag{30}$$

where x, y and z are the coördinates of the point under observation, t is the time, l, m and n are the cosines of the angles α, β and γ which determine the direction of the beam of light with reference to our system, and ω is a constant which determines the period of the light.

If now this same beam of light were examined by an observer in system S' which is moving past the original system in the X direction with the velocity V, we could write the light vector proportional to

$$\sin \omega' \left(t' - \frac{l'x' + m'y' + n'z'}{c} \right), \tag{31}$$

It is not difficult to show that the transformation equations which we have already developed must lead to the following relations between the measurements in the two systems*

$$\omega' = \omega\kappa\left(1 - l\,\frac{V}{c}\right),\qquad(32)$$

$$l' = \frac{l - \dfrac{V}{c}}{1 - l\,\dfrac{V}{c}},\qquad(33)$$

$$m' = \frac{m}{\kappa\left(1 - l\dfrac{V}{c}\right)},\qquad(34)$$

$$n' = \frac{n}{\kappa\left(1 - l\dfrac{V}{c}\right)}.\qquad(35)$$

---

*Methods for deriving the relation between the accented and unaccented quantities will be obvious to the reader. For example, consider the relation between ω and ω'. At the origin of coördinates $x = y = z = 0$ in system S, we shall have in accordance with expression (30) the light vector proportional to $\sin \omega t$, and hence similarly at the point O', which is the origin of coördinates in system S', we shall have the light vector proportional to $\sin \omega' t'$. But the point O' as observed from system S moves with the velocity V along the X axis and at any instant has the position $x = Vt$; hence substituting in expression (30) we have the light vector at the point O' as measured in system S proportional to

$$\sin \omega t\left(1 - l\,\frac{V}{c}\right),\qquad(36)$$

while as measured in system S' the intensity is proportional to

$$\sin \omega' t'.\qquad(37)$$

We have already obtained, however, a transformation equation for t', namely,

$$t' = \kappa\left(t - \frac{V}{c^2}\,x\right),$$

and further may place $x = Vt$. Making these substitutions and comparing expressions (36) and (37) we see that we must have the relation

$$\omega' = \omega\kappa\left(1 - l\,\frac{V}{c}\right).$$

Methods of obtaining the relation between the cosines l, m and n and the corresponding cosines l', m', and n' as measured in system S' may be left to the reader.

With the help of these equations we may now treat some important optical problems.

54. The Doppler Effect. At the origin of coördinates, $x = y = z = 0$, in system S we shall evidently have from expression (30) the light vector proportional to $\sin \omega t$. That means that the vector becomes zero whenever $\omega t = 2N\pi$, where N is any integer; in other words, the period of the light is $p = \dfrac{2\pi}{\omega}$ or the frequency

$$\nu = \frac{\omega}{2\pi}.$$

Similarly the frequency of the light as measured by an observer in system S' would be

$$\nu' = \frac{\omega'}{2\pi}.$$

Combining these two equations and substituting the equation connecting ω and ω' we have

$$\nu = \frac{\nu'}{\kappa \left(1 - l\dfrac{V}{c} \right)}.$$

This is the relation between the frequencies of a given beam of light as it appears to observers who are in relative motion.

If we consider a source of light at rest with respect to system S' and at a considerable distance from the observer in system S, we may substitute for ν' the frequency of the source itself, ν_0, and for l we may write $\cos \phi$, where ϕ is the angle between the line connecting source and observer and the direction of motion of the source, leading to the expression

$$\nu = \frac{\nu_0}{\kappa \left(1 - \cos \phi \dfrac{V}{c} \right)}. \tag{38}$$

This is the most general equation for the *Doppler effect.* When the source of light is moving directly in the line connecting source and observer, we have $\cos\phi = 1$, and the equation reduces to

$$\nu = \frac{\nu_0}{\kappa\left(1 - \dfrac{V}{c}\right)}, \tag{39}$$

which except for second order terms is identical with the older expressions for the Doppler effect, and hence agrees with experimental determinations.

We must also observe, however, that even when the source of light moves at right angles to the line connecting source and observer there still remains a second-order effect on the observed frequency, in contradiction to the predictions of older theories. We have in this case $\cos\phi = 0$,

$$\nu = \nu_0 \sqrt{1 - \frac{V^2}{c^2}}. \tag{40}$$

This is the change in frequency which we have already considered when we discussed the rate of a moving clock. The possibilities of direct experimental verification should not be overlooked (see Section 46).

55. The Aberration of Light. Returning now to our transformation equations, we see that equation (33) provides an expression for calculating the *aberration of light*. Let us consider that the source of light is stationary with respect to system S, and let there be an observer situated at the origin of coördinates of system S' and thus moving past the source with the velocity V in the X direction. Let ϕ be the angle between the X axis and the line connecting source of light and observer and let ϕ' be the same angle as it appears to the moving observer; then we can obviously substitute in equation (33), $\cos\phi = l$, $\cos\phi' = l'$, giving us

$$\cos\phi' = \frac{\cos\phi - \dfrac{V}{c}}{1 - \cos\phi\,\dfrac{V}{c}}. \tag{41}$$

This is a general equation for the aberration of light.

For the particular case that the direction of the beam of light is perpendicular to the motion of the observer we have $\cos \phi = 0$

$$\cos \phi' = -\frac{V}{c},\tag{42}$$

which, except for second-order differences, is identical with the familiar expression which makes the tangent of the angle of aberration numerically equal to V/c. The experimental verification of the formula by astronomical measurements is familiar.

56. Velocity of Light in Moving Media. It is also possible to treat very simply by kinematic methods the problem of the velocity of light in moving media. We shall confine ourselves to the particular case of a beam of light in a medium which is itself moving parallel to the light.

Let the medium be moving with the velocity V in the X direction, and let us consider the system of coördinates S' as stationary with respect to the medium. Now since the medium appears to be stationary with respect to observers in S' it is evident that the velocity of the light with respect to S' will be c/μ, where μ is index of refraction for the medium. If now we use our equation (26) for the addition of velocities we shall obtain for the velocity of light, as measured by observers in S,

$$u = \frac{\dfrac{c}{\mu} + V}{1 + \dfrac{V\dfrac{c}{\mu}}{c^2}}.\tag{43}$$

Carrying out the division and neglecting terms of higher order we obtain

$$u = \frac{c}{\mu} + \left(\frac{\mu^2 - 1}{\mu^2}\right)V.\tag{44}$$

The equation thus obtained is identical with that of Fresnel, the quantity $\left(\dfrac{\mu^2 - 1}{\mu^2}\right)$ being the well-known Fresnel coefficient. The empirical verification of this equation by the experiments of Fizeau and of Michelson and Morley is too well known to need further mention.

For the case of a dispersive medium we should obviously have to substitute in equation (44) the value of μ corresponding to the particular frequency, ν', which the light has in system S'. It should be noticed in this connection that the frequencies ν' and ν which the light has respectively in system S and system S', although nearly enough the same for the practical use of equation (44), are in reality connected by an expression which can easily be shown (see Section 54) to have the form

$$\nu' = \kappa \left(1 - \frac{V}{c} \right) \nu. \tag{45}$$

57. Group Velocity. In an entirely similar way we may treat the problem of group velocity and obtain the equation

$$G = \frac{G' + V}{1 + \dfrac{G'V}{c^2}}, \tag{46}$$

where G' is the group velocity as it appears to an observer who is stationary with respect to the medium. G' is, of course, an experimental quantity, connected with frequency and the properties of the medium, in a way to be determined by experiments on the stationary medium.

In conclusion we wish to call particular attention to the extraordinary simplicity of this method of handling the optics of moving media as compared with those that had to be employed before the introduction of the principle of relativity.

CHAPTER VI.

THE DYNAMICS OF A PARTICLE.

58. In this chapter and the two following, we shall present a system of "relativity mechanics" based on Newton's three laws of motion, the Einstein transformation equations for space and time, and the principle of the conservation of mass.

The Laws of Motion.

Newton's laws of motion may be stated in the following form:

I. Every particle continues in its state of rest or of uniform motion in a straight line, unless it is acted upon by an external force.

II. The rate of change of the momentum of the particle is equal to the force acting and is in the same direction.

III. For the action of every force there is an equal force acting in the opposite direction.

Of these laws the first two merely serve to define the concept of force, and their content may be expressed in mathematical form by the following equation of definition

$$\mathbf{F} = \frac{d}{dt}(m\mathbf{u}) = m\frac{d\mathbf{u}}{dt} + \frac{dm}{dt}\mathbf{u}, \tag{47}$$

where $\mathbf{F}$ is the force acting on a particle of mass m which has the velocity $\mathbf{u}$, and hence the momentum $m\mathbf{u}$.

Quite different in its nature from the first two laws, which merely give us a definition of force, the third law states a very definite physical postulate, since it requires for every change in the momentum of a body an equal and opposite change in the momentum of some other body. The truth of this postulate will of course be tested by comparing with experiment the results of the theory of mechanics which we base upon its assumption.

Difference between Newtonian and Relativity Mechanics.

59. Before proceeding we may point out the particular difference between the older Newtonian mechanics, which were based on the laws of motion and the *Galilean* transformation equations for space and time, and our new system of relativity mechanics based on those same laws of motion and the *Einstein* transformation equations.

In the older mechanics there was no reason for supposing that the mass of a body varied in any way with its velocity, and hence force could be defined interchangeably as the rate of change of momentum or as mass times acceleration, since the two were identical. In relativity mechanics, however, we shall be forced to conclude that the mass of a body increases in a perfectly definite way with its velocity, and hence in our new mechanics we must define force as equal to the total rate of change of momentum

$$\frac{d(m\mathbf{u})}{dt} = m\,\frac{d\mathbf{u}}{dt} + \frac{dm}{dt}\,\mathbf{u}$$

instead of merely as mass times acceleration $m\dfrac{d\mathbf{u}}{dt}$. If we should try to define force in "relativity mechanics" as merely equal to mass times acceleration, we should find that the application of Newton's third law of motion would then lead to very peculiar results, which would make the mass of a body different in different directions and force us to give up the idea of the conservation of mass.

The Mass of a Moving Particle.

60. In Section 31 we have already obtained in an elementary way an expression for the mass of a moving particle, by considering a collision between elastic particles and calculating how the resulting changes in velocity would appear to different observers who are themselves in relative motion. Since we now have at our command general formulæ for the transformation of velocities, we are now in a position to handle this problem much more generally, and *in particular to show that* *the expression obtained for the mass of a moving particle is entirely independent of the consideration of any particular type of collision.*

61. Transverse Collision. Let us first treat the case of a so-called "transverse" collision. Consider a system of coördinates and two exactly similar elastic particles, each having the mass m_0 when at rest, one moving in the X direction with the velocity $+u$ and the other with the velocity $-u$.

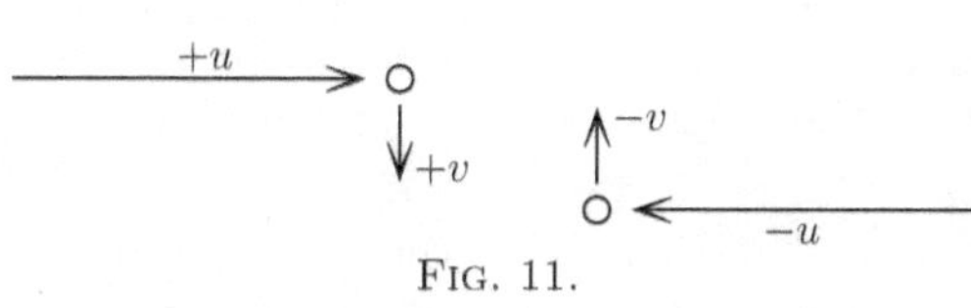

FIG. 11.

(See Fig. 11.) Besides the large components of velocity $+u$ and $-u$ which they have in the X direction let them also have small components of velocity in the Y direction, $+v$ and $-v$. The experiment is so arranged that the particles will just undergo a glancing collision as they pass each other and rebound with components of velocity in the Y direction of the same magnitude, v, which they originally had, but in the reverse direction. (It is evident from the symmetry of the arrangement that the experiment would actually occur as we have stated.)

We shall now be interested in the way this experiment would appear to an observer who is in motion in the X direction with the velocity V relative to our original system of coördinates.

From equation (14) for the transformation of velocities, it can be seen that this *new observer* would find for the X component velocities of the two particles the values

$$u_1 = \frac{u - V}{1 - \dfrac{uV}{c^2}} \qquad \text{and} \qquad u_2 = \frac{-u - V}{1 + \dfrac{uV}{c^2}} \tag{48}$$

and from equation (15) for the Y component velocities would find the values

$$v_1 = \pm\frac{v\sqrt{1 - \dfrac{V^2}{c^2}}}{1 - \dfrac{uV}{c^2}} \qquad \text{and} \qquad v_2 = \mp\frac{v\sqrt{1 - \dfrac{V^2}{c^2}}}{1 - \dfrac{uV}{c^2}}, \tag{49}$$

the signs depending on whether the velocities are measured before or after the collision.

Now from Newton's third law of motion (*i.e.*, the principle of the equality of action and reaction) it is evident that on collision the two particles must undergo the same numerical change in momentum.

For the experiment that we have chosen the only change in momentum is in the Y direction, and the observer whose measurements we are considering finds that one particle undergoes the total change in velocity

$$2v_1 = \frac{2v\sqrt{1 - \dfrac{V^2}{c^2}}}{1 - \dfrac{uV}{c^2}}$$

and that the other particle undergoes the change in velocity

$$2v_2 = \frac{2v\sqrt{1 - \dfrac{V^2}{c^2}}}{1 + \dfrac{uV}{c^2}}.$$

Since these changes in the velocities of the particles are not equal, it is evident that their masses must also be unequal if the principle of the equality of action and reaction is true for all observers, as we have assumed. This difference in the mass of the particles, each of which has the mass m_0 when at rest, arises from the fact that the mass of a particle is a function of its velocity and for the observer in question the two particles are not moving with the same velocity.

Using the symbols m_1 and m_2 for the masses of the particles, we may now write as a mathematical expression of the requirements of the third law of motion

$$\frac{2m_1 v \sqrt{1 - \dfrac{V^2}{c^2}}}{1 - \dfrac{uV}{c^2}} = \frac{2m_2 v \sqrt{1 - \dfrac{V^2}{c^2}}}{1 + \dfrac{uV}{c^2}} .$$

Simplifying, we obtain by direct algebraic transformation

$$\frac{m_1}{m_2} = \frac{1 - \dfrac{uV}{c^2}}{1 + \dfrac{uV}{c^2}} = \frac{\sqrt{1 - \dfrac{\left(\dfrac{-u - V}{1 + \frac{uV}{c^2}}\right)^2}{c^2}}}{\sqrt{1 - \dfrac{\left(\dfrac{u - V}{1 - \frac{uV}{c^2}}\right)^2}{c^2}}} ,$$

which on the substitution of equations (48) gives us

$$\frac{m_1}{m_2} = \frac{\sqrt{1 - \dfrac{{u_2}^2}{c^2}}}{\sqrt{1 - \dfrac{{u_1}^2}{c^2}}} . \tag{50}$$

This equation thus shows that the mass of a particle moving with the velocity u^* is inversely proportional to $\sqrt{1 - \dfrac{u^2}{c^2}}$, and, denoting the mass of the particle at rest by m_0, we may write as a *general expression*

---

*For simplicity of calculation we consider the case where the components of velocity in the Y direction are small enough to be negligible in their effect on the mass of the particles compared with the large components of velocity u_1 and u_2 in the X direction.

for the mass of a moving particle

$$m = \frac{m_0}{\sqrt{1 - \dfrac{u^2}{c^2}}}.\tag{51}$$

62. Mass the Same in All Directions. The method of derivation that we have just used to obtain this expression for the mass of a moving particle is based on the consideration of a so-called "transverse collision," and in fact the expression obtained has often been spoken of as that for the *transverse mass* of a moving particle, while a different expression, $\dfrac{m_0}{\left(1 - \dfrac{u^2}{c^2}\right)^{3/2}}$, has been used for the so-called *longitudinal mass* of the particle. These expressions $\dfrac{m_0}{\sqrt{1 - \dfrac{u^2}{c^2}}}$ and $\dfrac{m_0}{\left(1 - \dfrac{u^2}{c^2}\right)^{3/2}}$ are, as a matter of fact, the values of the electric force necessary to give a charged particle unit acceleration respectively at right angles and in the same direction as its original velocity, and hence such expressions would be proper for the mass of a moving particle if we should define force as mass times acceleration. As already stated, however, it has seemed preferable to retain, for force, Newton's original definition which makes it equal to the rate of change of momentum, and we shall presently see that this more suitable definition is in perfect accord with the idea that the mass of a particle is the same in all directions.

Aside from the unnecessary complexity which would be introduced, the particular reason making it unfortunate to have different expressions for mass in different directions is that under such conditions it would be impossible to retain or interpret the principle of the conservation of mass. And we shall now proceed to show that by introducing the principle of the conservation of mass, the consideration of a "longitudinal collision" will also lead to exactly the same expression, $\dfrac{m_0}{\sqrt{1 - \dfrac{u^2}{c^2}}}$, for the mass of a moving particle as we have already obtained from the consideration of a transverse collision.

63. Longitudinal Collision. Consider a system of coördinates and two elastic particles moving in the X direction with the velocities $+u$ and $-u$ so that a "longitudinal" (*i.e.*, head-on) collision will occur. Let the particles be exactly alike, each of them having the mass m_0 when at rest. On collision the particles will evidently come to rest, and then under the action of the elastic forces developed start up and move back over their original paths with the respective velocities $-u$ and $+u$ of the same magnitude as before.

Let us now consider how this collision would appear to an observer who is moving past the original system of coördinates with the velocity V in the X direction. Let u_1 and u_2 be the velocities of the particles as they appear to this new observer before the collision has taken place. Then, from our formula for the transformation of velocities (14), it is evident that we shall have

$$u_1 = \frac{u - V}{1 - \dfrac{uV}{c^2}} \qquad \text{and} \qquad u_2 = \frac{-u - V}{1 + \dfrac{uV}{c^2}}. \tag{52}$$

Since these velocities u_1 and u_2 are not of the same magnitude, the two particles which have the same mass when at rest do not have the same mass for this observer. Let us call the masses before collision m_1 and m_2.

Now during the collision the velocities of the particles will all the time be changing, but from the principle of the conservation of mass the sum of the two masses must all the time be equal to $m_1 + m_2$. When in the course of the collision the particles have come to relative rest, they will be moving past our observer with the velocity $-V$, and their momentum will be $-(m_1 + m_2)V$. But, from the principle of the equality of action and reaction, it is evident that this momentum must be equal to the original momentum before collision occurred. This gives us the equation $-(m_1 + m_2)V = m_1 u_1 + m_2 u_2$. Substituting our values (52) for u_1 and u_2 we have

$$\frac{m_1}{\left(1 - \frac{uV}{c^2}\right)} = \frac{m_2}{\left(1 + \frac{uV}{c^2}\right)},$$

and by direct algebraic transformation, as in the previous proof, this can be shown to be identical with

$$\frac{m_1}{m_2} = \frac{\sqrt{1 - \frac{u_2{}^2}{c^2}}}{\sqrt{1 - \frac{u_1{}^2}{c^2}}},$$

leading to the same expression that we obtained before for the mass of a moving particle, viz.:

$$m = \frac{m_0}{\sqrt{1 - \frac{u^2}{c^2}}}.$$

64. Collision of Any Type. We have derived this formula for the mass of a moving particle first from the consideration of a transverse and then of a longitudinal collision between particles which are elastic and have the same mass when at rest. It seems to be desirable to show, however, that the consideration of any type of collision between particles of any mass leads to the same formula for the mass of a moving particle.

For the mass m of a particle moving with the velocity u let us write the equation $m = m_0 F(u^2)$, where $F(\ )$ is the function whose form we wish to determine. The mass is written as a function of the square of the velocity, since from the homogeneity of space the mass will be independent of the direction of the velocity, and the mass is made proportional to the mass at rest, since a moving body may evidently be thought of as divided into parts without change in mass. It may be further remarked that the form of the function $F(\ )$ must be such that its value approaches unity as the variable approaches zero.

Let us now consider two particles having respectively the masses m_0 and n_0 when at rest, moving with the velocities u and w before collision, and with the velocities U and W after a collision has taken place.

From the principle of the conservation of mass we have

$$m_0 F(u_x{}^2 + u_y{}^2 + u_z{}^2) + n_0 F(w_x{}^2 + w_y{}^2 + w_z{}^2)$$
$$= m_0 F(U_x{}^2 + U_y{}^2 + U_z{}^2) + n_0 F(W_x{}^2 + W_y{}^2 + W_z{}^2), \quad (53)$$

and from the principle of the equality of action and reaction (*i.e.*, Newton's third law of motion)

$$m_0 F(u_x{}^2 + u_y{}^2 + u_z{}^2)u_x + n_0 F(w_x{}^2 + w_y{}^2 + w_z{}^2)w_x$$
$$= m_0 F(U_x{}^2 + U_y{}^2 + U_z{}^2)U_x + n_0 F(W_x{}^2 + W_y{}^2 + W_z{}^2)W_x, \quad (54)$$

$$m_0 F(u_x{}^2 + u_y{}^2 + u_z{}^2)u_y + n_0 F(w_x{}^2 + w_y{}^2 + w_z{}^2)w_y$$
$$= m_0 F(U_x{}^2 + U_y{}^2 + U_z{}^2)U_y + n_0 F(W_x{}^2 + W_y{}^2 + W_z{}^2)W_y, \quad (55)$$

$$m_0 F(u_x{}^2 + u_y{}^2 + u_z{}^2)u_z + n_0 F(w_x{}^2 + w_y{}^2 + w_z{}^2)w_z$$
$$= m_0 F(U_x{}^2 + U_y{}^2 + U_z{}^2)U_z + n_0 F(W_x{}^2 + W_y{}^2 + W_z{}^2)W_z. \quad (56)$$

These velocities, u_x, u_y, u_x, w_x, w_y, w_z, U_x, etc., are measured, of course, with respect to some definite system of "space-time" coördinates. An observer moving past this system of coördinates with the velocity V in the X direction would find for the corresponding component velocities the values

$$\frac{u_x - V}{1 - \dfrac{u_x V}{c^2}}, \quad \frac{\sqrt{1 - \dfrac{V^2}{c^2}}}{1 - \dfrac{u_x V}{c^2}} u_y, \quad \frac{\sqrt{1 - \dfrac{V^2}{c^2}}}{1 - \dfrac{u_x V}{c^2}} u_z, \quad \frac{w_x - V}{1 - \dfrac{w_x V}{c^2}}, \quad \text{etc.,}$$

as given by our transformation equations for velocity (14), (15), (16).

Since the law of the conservation of mass and Newton's third law of motion must also hold for the measurements of the new observer, we may write the following new relations corresponding to equations (53) to (56):

$$
m_0 F \left\{ \left(\frac{u_x - V}{1 - \frac{u_x V}{c^2}} \right)^2 + \left(\frac{\sqrt{1 - \frac{V^2}{c^2}}\, u_y}{1 - \frac{u_x V}{c^2}} \right)^2 + \left(\frac{\sqrt{1 - \frac{V^2}{c^2}}\, u_z}{1 - \frac{u_x V}{c^2}} \right)^2 \right\}
$$

$$
+ n_0 F \left\{ \left(\frac{w_x - V}{1 - \frac{w_x V}{c^2}} \right)^2 + \left(\frac{\sqrt{1 - \frac{V^2}{c^2}}\, w_y}{1 - \frac{w_x V}{c^2}} \right)^2 + \left(\frac{\sqrt{1 - \frac{V^2}{c^2}}\, w_z}{1 - \frac{w_x V}{c^2}} \right)^2 \right\}
$$

$$
= m_0 F \left\{ \left(\frac{U_x - V}{1 - \frac{U_x V}{c^2}} \right)^2 + \left(\frac{\sqrt{1 - \frac{V^2}{c^2}}\, U_y}{1 - \frac{U_x V}{c^2}} \right)^2 + \left(\frac{\sqrt{1 - \frac{V^2}{c^2}}\, U_z}{1 - \frac{U_x V}{c^2}} \right)^2 \right\}
$$

$$
+ n_0 F \left\{ \left(\frac{W_x - V}{1 - \frac{W_x V}{c^2}} \right)^2 + \left(\frac{\sqrt{1 - \frac{V^2}{c^2}}\, W_y}{1 - \frac{W_x V}{c^2}} \right)^2 + \left(\frac{\sqrt{1 - \frac{V^2}{c^2}}\, W_z}{1 - \frac{W_x V}{c^2}} \right)^2 \right\},
$$

$$\tag{53a}$$

$$
m_0 F \{ u_x \cdots \} \frac{u_x - V}{1 - \frac{u_x V}{c^2}} + n_0 F \{ w_x \cdots \} \frac{w_x - V}{1 - \frac{w_x V}{c^2}}
$$

$$
= m_0 F \{ U_x \cdots \} \frac{U_x - V}{1 - \frac{U_x V}{c^2}} + n_0 F \{ W_x \cdots \} \frac{W_x - V}{1 - \frac{W_x V}{c^2}},
$$

$$\tag{54a}$$

$$m_0 F\{u_x \cdots\} \frac{\sqrt{1 - \dfrac{V^2}{c^2}}\, u_y}{1 - \dfrac{u_x V}{c^2}} + n_0 F\{w_x \cdots\} \frac{\sqrt{1 - \dfrac{V^2}{c^2}}\, w_y}{1 - \dfrac{w_x V}{c^2}}$$

$$= m_0 F\{U_x \cdots\} \frac{\sqrt{1 - \dfrac{V^2}{c^2}}\, U_y}{1 - \dfrac{U_x V}{c^2}} + n_0 F\{W_x \cdots\} \frac{\sqrt{1 - \dfrac{V^2}{c^2}}\, W_y}{1 - \dfrac{W_x V}{c^2}}, \tag{55a}$$

$$m_0 F u_x \cdots \frac{\sqrt{1 - \dfrac{V^2}{c^2}}\, u_x}{1 - \dfrac{u_x V}{c^2}} + n_0 F w_x \cdots \frac{\sqrt{1 - \dfrac{V^2}{c^2}}\, w_x}{1 - \dfrac{w_x V}{c^2}}$$

$$= m_0 F U_x \cdots \frac{\sqrt{1 - \dfrac{V^2}{c^2}}\, U_x}{1 - \dfrac{U_x V}{c^2}} + n_0 F W_x \cdots \frac{\sqrt{1 - \dfrac{V^2}{c^2}}\, W_x}{1 - \dfrac{W_x V}{c^2}}. \tag{56a}$$

It is evident that these equations $(53a)$–$(56a)$ must be true no matter what the velocity between the new observer and the original system of coördinates, that is, true for all values of V. The velocities u_x, u_y, u_z, w_x, etc., are, however, perfectly definite quantities, measured with reference to a definite system of coördinates and entirely independent of V. If these equations are to be true for perfectly definite values of u_x, u_y, u_z, w_x, etc., and for all values of V, it is evident that the function $F(\ )$ must be of such a form that the equations are identities in V. As a matter of fact, it is found by trial that V can be cancelled from all the equations if we make $F(\ )$ of the form $\dfrac{1}{\sqrt{1 - \dfrac{(\ )}{c^2}}}$; and we see that the expected relation is a solution of the equations, although perhaps not necessarily a unique solution.

Before proceeding to use our formula for the mass of a moving particle for the further development of our system of mechanics, we may call attention in passing to the fact that the experiments of Kaufmann, Bucherer, and Hupka have in reality shown that the mass of the electron increases with its velocity according to the formula which we have just obtained. We shall consider the dynamics of the electron more in detail in the chapter devoted to electromagnetic theory. We wish to point out now, however, that in this derivation we have made no reference to any electrical charge which might be carried by the particle whose mass is to be determined. Hence we may reject the possibility of explaining the Kaufmann experiment by assuming that the charge of the electron decreases with its velocity, since the increase in mass is alone sufficient to account for the results of the measurement.

Transformation Equations for Mass.

65. Since the velocity of a particle depends on the particular system of coördinates chosen for the measurement, it is evident that the mass of the particle will also depend on our reference system of coördinates. For the further development of our system of dynamics, we shall find it desirable to obtain transformation equations for mass similar to those already obtained for velocity, acceleration, etc.

We have

$$m = \frac{m_0}{\sqrt{1 - \dfrac{u^2}{c^2}}},$$

where the velocity u is measured with respect to some definite system of coördinates, S. Similarly with respect to a system of coördinates S' which is moving relatively to S with the velocity V in the X direction we shall have

$$m' = \frac{m_0}{\sqrt{1 - \dfrac{u'^2}{c^2}}}.$$

We have already obtained, however, a transformation equation (17) for the function of the velocity occurring in these equations and on substitution we obtain the desired transformation equation

$$m' = \left(1 - \frac{u_x V}{c^2}\right) \kappa m, \tag{57}$$

where κ has the customary significance

$$\kappa = \frac{1}{\sqrt{1 - \dfrac{V^2}{c^2}}}.$$

By differentiation of (57) with respect to the time and simplification, we obtain the following transformation equation for the *rate at which the mass of a particle is changing* owing to change in velocity

$$\dot{m}' = \dot{m} - \frac{mV}{c^2}\left(1 - \frac{u_x V}{c^2}\right)^{-1}\frac{du_x}{dt}. \tag{58}$$

Equation for the Force Acting on a Moving Particle.

66. We are now in a position to return to our development of the dynamics of a particle. In the first place, the equation which we have now obtained for the mass of a moving particle will permit us to rewrite the original equation by which we defined force, in a number of ways which will be useful for future reference.

We have our equation of definition (47)

$$\mathbf{F} = \frac{d}{dt}(m\mathbf{u}) = m\frac{d\mathbf{u}}{dt} + \frac{dm}{dt}\mathbf{u},$$

which, on substitution of the expression for m, gives us

$$\mathbf{F} = \frac{d}{dt}\left[\frac{m_0}{\sqrt{1 - \dfrac{u^2}{c^2}}}\mathbf{u}\right] = \frac{m_0}{\sqrt{1 - \dfrac{u^2}{c^2}}}\frac{d\mathbf{u}}{dt} + \frac{d}{dt}\left[\frac{m_0}{\sqrt{1 - \dfrac{u^2}{c^2}}}\right]\mathbf{u} \tag{59}$$

or, carrying out the indicated differentiation,

$$\mathbf{F} = \frac{m_0}{\sqrt{1 - \dfrac{u^2}{c^2}}} \frac{d\mathbf{u}}{dt} + \frac{m_0}{\left(1 - \dfrac{u^2}{c^2}\right)^{3/2}} \frac{u}{c^2} \frac{du}{dt} \mathbf{u}. \tag{60}$$

Transformation Equations for Force.

67. We are also in position to obtain transformation equations for force. We have

$$\mathbf{F} = \frac{d}{dt}(m\mathbf{u}) = m\dot{\mathbf{u}} + \dot{m}\mathbf{u}$$

or

$$F_x = m\dot{u}_x + \dot{m}u_x,$$
$$F_y = m\dot{u}_y + \dot{m}u_y,$$
$$F_z = m\dot{u}_z + \dot{m}u_z.$$

We have transformation equations, however, for all the quantities on the right-hand side of these equations. For the velocities we have equations (14), (15) and (16), for the accelerations (18), (19) and (20), for mass, equation (57) and for rate of change of mass, equation (58). Substituting above we obtain as our *transformation equations for force*

$$F'_x = \frac{F_x - \dot{m}V}{1 - \dfrac{u_x V}{c^2}} = F_x - \frac{u_y V}{c^2 - u_x V} F_y - \frac{u_z V}{c^2 - u_x V} F_z, \tag{61}$$

$$F'_y = \frac{\kappa^{-1}}{1 - \dfrac{u_x V}{c^2}} F_y, \tag{62}$$

$$F'_z = \frac{\kappa^{-1}}{1 - \dfrac{u_x V}{c^2}} F_z. \tag{63}$$

We may now consider a few applications of the principles governing the dynamics of a particle.

The Relation between Force and Acceleration.

68. If we examine our equation (59) for the force acting on a particle

$$F = \frac{m_0}{\sqrt{1 - \dfrac{u^2}{c^2}}} \frac{d\mathbf{u}}{dt} + \frac{d}{dt}\left[\frac{m_0}{\sqrt{1 - \dfrac{u^2}{c^2}}}\right]\mathbf{u}, \tag{59}$$

we see that the force is equal to the sum of two vectors, one of which is in the direction of the acceleration $\dfrac{d\mathbf{u}}{dt}$ and the other in the direction of the existing velocity $\mathbf{u}$, so that *in general force and the acceleration it produces are not in the same direction.* We shall find it interesting to see, however, that if the force which does produce acceleration in a given direction be resolved perpendicular and parallel to the acceleration, the two components will be connected by a definite relation.

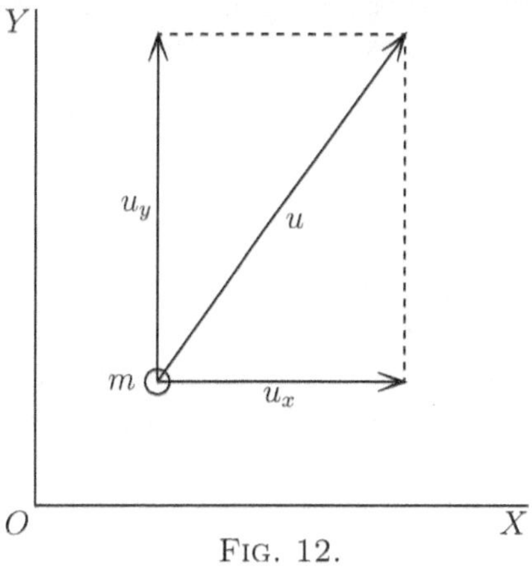

Consider a particle (Fig. 12) in plane space moving with the velocity

FIG. 12.

$$\mathbf{u} = u_x\mathbf{i} + u_y\mathbf{j}.$$

Let it be accelerated in the X direction by the action of the component forces F_x and F_y.

From our general equation (59) for the force acting on a particle we have for these component forces

$$F_x = \frac{m_0}{\sqrt{1 - \dfrac{u^2}{c^2}}}\frac{du_x}{dt} + \frac{d}{dt}\left[\frac{m_0}{\sqrt{1 - \dfrac{u^2}{c^2}}}\right]u_x, \tag{64}$$

$$F_y = \frac{m_0}{\sqrt{1 - \dfrac{u^2}{c^2}}}\frac{du_y}{dt} + \frac{d}{dt}\left[\frac{m_0}{\sqrt{1 - \dfrac{u^2}{c^2}}}\right]u_y. \tag{65}$$

Introducing the condition that all the acceleration is to be in the Y direction, which makes $\dfrac{du_x}{dt} = 0$, and further noting that $u^2 = u_x^2 + u_y^2$, by the division of equation (64) by (65), we obtain

$$\frac{F_x}{F_y} = \frac{u_x u_y}{c^2 - u_x{}^2},$$

$$F_x = \frac{u_x u_y}{c^2 - u_x{}^2}\,F_y. \tag{66}$$

Hence, in order to accelerate a particle in a given direction, we may apply any force F_y in the desired direction, but must at the same time apply at right angles another force F_x whose magnitude is given by equation (66).

Although at first sight this state of affairs might seem rather unexpected, a simple qualitative consideration will show the necessity of a component of force perpendicular to the desired acceleration. Refer again to Fig. 12; since the particle is being accelerated in the Y direction, its total velocity and hence its mass are increasing. This increasing mass is accompanied by increasing momentum in the X direction even when the velocity in that direction remains constant. The component force F_x is necessary for the production of this increase in X-momentum.

In a later paragraph we shall show an application of equation (66) in electrical theory.

Transverse and Longitudinal Acceleration.

69. An examination of equation (66) shows that there are two special cases in which the component force F_x disappears and the force and acceleration are in the same direction. F_x will disappear when either u_x or u_y is equal to zero, so that force and acceleration will be in the same direction when the force acts exactly at right angles to the line of motion of the particle, or in the direction of the motion (or of course also when u_x and u_y are both equal to zero and the particle is at rest). It is instructive to obtain simplified expressions for force for these two cases of transverse and longitudinal acceleration.

Let us again examine our equation (60) for the force acting on a particle

$$\mathbf{F} = \frac{m_0}{\sqrt{1 - \dfrac{u^2}{c^2}}} \frac{d\mathbf{u}}{dt} + \frac{m_0}{\left(1 - \dfrac{u^2}{c^2}\right)^{3/2}} \frac{u}{c^2} \frac{du}{dt} \mathbf{u}. \tag{60}$$

For the case of a *transverse acceleration* there is no component of force in the direction of the velocity $\mathbf{u}$ and the second term of the equation is equal to zero, giving us

$$\mathbf{F} = \frac{m_0}{\sqrt{1 - \dfrac{u^2}{c^2}}} \frac{d\mathbf{u}}{dt}. \tag{67}$$

For the case of *longitudinal acceleration*, the velocity $\mathbf{u}$ and the acceleration $\dfrac{d\mathbf{u}}{dt}$ are in the same direction, so that we may rewrite the second term of (60), giving us

$$\mathbf{F} = \frac{m_0}{\sqrt{1 - \dfrac{u^2}{c^2}}} \frac{d\mathbf{u}}{dt} + \frac{m_0}{\left(1 - \dfrac{u^2}{c^2}\right)^{3/2}} \frac{u^2}{c^2} \frac{d\mathbf{u}}{dt},$$

and on simplification this becomes

$$\mathbf{F} = \frac{m_0}{\left(1 - \dfrac{u^2}{c^2}\right)^{3/2}} \frac{d\mathbf{u}}{dt}. \tag{68}$$

An examination of this expression shows the reason why $\dfrac{m_0}{\left(1 - \dfrac{u^2}{c^2}\right)^{3/2}}$ is sometimes spoken of as the expression for the *longitudinal mass* of a particle.

The Force Exerted by a Moving Charge.

70. In a later chapter we shall present a consistent development of the fundamentals of electromagnetic theory based on the Einstein transformation equations for space and time and the four field equations. At this point, however, it may not be amiss to point out that the principles of mechanics themselves may sometimes be employed to obtain a simple and direct solution of electrical problems.

Suppose, for example, we wish to calculate the force with which a *point charge in uniform motion* acts on any other point charge. We can solve this problem by considering a system of coördinates which move with the same velocity as the charge itself. An observer making use of the new system of coördinates could evidently calculate the force exerted by the charge in question by Coulomb's familiar inverse square law for static charges, and the magnitude of the force as measured in the original system of coördinates can then be determined from our transformation equations for force. Let us proceed to the specific solution of the problem.

Consider a system of coördinates S, and a charge e in uniform motion along the X axis with the velocity V. We desire to know the force acting at the time t on any other charge e_1 which has any desired coördinates x, y, and z and any desired velocity u_x, u_y and u_z.

Assume a system of coördinates, S', moving with the same velocity as the charge e which is taken coincident with the origin. To an observer moving with the system S', the charge e appears to be always at rest and surrounded by a pure electrostatic field. Hence in system S' the force with which e acts on e_1 will be, in accordance with Coulomb's law*

$$\mathbf{F'} = \frac{ee_1\mathbf{r'}}{r'^3}$$

or

$$F'_x = \frac{ee_1x'}{(x'^2 + y'^2 + z'^2)^{3/2}}, \tag{69}$$

$$F'_y = \frac{ee_1x'}{(y'^2 + y'^2 + z'^2)^{3/2}}, \tag{70}$$

$$F'_z = \frac{ee_1x'}{(z'^2 + y'^2 + z'^2)^{3/2}}, \tag{71}$$

where x', y', and z' are the coördinates of the charge e_1 at the time t'. For simplicity let us consider the force at the time $t' = 0$; then from transformation equations (9), (10), (11), (12) we shall have

$$x' = \kappa^{-1}x, \qquad y' = y, \qquad z' = z.$$

Substituting in (69), (70), (71) and also using our transformation equations for force (61), (62), (63), we obtain the following equations for

---

*It should be noted that in its original form Coulomb's law merely stated that the force between two stationary charges was proportional to the product of the charges and inversely to the distance between them. In the present derivation we have extended this law to apply to the instantaneous force exerted by a stationary charge upon any other charge.

The fact that a charge of electricity appears the same to observers in all systems is obviously also necessary for the setting up of equations (69), (70), (71). That such is the case, however, is an evident consequence of the atomic nature of electricity. The charge e would appear of the same magnitude to observers both in system S and system S', since they would both count the same number of electrons on the charge. (See Section 157.)

the force acting on e_1, as it appears to an observer in system S:

$$F_x = \frac{ee_1 x'}{(x'^2 + y'^2 + z'^2)^{3/2}} \left(x + \frac{V}{c^2}\,\kappa^2(yu_y + zu_z) \right),\tag{72}$$

$$F_y = \frac{ee_1\left(1 - \frac{u_x V}{c^2}\right)\kappa y}{(\kappa^{-2}x'^2 + y'^2 + z'^2)^{3/2}},\tag{73}$$

$$F_z = \frac{ee_1\left(1 - \frac{u_x V}{c^2}\right)\kappa z}{(\kappa^{-2}x'^2 + y'^2 + z'^2)^{3/2}}.\tag{74}$$

These equations give the force acting on e_1 at the time t. From transformation equation (12) we have $t = \dfrac{V}{c^2}\,x$, since $t' = 0$. At this time the charge e, which is moving with the uniform velocity V along the X axis, will evidently have the position

$$x_e = \frac{V^2}{c^2}\,x, \qquad y_e = 0, \qquad z_e = 0.$$

For convenience we may now refer our results to a system of coördinates whose origin coincides with the position of the charge e at the instant under consideration. If X, Y and Z are the coördinates of e_1 with respect to this new system, we shall evidently have the relations

$$X = x - \frac{V^2}{c^2}\,x = \kappa^{-2}x, \qquad Y = y, \qquad Z = z,$$

$$U_x = u_x, \qquad U_y = u_y, \qquad U_z = u_z.$$

Substituting into (72), (73), (74) we obtain

$$F_x = \frac{ee_1}{s^3}\left(1 - \frac{V^2}{c^2}\right)\left(X + \frac{V}{c^2}(YU_y + ZU_z)\right),\tag{75}$$

$$F_y = \frac{ee_1}{s^3}\left(1 - \frac{V^2}{c^2}\right)\left(1 - \frac{U_x V}{c^2})\right)Y,\tag{76}$$

$$F_z = \frac{ee_1}{s^3}\left(1 - \frac{V^2}{c^2}\right)\left(1 - \frac{U_x V}{c^2})\right)Z,\tag{77}$$

where for simplicity we have placed

$$s = \sqrt{X^2 + \left(1 - \frac{V^2}{c^2}\right)(Y^2 + Z^2)}.$$

These are the same equations which would be obtained by substituting the well-known formulæ for the strength of the electric and magnetic field around a moving point charge into the fifth fundamental equation of the Maxwell-Lorentz theory, $\mathbf{f} = \rho \left(\mathbf{e} + \frac{1}{c}[\mathbf{u} \times \mathbf{h}]^*\right)$. They are really obtained in this way more easily, however, and are seen to come directly from Coulomb's law.

The Field around a Moving Charge. Evidently we may also use these considerations to obtain an expression for the electric field produced by a moving charge e, if we consider the particular case that the charge e_1 is stationary (*i.e.*, $U_x = U_y = U_z = 0$) and equal to unity. Making these substitutions in (75), (76), (77) we obtain the well-known expression for the electrical field in the neighborhood of a moving point charge

$$\mathbf{F} = e = \frac{\mathbf{e}}{s^3}\left(1 - \frac{V^2}{c^2}\right)\mathbf{r}, \tag{78}$$

where

$$\mathbf{r} = X\mathbf{i} + Y\mathbf{j} + Z\mathbf{k}.$$

71. Application to a Specific Problem. Equations (75), (76), (77) can also be applied in the solution of a rather interesting specific problem.

Consider a charge e constrained to move in the X direction with the velocity V and at the instant under consideration let it coincide with the origin of a system of stationary coördinates YeX (Fig. 13). Suppose now a second charge e_1, situated at the point $X = 0$, $Y = Y$ and moving in the X direction with the same velocity V as the charge e, and also having a component velocity in the Y direction U_y. Let us

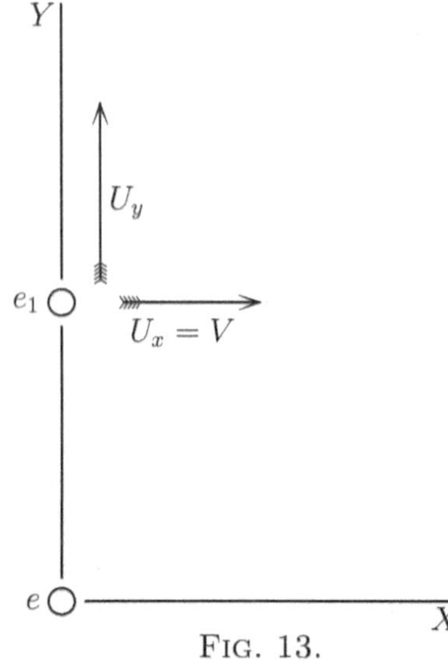

Fig. 13.

predict the nature of its motion under the influence of the charge e, it being otherwise unconstrained.

From the simple qualitative considerations placed at our disposal by the theory of relativity, it seems evident that the charge e_1 ought merely to increase its component of velocity in the Y direction and retain unchanged its component in the X direction, since from the point of view of an observer moving along with e the phenomenon is merely one of ordinary *electrostatic* repulsion.

Let us see whether our equations for the force exerted by a moving charge actually lead to this result. By making the obvious substitutions in equations (75) and (76) we obtain for the component forces on e_1

$$F_x = \frac{ee_1}{s^3}\left(1 - \frac{V^2}{c^2}\right)\frac{V}{c^2}YU_y, \tag{79}$$

$$F_x = \frac{ee_1}{s^3}\left(1 - \frac{V^2}{c^2}\right)^2 Y. \tag{80}$$

Now under the action of the component force F_x we might at first sight expect the charge e_1 to obtain an acceleration in the X direction, in contradiction to the simple qualitative prediction that we have just made on the basis of the theory of relativity. We remember, however, that equation (66) prescribes a definite ratio between the component forces F_x and F_y if the acceleration is to be in the Y direction, and dividing (79) by (80) we actually obtain the necessary relation

$$\frac{F_x}{F_y} = \frac{VU_y}{c^2 - V^2}.$$

Other applications of the new principles of dynamics to electrical, magnetic and gravitational problems will be evident to the reader.

Work.

72. Before proceeding with the further development of our theory of dynamics we shall find it desirable to define the quantities work, kinetic, and potential energy.

We have already obtained an expression for the force acting on a particle and shall define the work done on the particle as the integral of the force times the distance through which the particle is displaced. Thus

$$W = \int \mathbf{F} \cdot d\mathbf{r}, \tag{81}$$

where $\mathbf{r}$ is the radius vector determining the position of the particle.

Kinetic Energy.

73. When a particle is brought from a state of rest to the velocity $\mathbf{u}$ by the action of an unbalanced force $\mathbf{F}$, we shall define its kinetic energy as numerically equal to the work done in producing the velocity. Thus

$$K = W = \int \mathbf{F} \cdot d\mathbf{r}.$$

Since, however, the kinetic energy of a particle turns out to be entirely independent of the particular choice of forces used in producing the final velocity, it is much more useful to have an expression for kinetic energy in terms of the mass and velocity of the particle.

We have

$$K = \int \mathbf{F} \cdot d\mathbf{r} = \int \mathbf{F} \cdot \frac{d\mathbf{r}}{dt} \, dt = \int \mathbf{F} \cdot \mathbf{u} \, dt.$$

Substituting the value of $\mathbf{F}$ given by the equation of definition (47) we obtain

$$K = \int m \frac{d\mathbf{u}}{dt} \cdot \mathbf{u}\,dt + \int \frac{dm}{dt} \mathbf{u} \cdot \mathbf{u}\,dt$$
$$= \int m\,\mathbf{u} \cdot d\mathbf{u} + \int \mathbf{u} \cdot \mathbf{u}\,dm$$
$$= \int mu\,du + \int u^2\,dm.$$

Introducing the expression (51) for the mass of a moving particle $m = \dfrac{m_0}{\sqrt{1 - \dfrac{u^2}{c^2}}}$, we obtain

$$K = \int m_0 \frac{u}{\sqrt{1 - \dfrac{u^2}{c^2}}}\,du + \int \frac{m_0}{c^2} \frac{u^3}{\left(1 - \dfrac{u^2}{c^2}\right)^{3/2}}\,du$$

and on integrating and evaluating the constant of integration by placing the kinetic energy equal to zero when the velocity is zero, we easily obtain the desired expression for the kinetic energy of a particle:

$$K = m_0 c^2 \left[\frac{1}{\sqrt{1 - \dfrac{u^2}{c^2}}} - 1\right], \tag{82}$$
$$= c^2(m - m_0). \tag{83}$$

It should be noticed, as was stated above, that the kinetic energy of a particle *does* depend merely on its mass and final velocity and is entirely independent of the particular choice of forces which happened to be used in producing the state of motion.

It will also be noticed, on expansion into a series, that our expression (82) for the kinetic energy of a particle approaches at low velocities the form familiar in the older Newtonian mechanics,

$$K = \tfrac{1}{2}m_0 u^2.$$

Potential Energy.

74. When a moving particle is brought to rest by the action of a *conservative** force we say that its kinetic energy has been transformed into potential energy. The increase in the potential energy of the particle is equal to the kinetic energy which has been destroyed and hence equal to the work done by the particle against the force, giving us the equation

$$\Delta U = -W = -\int \mathbf{F} \cdot d\mathbf{r}. \tag{84}$$

The Relation between Mass and Energy.

75. We may now consider a very important relation between the mass and energy of a particle, which was first pointed out in our chapter on "Some Elementary Deductions."

When an isolated particle is set in motion, both its mass and energy are increased. For the increase in mass we may write

$$\Delta m = m - m_0,$$

---

*A conservative force is one such that any work done by displacing a system against it would be completely regained if the motion of the system should be reversed.

Since we believe that the forces which act on the ultimate particles and constituents of matter are in reality all of them conservative, we shall accept the general principle of the conservation of energy just as in Newtonian mechanics. (For a logical deduction of the principle of the conservation of energy in a system of particles, see the next chapter, Section 89.)

and for the increase in energy we have the expression for kinetic energy given in equation (83), giving us

$$\Delta E = c^2(m - m_0),$$

or, combining with the previous equation,

$$\Delta E = c^2 \Delta m. \tag{85}$$

Thus the increase in the kinetic energy of a particle always bears the same definite ratio (the square of the velocity of light) to its increase in mass. Furthermore, when a moving particle is brought to rest and thus loses both its kinetic energy and its extra ("kinetic") mass, there seems to be every reason for believing that this mass and energy which are associated together when the particle is in motion and leave the particle when it is brought to rest will still remain always associated together. For example, if the particle is brought to rest by collision with another particle, it is an evident consequence of our considerations that the energy and the mass corresponding to it do remain associated together since they are both passed on to the new particle. On the other hand, if the particle is brought to rest by the action of a conservative force, say for example that exerted by an elastic spring, the kinetic energy which leaves the particle will be transformed into the potential energy of the stretched spring, and since the mass which has undoubtedly left the particle must still be in existence, we shall believe that this mass is now associated with the potential energy of the stretched spring.

76. Such considerations have led us to believe that matter and energy may be best regarded as different names for the same fundamental entity: *matter*, the name which has been applied when we have been interested in the property of mass or inertia possessed by the entity, and *energy*, the name applied when we have been interested in the part taken by the entity in the production of motion and other changes in the physical universe. We shall find these ideas as to the relations between matter, energy and mass very fruitful in the simplification of physical reasoning, not only because it identifies the two laws of the conservation of mass and the conservation of energy, but also for its frequent application in the solution of specific problems.

77. We must call attention to the great difference in size between the two units, the gram and the erg, both of which are used for the measurement of the one fundamental entity, call it matter or energy as we please. Equation (85) gives us the relation

$$E = c^2 m, \tag{86}$$

where E is expressed in ergs and m in grams; hence, taking the velocity of light as 3×10^{10} centimeters per second, we shall have

$$1 \text{ gram} = 9 \times 10^{20} \text{ ergs.} \tag{87}$$

The enormous number of ergs necessary for increasing the mass of a system to the amount of a single gram makes it evident that experimental proofs of the relation between mass and energy will be hard to find, and outside of the experimental work on electrons at high velocities, already mentioned in Section 64 and the well-known relations between the energy and momentum of a beam of light, such evidence has not yet been forthcoming.

As to the possibility of obtaining further direct experimental evidence of the relation between mass and energy, we certainly cannot look towards thermal experiments with any degree of confidence, since even on cooling a body down to the absolute zero of temperature it loses but an inappreciable fraction of its mass at ordinary temperatures.* In the case of some radioactive processes, however, we may find a transfer of energy large enough to bring about measurable differences in mass. And making use of this point of view we might account for the lack of exact relations between the atomic weights of the successive products of radioactive decomposition.†

---

*It should be noticed that our theory points to the presence of enormous stores of interatomic energy which are still left in substances cooled to the absolute zero.

†See, for example, Comstock, *Philosophical Magazine*, vol. 15, p. 1 (1908).

78. Application to a Specific Problem. We may show an interesting application of our ideas as to the relation between mass and energy, in the treatment of a specific problem. Consider, just as in Section 63, two elastic particles both of which have the mass m_0 at rest, one moving in the X direction with the velocity $+u$ and the other with the velocity $-u$, in such a way that a head-on collision between the particles will occur and they will rebound over their original paths with the respective velocities $-u$ and $+u$ of the same magnitude as before.

Let us now consider how this collision would appear to an observer who is moving past the original system of coördinates with the velocity V in the X direction. To this new observer the particles will be moving before the collision with the respective velocities

$$u_1 = \frac{u - V}{1 - \dfrac{uV}{c^2}} \quad \text{and} \quad u_2 = \frac{-u - V}{1 - \dfrac{uV}{c^2}}, \tag{88}$$

as given by equation (14) for the transformation of velocities. Furthermore, when in the course of the collision the particles have come to relative rest they will obviously be moving past our observer with the velocity $-V$.

Let us see what the masses of the particles will be both before and during the collision. Before the collision, the mass of the first particle will be

$$\frac{m_0}{\sqrt{1 - \dfrac{u_1{}^2}{c^2}}} = \frac{m_0}{\sqrt{1 - \dfrac{\left[\dfrac{u - V}{1 - \frac{uV}{c^2}}\right]^2}{c^2}}} = \frac{m_0\left(1 - \dfrac{uV}{c^2}\right)}{\sqrt{\left(1 - \dfrac{V^2}{c^2}\right)\left(1 - \dfrac{u^2}{c^2}\right)}}$$

and the mass of the second particle will be

$$\frac{m_0}{\sqrt{1 - \dfrac{u_2{}^2}{c^2}}} = \frac{m_0}{\sqrt{1 - \dfrac{\left[\dfrac{-u - V}{1 + \frac{uV}{c^2}}\right]^2}{c^2}}} = \frac{m_0\left(1 + \dfrac{uV}{c^2}\right)}{\sqrt{\left(1 - \dfrac{V^2}{c^2}\right)\left(1 - \dfrac{u^2}{c^2}\right)}}.$$

Adding these two expressions, we obtain for the sum of the masses of the two particles before collision,

$$\frac{2m_0}{\sqrt{\left(1 - \dfrac{V^2}{c^2}\right)\left(1 - \dfrac{u^2}{c^2}\right)}}.$$

Now during the collision, when the two particles have come to relative rest, they will evidently both be moving past our observer with the velocity $-V$ and hence the sum of their masses at the instant of relative rest would appear to be

$$\frac{2m_0}{\sqrt{1 - \dfrac{V^2}{c^2}}},$$

a quantity which is smaller than that which we have just found for the sum of the two masses before the collision occurred. This apparent discrepancy between the total mass of the system before and during the collision, is removed, however, if we realize that when the particles have come to relative rest an amount of potential energy of elastic deformation has been produced, which is just sufficient to restore them to their original velocities, and the mass corresponding to this potential energy will evidently be just sufficient to make the total mass of the system the same as before collision.

In the following chapter on the dynamics of a system of particles we shall make further use of our ideas as to the mass corresponding to potential energy.

CHAPTER VII.

THE DYNAMICS OF A SYSTEM OF PARTICLES.

79. In the preceding chapter we discussed the laws of motion of a particle. With the help of those laws we shall now derive some useful general dynamical principles which describe the motions of a system of particles, and in the following chapter shall consider an application of some of these principles to the kinetic theory of gases.

The general dynamical principles which we shall present in this chapter will be similar *in form* to principles which are already familiar in the classical Newtonian mechanics. Thus we shall deduce principles corresponding to the principles of the conservation of momentum, of the conservation of moment of momentum, of least action and of *vis viva*, as well as the equations of motion in the Lagrangian and Hamiltonian (canonical) forms. For cases where the velocities of all the particles involved are slow compared with that of light, we shall find, moreover, that our principles become identical in content, as well as in form, with the corresponding principles of the classical mechanics. Where high velocities are involved, however, our new principles will differ from those of Newtonian mechanics. In particular we shall find among other differences that in the case of high velocities it will no longer be possible to define the Lagrangian function as the difference between the kinetic and potential energies of the system, nor to define the generalized momenta used in the Hamiltonian equations as the partial differential of the kinetic energy with respect to the generalized velocity.

On the Nature of a System of Particles.

80. Our purpose in this chapter is to treat dynamical systems consisting of a finite number of particles, each obeying the equation of motion which we have already written in the forms,

$$\mathbf{F} = \frac{d}{dt}(m\mathbf{u}) = m\frac{d\mathbf{u}}{dt} + \frac{dm}{dt}\mathbf{u}, \tag{47}$$

$$\mathbf{F} = \frac{d}{dt}\left[\frac{m_0}{\sqrt{1 - \dfrac{u^2}{c}}}\,\mathbf{u}\right] = \frac{m_0}{\sqrt{1 - \dfrac{u^2}{c}}}\frac{d\mathbf{u}}{dt} + \frac{d}{dt}\left[\frac{m_0}{\sqrt{1 - \dfrac{u^2}{c}}}\right]\mathbf{u}. \qquad (59)$$

It is not to be supposed, however, that the total mass of such a system can be taken as located solely in these particles. It is evident rather, since potential energy has mass, that there will in general be mass distributed more or less continuously throughout the space in the neighborhood of the particles. Indeed we have shown at the end of the preceding chapter (Section 78) that unless we take account of the mass corresponding to potential energy we can not maintain the principle of the conservation of mass, and we should also find it impossible to retain the principle of the conservation of momentum unless we included the momentum corresponding to potential energy.

For a continuous distribution of mass we may write for the force acting at any point on the material in a small volume, δV,

$$\mathbf{f}\,\delta V = \frac{d}{dt}(\mathbf{g}\,\delta V), \qquad (47A)$$

where $\mathbf{f}$ is the force per unit volume and $\mathbf{g}$ is the density of momentum. This equation is of course merely an equation of definition for the intensity of force at a point. We shall assume, however, that Newton's third law, that is, the principle of the equality of action and reaction, holds for forces of this type as well as for those acting on particles. In later chapters we shall investigate the way in which $\mathbf{g}$ depends on velocity, state of strain, etc., but for the purposes of this chapter we shall not need any further information as to the nature of the distributed momentum.

Let us proceed to the solution of our specific problems.

The Conservation of Momentum.

81. We may first show from Newton's third law of motion that the momentum of an isolated system of particles remains constant.

Considering a system of particles of masses m_1, m_2, m_3, etc., we may write in accordance with equation (47),

$$\mathbf{F}_1 + \mathbf{I}_1 = \frac{d}{dt}(m_1\mathbf{u}_1),$$

$$\mathbf{F}_2 + \mathbf{I}_2 = \frac{d}{dt}(m_2\mathbf{u}_2), \tag{89}$$

$$\text{etc.,}$$

where $\mathbf{F}_1$, $\mathbf{F}_2$, etc., are the external forces impressed on the individual particles from outside the system and $\mathbf{I}_1$, $\mathbf{I}_2$, etc., are the internal forces arising from mutual reactions within the interior of the system. Considering the distributed mass in the system, we may also write, in accordance with $(47A)$ the further equation

$$(\mathbf{f} + \mathbf{i})\,\delta V = \frac{d}{dt}(\mathbf{g}\,\delta V), \tag{90}$$

where $\mathbf{f}$ and $\mathbf{i}$ are respectively the external and internal forces acting *per unit volume* of the distributed mass. Integrating throughout the whole volume of the system V we have

$$\int (\mathbf{f} + \mathbf{i})\,dV = \frac{d\mathbf{G}}{dt}, \tag{91}$$

where $\mathbf{G}$ is the total distributed momentum in the system. Adding this to our previous equations (89) for the forces acting on the individual particles, we have

$$\sum \mathbf{F}_1 + \sum \mathbf{I}_1 + \int \mathbf{f}\,dV + \int \mathbf{i}\,dV = \frac{d}{dt}\sum m_1 u_1 + \frac{d\mathbf{G}}{dt}.$$

But from Newton's third law of motion (*i.e.*, the principle of the equality of action and reaction) it is evident that the sum of the internal forces, $\sum \mathbf{I}_1 + \int \mathbf{i}\,dV$, which arise from mutual reactions within the system must be equal to zero, which leads to the desired equation of momentum

$$\sum \mathbf{F}_1 + \int \mathbf{f}\, dv = \frac{d}{dt}\left(\sum m_1 u_1 + \mathbf{G}\right). \tag{92}$$

In words this equation states that at any given instant the vector sum of the external forces acting on the system is equal to the rate at which the total momentum of the system is changing.

For the particular case of an isolated system there are no external forces and our equation becomes a statement of the principle of the *conservation of momentum*.

The Equation of Angular Momentum.

82. We may next obtain an equation for the moment of momentum of a system about a point. Consider a particle of mass m_1 and velocity u_1. Let $\mathbf{r}_1$ be the radius vector from any given point of reference to the particle. Then for the moment of momentum of the particle about the point we may write

$$\mathbf{M}_1 = \mathbf{r}_1 \times m_1\mathbf{u}_1,$$

and summing up for all the particles of the system we may write

$$\sum \mathbf{M}_1 = \sum(\mathbf{r}_1 \times m_1\mathbf{u}_1). \tag{93}$$

Similarly, for the moment of momentum of the *distributed mass* we may write

$$\mathbf{M}_{\text{dist.}} = \int (\mathbf{r} \times \mathbf{g})\, dV, \tag{94}$$

where $\mathbf{r}$ is the radius vector from our chosen point of reference to a point in space where the density of momentum is $\mathbf{g}$ and the integration is to be taken throughout the whole volume, V, of the system.

Adding these two equations (93) and (94), we obtain for the total amount of momentum of the system about our chosen point

$$\mathbf{M} = \sum(\mathbf{r}_1 \times m_1\mathbf{u}_1) + \int (\mathbf{r} \times \mathbf{g})\, dV;$$

and differentiating with respect to the time we have, for the rate of change of the moment of momentum,

$$\frac{d\mathbf{M}}{dt} = \Sigma \left\{ \mathbf{r}_1 \times \frac{d}{dt}(m_1 \mathbf{u}_1) \right\} + \Sigma \left(\frac{d\mathbf{r}_1}{dt} \times m_1 \mathbf{u}_1 \right)$$
$$+ \int \left(\mathbf{r} \times \frac{d\mathbf{g}}{dt} \right) dV + \int \left(\frac{d\mathbf{r}}{dt} \times \mathbf{g} \right) dV;$$

or, making the substitutions given by equations (89) and (90), and writing $\dfrac{d\mathbf{r}_1}{dt} = \mathbf{u}_1$, etc., we have

$$\frac{d\mathbf{M}}{dt} = \Sigma(\mathbf{r}_1 \times \mathbf{F}_1) + \Sigma(\mathbf{r}_1 \times \mathbf{I}_1) + \Sigma(\mathbf{u}_1 \times m_1 \mathbf{u}_1)$$
$$+ \int (\mathbf{r} \times \mathbf{f}) \, dV + \int (\mathbf{r} \times \mathbf{i}) \, dV + \int (\mathbf{u} \times \mathbf{g}) \, dV.$$

To simplify this equation we may note that the third term is equal to zero because it contains the outer product of a vector by itself. Furthermore, if we accept the principle of the equality of action and reaction, together with the further requirement that forces are not only equal and opposite but that their points of application be in the same straight line, we may put the moment of all the internal forces equal to zero and thus eliminate the second and fifth terms. We obtain as the equation of angular momentum

$$\frac{d\mathbf{M}}{dt} = \Sigma(\mathbf{r}_1 \times \mathbf{F}_1) + \int (\mathbf{r} \times \mathbf{f}) \, dV + \int (\mathbf{u} \times \mathbf{g}) \, dV. \qquad (95)$$

We may call attention to the inclusion in this equation of the interesting term $\int (\mathbf{u} \times \mathbf{g}) \, dV$. If density of momentum and velocity should always be in the same direction this term would vanish, since the outer product of a vector by itself is equal to zero. In our consideration of the "Dynamics of Elastic Bodies," however, we shall find bodies with a component of momentum at right angles to their direction of motion and hence must include this term in a general treatment. For a completely isolated system it can be shown, however, that this term vanishes along with the external forces and we then have the principle of the *conservation of moment of momentum.*

The Function T.

83. We may now proceed to the definition of a function which will be needed in our treatment of the principle of least action.

One of the most valuable properties of the Newtonian expression, $\frac{1}{2}m_0u^2$, for kinetic energy was the fact that its derivative with respect to velocity is evidently the Newtonian expression for momentum, m_0u. It is not true, however, that the derivative of our new expression for kinetic energy (see Section 73), $m_0c^2\left[\dfrac{1}{\sqrt{1-\dfrac{u^2}{c^2}}}-1\right]$, with respect to velocity is equal to momentum, and for that reason in our non-Newtonian mechanics we shall find it desirable to define a new function, T, by the equation,

$$T = m_0c^2\left(1 - \sqrt{1 - \frac{u^2}{c^2}}\right). \tag{96}$$

For slow velocities (*i.e.*, small values of u) this reduces to the Newtonian expression for kinetic energy and at all velocities we have the relation,

$$\frac{dT}{du} = -m_0c^2\frac{d}{du}\sqrt{1 - \frac{u^2}{c^2}} = \frac{m_0u}{\sqrt{1 - \dfrac{u^2}{c^2}}} = mu, \tag{97}$$

showing that the differential of T with respect to velocity is momentum.

For a system of particles we shall define T as the summation of the values for the individual particles:

$$T = \sum m_0 c^2 \left(1 - \sqrt{1 - \frac{u^2}{c^2}} \right). \tag{98}$$

The Modified Lagrangian Function.

84. In the older mechanics the Lagrangian function for a system of particles was defined as the difference between the kinetic and potential energies of the system. The value of the definition rested, however, on the fact that the differential of the kinetic energy with respect to velocity was equal to momentum, so that we shall now find it advisable to define the Lagrangian function with the help of our new function T in accordance with the equation

$$L = T - U. \tag{99}$$

The Principle of Least Action.

85. We are now in a position to derive a principle corresponding to that of least action in the older mechanics. Consider the path by which our dynamical system actually moves from state (1) to state (2). The motion of any particle in the system of mass m will be governed by the equation

$$\mathbf{F} = \frac{d}{dt}(m\mathbf{u}). \tag{100}$$

Let us now compare the actual path by which the system moves from state (1) to state (2) with a slightly displaced path in which the laws of motion are not obeyed, and let the displacement of the particle at the instant in question be $\delta\mathbf{r}$.

Let us take the inner product of both sides of equation (100) with $\delta\mathbf{r}$; we have

$$
\begin{aligned}
\mathbf{F} \cdot \delta\mathbf{r} &= \frac{d}{dt}(m\mathbf{u}) \cdot \delta\mathbf{r} \\
&= \frac{d}{dt}(m\mathbf{u} \cdot \delta\mathbf{r}) - m\mathbf{u} \cdot \frac{d\,\delta\mathbf{r}}{dt} \\
&= \frac{d}{dt}(m\mathbf{u} \cdot \delta\mathbf{r}) - m\mathbf{u} \cdot \delta\mathbf{u}) \\
(m\mathbf{u} \cdot \delta\mathbf{u} &+ \mathbf{F} \cdot \delta\mathbf{r})\,dt = d(m\mathbf{u} \cdot \delta\mathbf{r}).
\end{aligned}
$$

Summing up for all the particles of the system and integrating between the limits t_1 and t_2, we have

$$
\int_{t_1}^{t_2} \left(\sum m\mathbf{u} \cdot \delta\mathbf{u} + \sum \mathbf{F} \cdot \delta\mathbf{r} \right) dt = \left[\sum m\mathbf{u} \cdot \delta\mathbf{r} \right]_{t_1}^{t_2}.
$$

Since t_1 and t_2 are the times when the actual and displaced motions coincide, we have at these times $\delta\mathbf{r} = 0$; furthermore we also have $\mathbf{u} \cdot \delta\mathbf{u} = u\,\delta u$, so that we may write

$$
\int_{t_1}^{t_2} \left(\sum m u\,\delta u + \mathbf{F} \cdot \delta\mathbf{r} \right) dt = 0.
$$

With the help of equation (97), however, we see that $\sum m u\,\delta u = \delta T$, giving us

$$
\int_{t_1}^{t_2} (\delta T + \mathbf{F} \cdot \delta r)\,dt = 0. \tag{101}
$$

If the forces F are conservative, we may write $\mathbf{F} \cdot \delta r = -\delta U$, where δU is the difference between the potential energies of the displaced and the actual configurations. This gives us

$$
\delta \int_{t_1}^{t_2} (T - U)\,dt = 0
$$

or

$$\delta \int_{t_1}^{t_2} L \, dt = 0, \tag{102}$$

which is the modified principle of least action. The principle evidently requires that for the actual path by which the system goes from state (1) to state (2), the quantity $\int_{t_1}^{t_2} L \, dt$ shall be a minimum (or maximum).

Lagrange's Equations.

86. We may now derive the Lagrangian equations of motion from the above principle of least action. Let us suppose that the position of each particle of the system under consideration is completely determined by n *independent* generalized coördinates $\phi_1,\ \phi_2,\ \phi_3 \cdots \phi_n$ and hence that L is some function of $\phi_1,\ \phi_2,\ \phi_3 \cdots \phi_n,\ \dot{\phi}_1,\ \dot{\phi}_2,\ \dot{\phi}_3 \cdots \dot{\phi}_n,$ where for simplicity we have put $\dot{\phi}_1 = \dfrac{d\phi_1}{dt},\ \dot{\phi}_2 = \dfrac{d\phi_2}{dt}$, etc.

From equation (102) we have

$$\int_{t_1}^{t_2} (\delta L) \, dt = \int_{t_1}^{t_2} \left(\sum_{1}^{n} \frac{\partial L}{\partial \phi_i} \delta\phi_i + \sum_{1}^{n} \frac{\partial L}{\partial \dot{\phi}_i} \delta\dot{\phi}_i \right) dt = 0. \tag{103}$$

But

$$\delta\dot{\phi}_i = \frac{d}{dt}(\delta\phi_i),$$

which gives us

$$\int_{t_1}^{t_2} \frac{\partial L}{\partial \dot{\phi}_i} \delta\dot{\phi}_i \, dt = \int_{t_1}^{t_2} \frac{\partial L}{\partial \dot{\phi}_i} \frac{d}{dt}(\delta\phi_i) \, dt$$

$$= \left[\frac{\partial L}{\partial \dot{\phi}_i} \delta\phi_i \right]_{t_1}^{t_2} - \int_{t_1}^{t_2} \delta\phi_i \frac{d}{dt}\left(\frac{\partial L}{\partial \dot{\phi}_i} \right) dt$$

or, since at times t_1 and t_2, $\delta\phi_i$ is zero, the first term in this expression disappears and on substituting in equation (103) we obtain

$$\int_{t_1}^{t_2} \left[\sum_{1}^{n} \delta\phi_i \left\{ \frac{\partial L}{\partial \phi_i} - \frac{d}{dt}\left(\frac{\partial L}{\partial \dot{\phi}_i} \right) \right\} \right] dt = 0.$$

Since, however, the limits t_1 and t_2 are entirely at our disposal we must have at every instant

$$\sum_1^n \delta\phi_i \left\{ \frac{\partial L}{\partial \phi_i} - \frac{d}{dt}\left(\frac{\partial L}{\partial \dot\phi_i}\right) \right\} = 0.$$

Finally, moreover, since the ϕ's are independent parameters, we can assign perfectly arbitrary values to $\delta\phi_1$, $\delta\phi_2$, etc., and hence must have the series of equations

$$\frac{d}{dt}\left(\frac{\partial L}{\partial \dot\phi_1}\right) - \frac{\partial L}{\partial \phi_1} = 0,$$

$$\frac{d}{dt}\left(\frac{\partial L}{\partial \dot\phi_2}\right) - \frac{\partial L}{\partial \phi_2} = 0, \qquad (104)$$

etc.

These correspond to Lagrange's equations in the older mechanics, differing only in the definition of L.

Equations of Motion in the Hamiltonian Form.

87. We shall also find it desirable to obtain equations of motion in the Hamiltonian or canonical form.

Let us define the *generalized momentum* ψ_i corresponding to the coördinate ϕ_i by the equation,

$$\psi_i = \frac{\partial T}{\partial \dot\phi_i}. \qquad (105)$$

It should be noted that the generalized momentum is not as in ordinary mechanics the derivative of the kinetic energy with respect to the generalized velocity but approaches that value at low velocities.

Consider now a function T' defined by the equation

$$T' = \psi_1 \dot\phi_1 + \psi_2 \dot\phi_2 + \cdots - T. \qquad (106)$$

Differentiating we have

$$dT' = \psi_1 \, d\dot{\phi}_1 + \psi_2 \, d\dot{\phi}_2 + \cdots$$
$$+ \dot{\phi}_1 \, d\psi_1 + \dot{\phi}_2 \, d\psi_2 + \cdots$$
$$- \frac{\partial T}{\partial \phi_1} \, d\phi_1 - \frac{\partial T}{\partial \phi_2} \, d\phi_2 - \cdots$$
$$- \frac{\partial T}{\partial \dot{\phi}_1} \, d\dot{\phi}_1 - \frac{\partial T}{\partial \dot{\phi}_2} \, d\dot{\phi}_2 - \cdots ,$$

and this, by the introduction of (105), becomes

$$dT' = \dot{\phi}_1 \, d\psi_1 + \dot{\phi}_2 \, d\psi_2 + \cdots - \frac{\partial T}{\partial \phi_1} \, d\phi_1 - \frac{\partial T}{\partial \phi_2} \, d\phi_2 - \cdots . \tag{107}$$

Examining this equation we have

$$\frac{\partial T'}{\partial \phi_i} = -\frac{\partial T}{\partial \phi_i}, \tag{108}$$

$$\frac{\partial T'}{\partial \psi_i} = \dot{\phi}_i. \tag{109}$$

In Lagrange's equations we have

$$\frac{d}{dt}\left\{ \frac{\partial}{\partial \dot{\phi}_i}(T - U) \right\} - \frac{\partial}{\partial \phi_i}(T - U) = 0.$$

But since U is independent of $\dot{\psi}_i$ we may write

$$\frac{\partial (T - U)}{\partial \dot{\phi}_i} = \frac{\partial T}{\partial \dot{\phi}_i} = \psi_i,$$

and furthermore by (108),

$$\frac{\partial T}{\partial \phi_i} = -\frac{\partial T'}{\partial \phi_i}.$$

Substituting these two expressions in Lagrange's equations we obtain

$$\frac{d\psi_i}{dt} = -\frac{\partial(T'+U)}{\partial\phi_i}$$

or, writing $T' + U = E$, we have

$$\frac{d\psi_i}{dt} = -\frac{\partial E}{\partial\phi_i} \tag{110}$$

and since U is independent of ψ_i we may rewrite equation (109) in the form

$$\frac{d\phi_i}{dt} = \frac{\partial E}{\partial\psi_i}. \tag{111}$$

The set of equations corresponding to (110) and (111) for all the coördinates ϕ_1, ϕ_2, $\phi_3, \cdots \phi_n$ and the momenta ψ_1, ψ_2, $\psi_3, \cdots \psi_n$ are the desired equations of motion in the canonical form.

88. Value of the Function T'. We have given the symbol E to the quantity $T' + U$, since T' actually turns out to be identical with the expression by which we defined kinetic energy, thus making $E = T' + U$ the sum of the kinetic and potential energies of the system.

To show that T' is equal to K, the kinetic energy, we have by the equation of definition (106)

$$T' = \phi_1\psi_1 + \phi_2\psi_2 + \cdots - T,$$
$$= \phi_1\frac{\partial T}{\partial\dot\phi_1} + \phi_2\frac{\partial T}{\partial\dot\phi_2} + \cdots - T.$$

But T by definition, equation (98), is

$$T = \sum c^2 m_0\left(1 - \sqrt{1 - \frac{u^2}{c^2}}\right),$$

which gives us

$$\frac{\partial T}{\partial \dot{\phi}_i} = \sum m_0 \left(1 - \frac{u^2}{c^2}\right)^{-1/2} u \frac{\partial u}{\partial \dot{\phi}_i}$$

$$= \sum m u \frac{\partial u}{\partial \dot{\phi}_i}$$

and substituting we obtain

$$T' = \dot{\phi}_1 \sum m u \frac{\partial u}{\partial \dot{\phi}_1} + \dot{\phi}_2 \sum m u \frac{\partial u}{\partial \dot{\phi}_2} + \cdots - T$$

$$= \sum m u \left\{ \dot{\phi}_1 \frac{\partial u}{\partial \dot{\phi}_1} + \dot{\phi}_2 \frac{\partial u}{\partial \dot{\phi}_2} + \cdots \right\} - T. \tag{112}$$

We can show, however, that the term in parenthesis is equal to u. If the coördinates x, y, z determine the position of the particle in question, we have,

$$x = f(\phi_1 \phi_2 \phi_3 \cdots \phi_n),$$

$$\dot{x} = \frac{dx}{dt} = \dot{\phi}_1 \frac{\partial f(\ )}{\partial \phi_1} + \dot{\phi}_2 \frac{\partial f(\ )}{\partial \phi_2} + \dot{\phi}_3 \frac{\partial f(\ )}{\partial \phi_3} + \cdots$$

and differentiating with respect to the $\dot{\phi}$'s, we obtain,

$$\frac{\partial \dot{x}}{\partial \dot{\phi}_1} = \frac{\partial f(\ )}{\partial \phi_1} = \frac{\partial x}{\partial \phi_1}, \quad \frac{\partial \dot{x}}{\partial \dot{\phi}_2} = \frac{\partial x}{\partial \phi_2}, \quad \frac{\partial \dot{x}}{\partial \dot{\phi}_3} = \frac{\partial x}{\partial \phi_3}, \quad \text{etc.}$$

Similarly

$$\frac{\partial \dot{y}}{\partial \dot{\phi}_1} = \frac{\partial y}{\partial \phi_1}, \quad \frac{\partial \dot{y}}{\partial \dot{\phi}_2} = \frac{\partial y}{\partial \phi_2}, \quad \text{etc.,}$$

$$\frac{\partial \dot{z}}{\partial \dot{\phi}_1} = \frac{\partial z}{\partial \phi_1}, \quad \frac{\partial \dot{z}}{\partial \dot{\phi}_2} = \frac{\partial z}{\partial \phi_2}, \quad \text{etc.,}$$

Let us write now

$$u = \sqrt{\dot{x}^2 + \dot{y}^2 + \dot{z}^2},$$

$$\frac{\partial u}{\partial \dot{\phi}_i} = \frac{1}{\sqrt{\dot{x}^2 + \dot{y}^2 + \dot{z}^2}}\left(\dot{x}\,\frac{\partial \dot{x}}{\partial \dot{\phi}_i} + \dot{y}\,\frac{\partial \dot{y}}{\partial \dot{\phi}_i} + \dot{z}\,\frac{\partial \dot{z}}{\partial \dot{\phi}_i}\right),$$

or making the substitutions for $\dfrac{\partial \dot{x}}{\partial \dot{\phi}_i}, \dfrac{\partial \dot{y}}{\partial \dot{\phi}_i}$, etc., given above, we have,

$$\frac{\partial u}{\partial \dot{\phi}_i} = \frac{1}{u}\left(\dot{x}\,\frac{\partial x}{\partial \phi_i} + \dot{y}\,\frac{\partial y}{\partial \phi_i} + \dot{z}\,\frac{\partial z}{\partial \phi_i}\right).$$

Substituting now in (112) we shall obtain,

$$T' = \sum mu\left\{\frac{\dot{x}}{u}\left(\phi_1 \frac{\partial x}{\partial \phi_1} + \phi_2 \frac{\partial x}{\partial \phi_2} + \cdots\right) + \frac{\dot{y}}{u}\left(\phi_1 \frac{\partial y}{\partial \phi_1} + \phi_2 \frac{\partial y}{\partial \phi_2} + \cdots\right)\right.$$

$$\left.+ \frac{\dot{z}}{u}\left(\phi_1 \frac{\partial z}{\partial \phi_1} + \phi_2 \frac{\partial z}{\partial \phi_2} + \cdots\right)\right\} - T$$

$$= \sum mu^2 - T$$

or, introducing the value of T given by equation (98), we have

$$T' = \sum \frac{m_0}{\sqrt{1 - \dfrac{u^2}{c^2}}}\left\{u^2 - c^2\sqrt{1 - \frac{u^2}{c^2}} + c^2\left(1 - \frac{u^2}{c^2}\right)\right\}$$

$$= \sum c^2(m - m_0),$$

which is the expression (83) for kinetic energy.

Hence we see that the Hamiltonian function $E = T' + U$ is the sum of the kinetic and potential energies of the system as in Newtonian mechanics.

The Principle of the Conservation of Energy.

89. We may now make use of our equations of motion in the canonical form to show that the total energy of a system of interacting particles remains constant. If such were not the case it is obvious that our definitions of potential and kinetic energy would not be very useful.

Since $E = T' + U$ is a function of ϕ_1, ϕ_2, ϕ_3, $\cdots$ ψ_1, ψ_2, ψ_3, $\cdots$, we may write

$$\frac{dE}{dt} = \frac{\partial E}{\partial \phi_1}\dot{\phi}_1 + \frac{\partial E}{\partial \phi_2}\dot{\phi}_2 + \cdots$$
$$+ \frac{\partial E}{\partial \psi_1}\dot{\psi}_1 + \frac{\partial E}{\partial \psi_2}\dot{\psi}_2 + \cdots .$$

Substituting the values of $\dfrac{\partial E}{\partial \phi_1}$, $\dfrac{\partial E}{\partial \psi_1}$, etc., given by the canonical equations of motion (110) and (111), we have

$$\frac{dE}{dt} = -\dot{\psi}_1\dot{\phi}_1 - \dot{\psi}_2\dot{\phi}_2 - \cdots$$
$$+ \dot{\psi}_1\dot{\phi}_1 + \dot{\psi}_2\dot{\phi}_2 + \cdots$$
$$= 0,$$

which gives us the desired proof that just as in the older Newtonian mechanics the total energy of an isolated system of particles is a conservative quantity.

On the Location of Energy in Space.

90. This proof of the conservation of energy in a system of interacting particles justifies us in the belief that the concept of energy will not fail to retain in the newer mechanics the position of great importance which it gradually acquired in the older systems of physical theory. Indeed, our newer considerations have augmented the important rôle of energy by adding to its properties the attribute of mass or inertia, and thus leading to the further belief that matter and energy are in reality different names for the same fundamental entity.

The importance of this entity, energy, makes it very interesting to consider the possibility of ascribing a definite location in space to any given quantity of energy. In the older mechanics we had a hazy notion that the kinetic energy of a moving body was probably located in some way in the moving body itself, and possibly a vague idea that the potential energy of a raised weight might be located in the space between the weight and the earth. Our discovery of the relation between mass and energy has made it possible, however, to give a much more definite, although not a complete, answer to inquiries of this kind.

In our discussions of the dynamics of a particle (Chapter VI, Section 61) we saw that an acceptance of Newton's principle of the equality of action and reaction forced us to ascribe an increased mass to a moving particle over that which it has at rest. This increase in the mass of the moving particle is necessarily located either in the particle itself or distributed in the surrounding space in such a way that its center of mass always coincides with the position of the particle, and since the kinetic energy of the particle is the energy corresponding to this increased mass we may say that *the kinetic energy of a moving particle is so distributed in space that its center of mass always coincides with the position of the particle.*

If now we consider the transformation of kinetic energy into potential energy we can also draw somewhat definite conclusions as to the location of potential energy. By the principle of the conservation of mass we shall be able to say that the mass of any potential energy formed is just equal to the "kinetic" mass which has disappeared, and by the principle of the conservation of momentum we can say that the velocity of this potential energy is just that necessary to keep the total momentum of the system constant. Such considerations will often permit us to reach a good idea as to the location of potential energy.

Consider, for example, a pair of similar attracting particles which are moving apart from each other with the velocities $+u$ and $-u$ and are gradually coming to rest under the action of their mutual attraction, their kinetic energy thus being gradually changed into potential energy. Since the total momentum of the system must always remain zero, we may think of the potential energy which is formed as left stationary in the space between the two particles.

CHAPTER VIII.

THE CHAOTIC MOTION OF A SYSTEM OF PARTICLES.

The discussions of the previous chapter have placed at our disposal generalized equations of motion for a system of particles similar in form to those familiar in the classical mechanics, and differing only in the definition of the Lagrangian function. With the help of these equations it is possible to carry out investigations parallel to those already developed in the classical mechanics, and in the present chapter we shall discuss the chaotic motion of a system of particles. This problem has received much attention in the classical mechanics because of the close relations between the theoretical behavior of such an ideal system of particles and the actual behavior of a monatomic gas. We shall find no more difficulty in handling the problem than was experienced in the older mechanics, and our results will of course reduce to those of Newtonian mechanics in the case of slow velocities. Thus we shall find a distribution law for momenta which reduces to that of Maxwell for slow velocities, and an equipartition law for the average value of a function which at low velocities becomes identical with the kinetic energy of the particles.

91. The Equations of Motion. It has been shown that the Hamiltonian equations of motion

$$\frac{\partial E}{\partial \phi_1} = -\frac{d\psi_1}{dt} = -\dot{\psi}_1,$$

$$\frac{\partial E}{\partial \psi_1} = \frac{d\phi_1}{dt} = \dot{\phi}_1, \tag{113}$$

etc.,

will hold in relativity mechanics provided we define the generalized momenta ψ_1, ψ_2, etc., *not* as the differential of the kinetic energy with respect to the generalized velocities $\dot{\phi}_1$, $\dot{\phi}_2$, etc., but as the differential with respect to $\dot{\phi}_1$, $\dot{\phi}_2$, etc., of a function

$$T = \sum m_0 c^2 \left(1 - \sqrt{1 - \frac{u^2}{c^2}} \right),$$

where m_0 is the mass of a particle having the velocity u and the summation $\sum$ extends over all the particles of the system.

92. Representation in Generalized Space. Consider now a system defined by the n generalized coördinates ϕ_1, ϕ_2, $\phi_3, \cdots, \phi_n$, and the corresponding momenta ψ_1, ψ_2, $\psi_3, \cdots, \psi_n$. Employing the methods so successfully used by Jeans,[*] we may think of the state of the system at any instant as determined by the position of a point plotted in a $2n$-dimensional space. Suppose now we had a large number of systems of the same structure but differing in state, then for each system we should have at any instant a corresponding point in our $2n$-dimensional space, and as the systems changed their state, in the manner required by the laws of motion, the points would describe stream lines in this space.

93. Liouville's Theorem. Suppose now that the points were originally distributed in the generalized space with the uniform density ρ. Then it can be shown by familiar methods that, just as in the classical mechanics, the density of distribution remains uniform.

Take, for example, some particular cubical element of our generalized space $d\phi_1\, d\phi_2\, d\phi_3 \ldots d\psi_1\, d\psi_2\, d\psi_3 \ldots$. The density of distribution will evidently remain uniform if the number of points entering any such cube per second is equal to the number leaving. Consider now the two parallel bounding surfaces of the cube which are perpendicular to the ϕ_1 axis, one cutting the axis at the point ϕ_1 and the other at the point $\phi_1 + d\phi_1$. The area of each of these surfaces is $d\phi_2\, d\phi_3 \ldots d\psi_1\, d\psi_2\, d\psi_3 \ldots$, and hence, if $\dot{\phi}_1$ is the component of velocity which the points have parallel to the ϕ_1 axis, and $\dfrac{\partial \dot{\phi}_1}{\partial \phi_1}$ is the rate at

---

[*]Jeans, *The Dynamical Theory of Gases*, Cambridge, 1916.

which this component is changing as we move along the axis, we may obviously write the following expression for the difference between the number of points leaving and entering per second through these two parallel surfaces

$$\rho \left[\left(\frac{\partial \dot{\phi}_1}{\partial \phi_1} \right) d\phi_1 \right] d\phi_2 \, d\phi_3 \ldots d\psi_1 \, d\psi_2 \, d\psi_3 \cdots = \rho \frac{\partial \dot{\phi}_1}{\partial \phi_1} \, dV.$$

Finally, considering all the pairs of parallel bounding surfaces, we find for the total decrease per second in the contents of the element

$$\rho \left(\frac{\partial \dot{\phi}_1}{\partial \phi_1} + \frac{\partial \dot{\phi}_2}{\partial \phi_2} + \frac{\partial \dot{\phi}_3}{\partial \phi_3} + \cdots + \frac{\partial \dot{\psi}_1}{\partial \psi_1} + \frac{\partial \dot{\psi}_2}{\partial \psi_2} + \frac{\partial \dot{\psi}_3}{\partial \psi_3} + \cdots \right) dV.$$

But the motions of the points are necessarily governed by the Hamiltonian equations (113) given above, and these obviously lead to the relations

$$\frac{\partial \dot{\phi}_1}{\partial \phi_1} + \frac{\partial \dot{\psi}_1}{\partial \psi_1} = 0,$$

$$\frac{\partial \dot{\phi}_2}{\partial \phi_2} + \frac{\partial \dot{\psi}_2}{\partial \psi_2} = 0,$$

etc.

So that our expression for the change per second in the number of points in the cube becomes equal to zero, the necessary requirement for preserving uniform density.

This maintenance of a uniform distribution means that there is no tendency for the points to crowd into any particular region of the generalized space, and hence if we start some one system going and plot its state in our generalized space, we may *assume* that, after an indefinite lapse of time, the point is equally likely to be in any one of the little elements dV. *In other words, the different states of a system, which we* *can specify by stating the region $d\phi_1\,d\phi_2\,d\phi_3\ldots d\psi_1\,d\psi_2\,d\psi_3\ldots$ in which the values of the coördinates and momenta of the system fall, are all equally likely to occur.*[*]

94. A System of Particles. Consider now a system containing N_a particles which have the mass m_a when at rest, N_b particles which have the mass m_b, N_c particles which have the mass m_c, etc. If at any given instant we specify the particular differential element $dx\,dy\,dz\,d\psi_x\,d\psi_y\,d\psi_z$ which contains the coördinates x, y, z, and the corresponding momenta ψ_x, ψ_y, ψ_z for *each* particle, we shall thereby completely determine what Planck[†] has well called the *microscopic* state of the system, and by the previous paragraph any microscopic state of the system in which we thus specify the six-dimensional position of each particle is just as likely to occur as any other microscopic state.

It must be noticed, however, that many of the possible microscopic states which are determined by specifying the six-dimensional position of each individual particle are in reality completely identical, since if all the particles having a given mass m_a are alike among themselves, it makes no difference which particular one of the various available identical particles we pick out to put into a specified range $dx\,dy\,dz\,d\psi_x\,d\psi_y\,d\psi_z$.

For this reason we shall usually be interested in specifying the *statistical* state[‡] of the system, for which purpose we shall merely state the number of particles of a given kind which have coördinates falling in a given range $dx\,dy\,dz\,d\psi_x\,d\psi_y\,d\psi_z$. We see that corresponding to any given statistical state there will be in general a large number of microscopic states.

---

[*]The criterion here used for determining whether or not the states are equally liable to occur is obviously a necessary requirement, although it is not so evident that it is a sufficient requirement for equal probability.

[†]Planck, *Wärmestrahlung*, Leipzig, 1913.

[‡]What we have here defined as the *statistical* state is what Planck calls the *macroscopic* state of the system. The word macroscopic is unfortunate, however, in implying a less minute observation as to the size of the elements $dx\,dy\,dz\,d\psi_x\,d\psi_y\,d\psi_z$ in which the representative points are found.

95. Probability of a Given Statistical State. We shall now be particularly interested in the probability that the system of particles will actually be in some specified *statistical* state, and since Liouville's theorem has justified our belief that all *microscopic* states are equally likely to occur, we see that the probability of a given statistical state will be proportional to the number of microscopic states which correspond to it.

For the system under consideration let a particular statistical state be specified by stating that $N_a{}'$, $N_a{}''$, $N_a{}'''$, $\cdots$, $N_b{}'$, $N_b{}''$, $N_b{}'''$, $\cdots$, etc., are the number of particles of the corresponding masses m_a, m_b, etc., which fall in the specified elementary regions $dx\,dy\,dz\,d\psi_x\,d\psi_y\,d\psi_z$, Nos. $1a$, $2a$, $3a$, $\cdots$, $1b$, $2b$, $3b$, $\cdots$, etc. By familiar methods of calculation it is evident that the number of arrangements by which the particular distribution of particles can be effected, that is, in other words, the number of microscopic states, W, which correspond to the given statistical state, is given by the expression

$$W = \frac{N_a!\,N_b!\,N_c!\,\cdots}{N_a{}'!\,N_a{}''!\,N_a{}'''!\,\cdots\,N_b{}'!\,N_b{}''!\,N_b{}'''!\,\cdots}$$

and this number W is proportional to the probability that the system will be found in the particular statistical state considered.

If now we assume that each of the regions

$$dx\,dy\,dz\,d\psi_x\,d\psi_y\,d\psi_z, \quad \text{Nos. } 1a,\ 2a,\ 3a,\ \cdots,\ 1b,\ 2b,\ 3b,\ \cdots \text{ etc.}$$

is great enough to contain a large number of particles,* we may apply the Stirling formula

$$N! = \sqrt{2\pi N}\left(\frac{N}{\epsilon}\right)^{N}$$

---

*The idea of successive orders of infinitesimals which permit the differential region $dx\,dy\,dz\,d\psi_x\,d\psi_y\,d\psi_z$, to contain a large number of particles is a familiar one in mathematics.

for evaluating $N_a!$, $N_b!$, etc., and omitting negligible terms, shall obtain for $\log W$ the result

$$\log W = -N_a \left(\frac{N_a{}'}{N_a} \log \frac{N_a{}'}{N_a} + \frac{N_a{}''}{N_a} \log \frac{N_a{}''}{N_a} + \frac{N_a{}'''}{N_a} \log \frac{N_a{}'''}{N_a} + \cdots \right)$$

$$- N_b \left(\frac{N_b{}'}{N_b} \log \frac{N_b{}'}{N_b} + \frac{N_b{}''}{N_b} \log \frac{N_b{}''}{N_b} + \frac{N_b{}'''}{N_b} \log \frac{N_b{}'''}{N_b} + \cdots \right),$$

etc.

For simplicity let us denote the ratios $\dfrac{N_a{}'}{N_a}$, $\dfrac{N_a{}''}{N_a}$, etc., by the symbols $w_a{}'$, $w_a{}''$, etc. These quantities $w_a{}'$, $w_a{}''$, etc., are evidently the probabilities, in the case of this particular statistical state, that any given particle m_a will be found in the respective regions Nos. $1a$, $2a$, etc.

We may now write

$$\log W = -N_a \sum w_a \log w_a - N_b \sum w_b \log w_b - , \quad \text{etc.,}$$

where the summation extends over all the regions Nos. $1a$, $2a$, $\cdots 1b$, $2b$, etc.

96. Equilibrium Relations. Let us now suppose that the system of particles is contained in an enclosed space and has the definite energy content E. Let us find the most probable distribution of the particles. For this the necessary condition will be

$$\delta \log W = -N_a \sum (\log w_a + 1)\, \delta w_a$$

$$- N_b \sum (\log w_b + 1)\, \delta w_b \cdots = 0. \quad (114)$$

In carrying out our variation, however, the number of particles of each kind must remain constant so that we have the added relations

$$\sum \delta w_a = 0, \qquad \sum \delta w_b = 0, \qquad \text{etc.} \quad (115)$$

Finally, since the energy is to have a definite value E, it must also remain constant in the variation, which will provide still a further relation. Since the energy of a particle will be a definite function of its position and momentum,* let us write the energy of the system in the form

$$E = N_a \sum w_a E_a + N_b \sum w_b E_b + \cdots ,$$

where E_a is the energy of a particle in the region $1a$, etc.

Since in carrying out our variation the energy is to remain constant, we have the relation

$$E = N_a \sum E_a \, \delta w_a + N_b \sum E_b \, \delta w_b + \cdots = 0. \tag{116}$$

Solving the simultaneous equations (114), (115), (116) by familiar methods we obtain

$$\log w_a + 1 + \lambda E_a + \mu_b = 0,$$
$$\log w_b + 1 + \lambda E_b + \mu_b = 0,$$
$$\text{etc.,}$$

where λ, μ_a, μ_b, etc., are undetermined constants. (It should be specially noticed that λ is the same constant in each of the series of equations.)

Transforming we have

$$w_a = \alpha_a \, e^{-hE_a},$$
$$w_b = \alpha_b \, e^{-hE_b}, \tag{117}$$
$$\text{etc.,}$$

as the expressions which determine the chance that a given particle of mass m_a, m_b, etc., will fall in a given region $dx\,dy\,dz\,d\psi_x\,d\psi_y\,d\psi_z$, when we have the distribution of maximum probability. It should be noticed that h, which corresponds to the λ of the preceding equations, is the same constant in all of the equations, while α_a, α_b, etc., are different constants, depending on the mass of the particles m_a, m_b, etc.

---

*We thus exclude from our considerations systems in which the potential energy depends appreciably on the *relative* positions of the independent particles.

97. The Energy as a Function of the Momentum. E_a, E_b, etc., are of course functions of x, y, z, ψ_x, ψ_y, ψ_z. Let us now obtain an expression for E_a in terms of these quantities. If there is no external field of force acting, the energy of a particle E_a will be independent of x, y, and z, and will be determined entirely by its velocity and mass. In accordance with the theory of relativity we shall have*

$$E_a = \frac{m_a c^2}{\sqrt{1 - \dfrac{u^2}{c^2}}}, \tag{118}$$

where m_a is the mass of the particle at rest.

Let us now express E_a as a function of ψ_x, ψ_y, ψ_z.

We have from our equations (105) and (98), which were used for defining momentum

$$\begin{aligned}
\psi_x &= \frac{\partial}{\partial \dot{x}} m_a \left(1 - \sqrt{1 - \frac{u^2}{c^2}} \right) \\
&= \frac{\partial}{\partial \dot{x}} m_a \left(1 - \sqrt{1 - \frac{\dot{x}^2 + \dot{y}^2 + \dot{z}^2}{c^2}} \right) \\
&= \frac{m_0 \dot{x}}{\sqrt{1 - \dfrac{u^2}{c^2}}}.
\end{aligned}$$

---

*This expression is that for the total energy of the particle, including that internal energy $m_0 c^2$ which, according to relativity theory, the particle has when it is at rest. (See Section 75.) It would be just as correct to substitute for E_a in equation (117) the value of the kinetic energy $m_a c^2 \left(\dfrac{1}{\sqrt{1 - \dfrac{u^2}{c^2}}} - 1 \right)$ instead of the total energy $\dfrac{m_a c^2}{\sqrt{1 - \dfrac{u^2}{c^2}}}$, since the two differ merely by a constant $m_a c^2$ which would be taken care of by assigning a suitable value to α_a.

Constructing the similar expressions for ψ_y and ψ_z we may write the relation

$$\psi^2 = \psi_x^2 + \psi_y^2 + \psi_z^2 = \frac{m_a^2(\dot{x}^2 + \dot{y}^2 + \dot{z}^2)}{1 - \dfrac{u^2}{c^2}} = \frac{m_a^2 u^2}{1 - \dfrac{u^2}{c^2}}, \qquad (119)$$

which also defines ψ^2.

By simple transformations and the introduction of equation (118) we obtain the desired relation

$$E_a = c\sqrt{\psi^2 + m_a{}^2 c^2}. \qquad (120)$$

98. The Distribution Law. We may now rewrite equations (117) in the form

$$w_a = \alpha_a \, e^{-hc\sqrt{\psi^2 + m_a{}^2 c^2}},$$

$$w_b = \alpha_b \, e^{-hc\sqrt{\psi^2 + m_b{}^2 c^2}}, \qquad (121)$$

etc.

These expressions determine the probability that a given particle of mass m_a, m_b, etc., will fall in a given region $dx\,dy\,dz\,d\psi_x\,d\psi_y\,d\psi_z$, and correspond to Maxwell's distribution law in ordinary mechanics. We see that these probabilities are independent of the position x, y, z^* but dependent on the momentum.

$\alpha_a \, e^{-hc\sqrt{\psi^2 + m_a{}^2 c^2}}$ is the probability that a given particle will fall in a particular six-dimensional cube of volume $dx\,dy\,dz\,d\psi_x\,d\psi_y\,d\psi_z$. Let us now introduce, for convenience, a new quantity $a_a \, e^{-hc\sqrt{\psi^2 + m_a{}^2 c^2}}$ which will be the probability per *unit* volume that a given particle will have the six dimensional location in question, the constants α_a and a_a standing in the same ratio as the volumes $dx\,dy\,dz\,d\psi_x\,d\psi_y\,d\psi_z$ and unity.

---

*This is true only when, as assumed, no external field of force is acting.

We may then write

$$w_a = \alpha_a\, e^{-hc\sqrt{\psi^2+m_a{}^2c^2}} = a_a\, e^{-hc\sqrt{\psi^2+m_a{}^2c^2}}\, dx\, dy\, dz\, d\psi_x\, d\psi_y\, d\psi_z$$

$$w_b = \alpha_b\, e^{-hc\sqrt{\psi^2+m_b{}^2c^2}} = a_b\, e^{-hc\sqrt{\psi^2+m_b{}^2c^2}}\, dx\, dy\, dz\, d\psi_x\, d\psi_y\, d\psi_z$$

etc.

Since every particle must have components of momentum lying between minus and plus infinity, and lie somewhere in the whole volume V occupied by the mixture, we have the relation

$$V \int_{-\infty}^{+\infty} \int_{-\infty}^{+\infty} \int_{-\infty}^{+\infty} a_a\, e^{-hc\sqrt{\psi^2+m_a{}^2c^2}}\, d\psi_x\, d\psi_y\, d\psi_z = 1. \qquad (122)$$

It is further evident that the average value of any quantity A which depends on the momentum of the particles is given by the expression

$$[A]_{\text{av.}} = V \int_{-\infty}^{+\infty} \int_{-\infty}^{+\infty} \int_{-\infty}^{+\infty} a_a\, e^{-hc\sqrt{\psi^2+m_a{}^2c^2}}\, A\, d\psi_x\, d\psi_y\, d\psi_z, \qquad (123)$$

where A is some function of ψ_x, ψ_y, and ψ_z.

99. Polar Coördinates. We may express relations corresponding to (122) and (123) more simply if we make use of polar coördinates. Consider instead of the elementary volume $d\psi_x\, d\psi_y\, d\psi_z$ the volume $\psi^2 \sin\theta\, d\theta\, d\phi\, d\psi$ expressed in polar coördinates, where

$$\psi^2 = \psi_x{}^2 + \psi_y{}^2 + \psi_z{}^2.$$

The probability that a particle m_a will fall in the region

$$dx\, dy\, dz\, \psi^2 \sin\theta\, d\theta\, d\phi\, d\psi$$

will be

$$a_a\, e^{-hc\sqrt{\psi^2+m_a{}^2c^2}}\, dx\, dy\, dz\, \psi^2 \sin\theta\, d\theta\, d\phi\, d\psi,$$

and since each particle must fall somewhere in the space $x\,y\,z\,\psi_x\,\psi_y\,\psi_z$ we shall have corresponding to (122) the relation

$$V \int_0^\pi \int_0^{2\pi} \int_0^\infty a_a\, e^{-hc\sqrt{\psi^2+m_a{}^2c^2}}\, \psi^2 \sin\theta\, d\theta\, d\phi\, d\psi = 1,$$

$$4\pi V \int_0^\infty a_a\, e^{-hc\sqrt{\psi^2+m_a{}^2c^2}}\, \psi^2\, d\psi = 1. \tag{124}$$

Corresponding to equation (123), we also see that the average value of any quantity A, which is dependent on the momentum of the molecules of mass m_a, will be given by the expression

$$[A]_{\text{av.}} = 4\pi V \int_0^\infty a_a\, e^{-hc\sqrt{\psi^2+m_a{}^2c^2}}\, A\, \psi^2\, d\psi. \tag{125}$$

100. The Law of Equipartition. We may now obtain a law which corresponds to that of the equipartition of *vis viva* in the classical mechanics. Considering equation (124) let us integrate by parts, we obtain

$$\left[4\pi V a_a\, e^{-hc\sqrt{\psi^2+m_a{}^2c^2}}\, \frac{\psi^3}{3} \right]_{\psi=0}^{\psi=\infty}$$

$$- 4\pi V \int_0^\infty \frac{\psi^3}{3}\, a_a\, e^{-hc\sqrt{\psi^2+m_a{}^2c^2}}\, (-hc)\, \frac{\psi}{\sqrt{\psi^2+m_a{}^2c^2}}\, d\psi = 1.$$

Substituting the limits into the first term we find that it becomes zero and may write

$$4\pi V \int_0^\infty a_a\, e^{-hc\sqrt{\psi^2+m_a{}^2c^2}}\, \frac{\psi^2 c}{\sqrt{\psi^2+m_a{}^2c^2}}\, \psi^2\, d\psi = \frac{3}{h}.$$

But by equation (125) the left-hand side of this relation is the average value of $\dfrac{\psi^2 c}{\sqrt{\psi^2+m_a{}^2c^2}}$ for the particles of mass m_a. We have

$$\left[\frac{\psi^2 c}{\sqrt{\psi^2+m_a{}^2c^2}} \right]_{\text{av.}} = \frac{3}{h}.$$

Introducing equation (119) which defines ψ^2, we may transform this expression into

$$\left[\frac{m_a u^2}{\sqrt{1-\dfrac{u^2}{c^2}}}\right]_{\text{av.}} = \frac{3}{h}. \tag{126}$$

Since we have shown that h is independent of the mass of the parti-cles, *we see that the average value of* $\dfrac{m_0 u^2}{\sqrt{1-\dfrac{u^2}{c^2}}}$ *is the same for particles of all different masses.* This is the principle in relativity mechanics that corresponds to the law of the equipartition of *vis viva* in the classical mechanics. Indeed, for low velocities the above expression reduces to $m_0 u^2$, the *vis viva* of Newtonian mechanics, a fact which affords an illustration of the general principle that the laws of Newtonian mechanics are always the limiting form assumed at low velocities by the more exact formulations of relativity mechanics.

We may now call attention in passing to the fact that this quantity $\dfrac{m_0 u^2}{\sqrt{1-\dfrac{u^2}{c^2}}}$, whose value is the same for particles of different masses, is not the relativity expression for kinetic energy, which is given rather by the formula $c^2\left[\dfrac{m_0}{\sqrt{1-\dfrac{u^2}{c^2}}}-m_0\right]$. So that in relativity mechanics the principle of the equipartition of energy is merely an approximation. We shall later return to this subject.

101. Criterion for Equality of Temperature. For a system of particles of masses m_a, m_b, etc., enclosed in the volume V, and having the definite energy content E, we have shown that

$$4\pi V\, a_a\, e^{-hc\sqrt{\psi^2 + m_a^2 c^2}}\, \psi^2\, d\psi$$

and

$$4\pi V\, a_b\, e^{-hc\sqrt{\psi^2 + m_b{}^2 c^2}}\, \psi^2\, d\psi$$

are the respective probabilities that given particles of mass m_a or mass m_b will have momenta between ψ and $\psi + d\psi$. Suppose now we consider a differently arranged system in which we have N_a particles of mass m_a by themselves in a space of volume V_a and N_b particles of mass m_b in a contiguous space of volume V_b, separated from V_a by a partition which permits a transfer of energy, and let the total energy of the double system be, as before, a definite quantity E (the energy content of the partition being taken as negligible). Then, by reasoning entirely similar to that just employed, we can obviously show that

$$4\pi V_a\, a_a\, e^{-hc\sqrt{\psi^2 + m_a{}^2 c^2}}\, \psi^2\, d\psi$$

and

$$4\pi V_b\, a_b\, e^{-hc\sqrt{\psi^2 + m_b{}^2 c^2}}\, \psi^2\, d\psi$$

are now the respective probabilities that given particles of mass m_a or mass m_b will have momenta between ψ and $\psi + d\psi$, the only changes in the expressions being the substitution of the volumes V_a and V_b in the place of the one volume V. Furthermore, this distribution law will evidently lead as before to the equality of the average values of

$$\frac{m_a u^2}{\sqrt{1 - \dfrac{u^2}{c^2}}} \quad \text{and} \quad \frac{m_b u^2}{\sqrt{1 - \dfrac{u^2}{c^2}}}.$$

Since, however, the spaces containing the two kinds of particles are in thermal contact, their temperature is the same. Hence we find that *the equality of the average values of* $\dfrac{m_0 u^2}{\sqrt{1 - \dfrac{u^2}{c^2}}}$ *is the necessary condition for equality of temperature.*

The above distribution law also leads to the important corollary that for any given system of particles at a definite temperature the momenta and hence the total energy content is independent of the volume.

We may now proceed to the derivation of relations which will permit us to show that the important quantity $\dfrac{m_0 u^2}{\sqrt{1 - \dfrac{u^2}{c^2}}}$ is directly proportional to the temperature as measured on the absolute thermodynamic temperature scale.

102. Pressure Exerted by a System of Particles. We first need to obtain an expression for the pressure exerted by a system of N particles enclosed in the volume V. Consider an element of surface dS perpendicular to the X axis, and let the pressure acting on it be p. The total force which the element dS exerts on the particles that impinge will be $p\,dS$, and this will be equal to the rate of change of the momenta in the X direction of these particles.*

Now by equation (122) the total number of particles having momenta between ψ_x and $\psi_x + d\psi_x$ in the *positive* direction is

$$NV \int_{\psi_x}^{\psi_x + d\psi_x} \int_{-\infty}^{+\infty} \int_{-\infty}^{+\infty} a\, e^{-hc\sqrt{\psi^2 + m_0^2 c^2}}\, d\psi_x\, d\psi_y\, d\psi_z.$$

But $\dot{x}\,dS$ gives us the volume which contains the number of particles having momenta between ψ_x and $\psi_x + d\psi_x$ which will reach dS in a second. Hence the number of such particles which impinge per second will be

$$NV \frac{\dot{x}\,dS}{V} \int_{\psi_x}^{\psi_x + d\psi_x} \int_{-\infty}^{+\infty} \int_{-\infty}^{+\infty} a\, e^{-hc\sqrt{\psi^2 + m_0^2 c^2}}\, d\psi_x\, d\psi_y\, d\psi_z.$$

and their change in momentum, allowing for the effect of the rebound,

---

*The system is considered dilute enough for the mutual attractions of the particles to be negligible in their effect on the external pressure.

will be

$$2N\,dS \int_{\psi_x}^{\psi_x+d\psi_x} \int_{-\infty}^{+\infty} \int_{-\infty}^{+\infty} a\,e^{-hc\sqrt{\psi^2+m_0^2c^2}}\,\psi_x\,\dot{x}\,d\psi_x\,d\psi_y\,d\psi_z.$$

Finally, the total change in momentum per second for all particles can be found by integrating for all possible positive values of ψ_x. Equating this to the total force $p\,dS$ we have

$$p\,dS = 2N\,dS \int_0^\infty \int_{-\infty}^{+\infty} \int_{-\infty}^{+\infty} a\,e^{-hc\sqrt{\psi^2+m_0^2c^2}}\,\psi_x\,\dot{x}\,d\psi_x\,d\psi_y\,d\psi_z.$$

Cancelling dS, multiplying both sides of the equation by the volume V, changing the limits of integration and substituting $\dfrac{m_0\dot{x}}{\sqrt{1+\dfrac{u^2}{c^2}}}$ for ψ_x, we have

$$pV = NV \int_{-\infty}^{+\infty} \int_{-\infty}^{+\infty} \int_{-\infty}^{+\infty} a\,e^{-hc\sqrt{\psi^2+m_0^2c^2}}\,\frac{m_0\dot{x}^2}{\sqrt{1-\dfrac{u^2}{c^2}}}\,d\psi_x\,d\psi_y\,d\psi_z.$$

But this by equation (123) reduces to

$$pV = N\left[\frac{m_0\dot{x}^2}{\sqrt{1-\dfrac{u^2}{c^2}}}\right]_{\text{av.}}$$

or, since

$$\frac{m_0u^2}{\sqrt{1-\dfrac{u^2}{c^2}}} = \frac{m_0\dot{x}^2}{\sqrt{1-\dfrac{u^2}{c^2}}} + \frac{m_0\dot{y}^2}{\sqrt{1-\dfrac{u^2}{c^2}}} + \frac{m_0\dot{z}^2}{\sqrt{1-\dfrac{u^2}{c^2}}},$$

we have from symmetry

$$pV = \frac{N}{3}\left[\frac{m_0u^2}{\sqrt{1-\dfrac{u^2}{c^2}}}\right]_{\text{av.}} \tag{127}$$

Since at a given temperature we have seen that the term in parenthesis is independent of the volume and the nature of the particles, we see that the laws of Boyle and Avogadro hold also in relativity mechanics for a system of particles.

For slow velocities equation (127) reduces to the familiar expression

$$pV = \frac{N}{3}\,(m_0 u^2)_{av.}.$$

103. The Relativity Expression for Temperature. We are now in a position to derive the relativity expression for temperature. The thermodynamic scale of temperature may be defined in terms of the efficiency of a heat engine. Consider a four-step cycle performed with a working substance contained in a cylinder provided with a piston. In the first step let the substance expand isothermally and reversibly, absorbing the heat Q_2 from a reservoir at temperature T_2; in the second step cool the cylinder down at constant volume to T_1; in the third step compress to the original volume, giving out the heat Q_1 at temperature T_1, and in the fourth step heat to the original temperature. Now if the working substance is of such a nature that the heat given out in the second step could be used for the *reversible* heating of the cylinder in the fourth step, we may define the absolute temperatures T_2 and T_1 by the relation $\dfrac{T_2}{T_1} = \dfrac{Q_2}{Q_1}.$*

Consider now such a cycle performed on a cylinder which contains one of our systems of particles. Since we have shown (Section 101) that at a definite temperature the energy content of such a system is independent of the volume, it is evident that our working substance fulfils the requirement that the heat given out in the second step shall be sufficient for the reversible heating in the last step. Hence, in accordance with the thermodynamic scale, we may measure the temperatures of the two heat reservoirs by the relation $\dfrac{T_2}{T_1} = \dfrac{Q_2}{Q_1}$ and may proceed to

---

*We have used this cycle for defining the thermodynamic temperature scale instead of the familiar Carnot cycle, since it avoids the necessity of obtaining an expression for the relation between pressure and volume in an adiabatic expansion.

obtain expressions for Q_2 and Q_1.

In order to obtain these expressions we may again make use of the principle that the energy content at a definite temperature is independent of the volume. This being true, we see that Q_2 and Q_1 must be equal to the work done in the changes of volume that take place respectively at T_2 and T_1, and we may write the relations

$$Q_2 = \int_V^{V'} p\, dV \quad (\text{at } T_2),$$

$$Q_1 = \int_V^{V'} p\, dV \quad (\text{at } T_1).$$

But equation (127) provides an expression for p in terms of V, leading on integration to the relations

$$Q_2 = \frac{N}{3}\left[\frac{m_0 u_2{}^2}{\sqrt{1 - \frac{u_2{}^2}{c^2}}}\right]_{\text{av.}} \log\frac{V'}{V},$$

$$Q_1 = \frac{N}{3}\left[\frac{m_0 u_1{}^2}{\sqrt{1 - \frac{u_1{}^2}{c^2}}}\right]_{\text{av.}} \log\frac{V'}{V},$$

which gives us on division

$$\frac{T_2}{T_1} = \frac{Q_2}{Q_1} = \frac{\left[\dfrac{m_0 u_2{}^2}{\sqrt{1 - \frac{u_2{}^2}{c^2}}}\right]_{\text{av.}}}{\left[\dfrac{m_0 u_1{}^2}{\sqrt{1 - \frac{u_1{}^2}{c^2}}}\right]_{\text{av.}}}.$$

We see that the absolute temperature measured on the thermodynamic scale is proportional to the average value of $\dfrac{m_0 u^2}{\sqrt{1 - \frac{u^2}{c^2}}}$.

We may finally express our temperature in the same units customarily employed by comparing equation (127)

$$pV = \frac{N}{3}\left[\frac{m_0 u^2}{\sqrt{1 - \dfrac{u^2}{c^2}}}\right]_{av.},$$

with the ordinary form of the gas law

$$pV = nRT,$$

where n is the number of mols of gas present.

We evidently obtain

$$nRT = \frac{N}{3}\left[\frac{m_0 u^2}{\sqrt{1 - \dfrac{u^2}{c^2}}}\right]_{av.},$$

$$T = \frac{N}{3nR}\left[\frac{m_0 u^2}{\sqrt{1 - \dfrac{u^2}{c^2}}}\right]_{av.} = \frac{1}{3k}\left[\frac{m_0 u^2}{\sqrt{1 - \dfrac{u^2}{c^2}}}\right]_{av.},$$

$$(128)$$

where the quantity $\dfrac{nR}{N}$, which may be called the gas constant for a single molecule, has been denoted, as is customary, by the letter k.

Remembering the relation $\left[\dfrac{m_0 \dot{x}^2}{\sqrt{1 - \dfrac{u^2}{c^2}}}\right]_{av.} = \dfrac{3}{h}$, we have

$$kT = \frac{1}{h}. \qquad (129)$$

104. The Partition of Energy. We have seen that our new equipartition law precludes the possibility of an exact equipartition of energy. It becomes very important to see what the average energy of a particle of a given mass does become at any temperature.

Equation (125) provides a general expression for the average value of any property of the particles. For the average value of the energy $c\sqrt{\psi^2 + m_0{}^2c^2}$ of particles of mass m_0 (see equation 120) we shall have

$$[E]_{\text{av.}} = 4\pi V \int_0^\infty a\, e^{-hc\sqrt{\psi^2 + m_0{}^2c^2}}\, c\,\sqrt{\psi^2 + m_0{}^2c^2}\; \psi^2\, d\psi.$$

The unknown constant a may be eliminated with the help of the relation (124)

$$4\pi V \int_0^\infty a\, e^{-hc\sqrt{\psi^2 + m_0{}^2c^2}}\, \psi^2\, d\psi = 1$$

and for h we may substitute the value given by (129), which gives us the desired equation

$$[E]_{\text{av.}} = \frac{\displaystyle\int_0^\infty e^{-(c/kT)\sqrt{\psi^2 + m_0{}^2c^2}}\, c\,\sqrt{\psi^2 + m_0{}^2c^2}\; \psi^2\, d\psi}{\displaystyle\int_0^\infty e^{-(c/kT)\sqrt{\psi^2 + m_0{}^2c^2}}\, \psi^2\, d\psi}. \tag{130}$$

105. Partition of Energy for Zero Mass. Unfortunately, no general method for the evaluation of this expression seems to be available. For the particular case that the mass m_0 of the particles approaches zero compared to the momentum, the expression reduces to

$$[E]_{\text{av.}} = \frac{c\displaystyle\int_0^\infty e^{-(c\psi/kT)}\, \psi^3\, d\psi}{\displaystyle\int_0^\infty e^{-(c\psi/kT)}\, \psi^2\, d\psi}$$

in terms of integrals whose values are known. Evaluating, we obtain

$$[E]_{\text{av.}} = 3kT.$$

For the total energy of N such particles we obtain

$$E = 3NkT,$$

and introducing the relation $k = \dfrac{nR}{N}$ by which we defined k we have

$$E = 3nRT \tag{131}$$

as the expression for the energy of n mols of particles if their value of m_0 is small compared with their momentum.

It is instructive to compare this with the ordinary expression of Newtonian mechanics

$$E = \frac{3}{2} nRT,$$

which undoubtedly holds when the masses are so large and the velocities so small that no appreciable deviations from the laws of Newtonian mechanics are to be expected. We see that for particles of very small mass the average kinetic energy at any temperature is twice as large as that for large particles at the same temperature. It is also interesting to note that in accordance with equation (131) a mol of particles which approach zero mass at the absolute zero, would have a mass of

$$\frac{3 \times 8.31 \times 10^7 \times 300}{10^{21}} = 7.47 \times 10^{-11}$$

grams at room temperature (300° absolute). This suggests a field of fascinating if profitless speculation.

106. Approximate Partition of Energy for Particles of any Desired Mass. For particles of any desired mass we may obtain an approximate idea of the relation between energy and temperature by expanding the expression for kinetic energy into a series. For the average kinetic energy of a particle we have

$$[K]_{\text{av.}} = c^2 \left[\frac{m_0}{\sqrt{1 - \dfrac{u^2}{c^2}}} - m_0 \right]_{\text{av.}}.$$

Expanding into a series we obtain for the total kinetic energy of N particles

$$K = Nm_0 \left(\frac{1}{2}\mathbf{u}^2 + \frac{3}{8}\frac{\mathbf{u}^4}{c^2} + \frac{15}{48}\frac{\mathbf{u}^6}{c^4} + \frac{105}{384}\frac{\mathbf{u}^8}{c^6} + \cdots \right), \tag{132}$$

where $\mathbf{u}^2$, $\mathbf{u}^4$, etc., are the average values of u^2, u^4, etc., for the individual particles.

To determine approximately how the value of K varies with the temperature we may also expand our expression (128) for temperature,

$$T = \frac{1}{3k}\left[\frac{m_0 u^2}{\sqrt{1 - \dfrac{u^2}{c^2}}}\right]_{\mathrm{Av.}},$$

into a series; we obtain

$$\frac{3}{2}kNT = \frac{3}{2}nRT = Nm_0\left(\frac{1}{2}\mathbf{u}^2 + \frac{1}{4}\frac{\mathbf{u}^4}{c^2} + \frac{3}{16}\frac{\mathbf{u}^6}{c^4} + \frac{15}{96}\frac{\mathbf{u}^8}{c^6} + \cdots\right). \quad (133)$$

Combining expressions (132) and (133) by subtraction and transposition, we obtain

$$K = \frac{3}{2}nRT + Nm_0\left(\frac{1}{8}\frac{\mathbf{u}^4}{c^2} + \frac{1}{8}\frac{\mathbf{u}^6}{c^4} + \frac{15}{128}\frac{\mathbf{u}^8}{c^6} + \cdots\right). \quad (134)$$

For the case of velocities low enough so that $\mathbf{u}^4$ and higher powers can be neglected, this reduces to the familiar expression of Newtonian mechanics, $K = \dfrac{3}{2}nRT$.

In case we neglect in expression (134) powers higher than $\mathbf{u}^4$ we have the approximate relation

$$\frac{Nm_0\mathbf{u}^4}{8c^2} = \frac{1}{2Nm_0c^2}\left(\frac{Nm_0\mathbf{u}^2}{2}\right)^2,$$

the left-hand term really being the larger, since the average square of a quantity is greater than the square of its average. Since $\left(\dfrac{Nm_0\mathbf{u}^2}{2}\right)^2$ is approximately equal to $\left(\dfrac{3}{2}nRT\right)^2$, we may write the approximation

$$K = \frac{3}{2}nRT + \frac{1}{2Nm_0c^2}\left(\frac{3}{2}nRT\right)^2,$$

or, noting that $Nm_0 = M$, the total mass of the system at the absolute zero, we have

$$K = \frac{3}{2} nRT + \frac{9}{8} \frac{n^2 R^2}{Mc^2} T^2.$$

If we use the erg as our unit of energy, R will be 8.31×10^7; expressing velocities in centimeters per second, c^2 will be 10^{21}, and M will be the mass of the system in grams.

For one mol of a monatomic gas we should have in ergs

$$K = 12.4 \times 10^7 T + \frac{7.77}{M} 10^{-6} T^2.$$

In the case of the electron M may be taken as approximately $1/1800$. At room temperature the second term of our equation would be entirely negligible, being only 3.5×10^{-6} per cent of the first, and still be only 3.5×10^{-4} per cent in a fixed star having a temperature of $30,000°$. Hence at all ordinary temperatures we may expect the law of the equipartition of energy to be substantially exact for particles of mass as small as the electron.

Our purpose in carrying through the calculations of this chapter has been to show that a very important and interesting problem in the classical mechanics can be handled just as easily in the newer mechanics, and also to point out the nature of the modifications in existing theory which will have to be introduced if the later developments of physics should force us to consider equilibrium relations for particles of mass much smaller than that of the electron.

We may also call attention to the fact that we have here considered a system whose equations of motion agree with the principles of dynamics and yet do not lead to the equipartition of energy. This is of particular interest at a time when many scientists have thought that the failure of equipartition in the hohlraum stood in necessary conflict with the principles of dynamics.

CHAPTER IX.

THE PRINCIPLE OF RELATIVITY AND THE PRINCIPLE OF LEAST ACTION.

It has been shown by the work of Helmholtz, J. J. Thomson, Planck and others that the principle of least action is applicable in the most diverse fields of physical science, and is perhaps the most general dynamical principle at our disposal. Indeed, for any system whose future behavior is determined by the instantaneous values of a number of coördinates and their time rate of change, it seems possible to throw the equations describing the behavior of the system into the form prescribed by the principle of least action. This generality of the principle of least action makes it very desirable to develop the relation between it and the principle of relativity, and we shall obtain in this way the most important and most general method for deriving the consequences of the theory of relativity. We have already developed in Chapter VII the particular application of the principle of least action in the case of a system of particles, and with the help of the more general development which we are about to present, we shall be able to apply the principle of relativity to the theories of elasticity, of thermodynamics and of electricity and magnetism.

107. The Principle of Least Action. For our purposes the principle of least action may be most simply stated by the equation

$$\int_{t_1}^{t_2} (\delta H + W)\, dt = 0. \tag{135}$$

This equation applies to any system whose behavior is determined by the values of a number of independent coördinates $\phi_1 \phi_2 \phi_3 \cdots$ and their rate of change with the time $\dot{\phi}_1 \dot{\phi}_2 \dot{\phi}_3 \cdots$, and the equation describes the path by which the system travels from its configuration at any time t_1 to its configuration at any subsequent time t_2.

H is the so-called kinetic potential of the system and is a function of the coördinates and their generalized velocities:

$$H = F(\phi_1 \phi_2 \phi_3 \cdots \dot\phi_1 \dot\phi_2 \dot\phi_3 \cdots). \tag{136}$$

δH is the variation of H at any instant corresponding to a slightly displaced path by which the system might travel from the same initial to the same final state in the same time interval, and W is the external work corresponding to the variation δ which would be done on the system by the external forces if at the instant in question the system should be displaced from its actual configuration to its configuration on the displaced path. Thus

$$W = \Phi_1 \, \delta\phi_1 + \Phi_2 \, \delta\phi_2 + \Phi_3 \, \delta\phi_3 + \cdots , \tag{137}$$

where Φ_1, Φ_2, etc., are the so-called generalized external forces which act in such a direction as to increase the values of the corresponding coördinates.

The form of the function which determines the kinetic potential H depends on the particular nature of the system to which the principle of least action is being applied, and it is one of the chief tasks of general physics to discover the form of the function in the various fields of mechanical, electrical and thermodynamic investigation. As soon as we have found out experimentally what the form of H is for any particular field of investigation, the principle of least action, as expressed by equation (135), becomes the basic equation for the mathematical development of the field in question, a development which can then be carried out by well-known methods.

The special task for the theory of relativity will be to find a general relation applicable to any kind of a system, which shall connect the value of the kinetic potential H as measured with respect to a set of coördinates S with its value H' as measured with reference to another set of coördinates S' which is in motion relative to S. This relation will of course be of such a nature as to agree with the principle of the relativity of motion, and in this way we shall introduce the principle of relativity at the very start into the fundamental equation for all fields of dynamics.

Before proceeding to the solution of that problem we may put the principle of least action into another form which is sometimes more convenient, by obtaining the equations for the motion of a system in the so-called Lagrangian form.

108. The Equations of Motion in the Lagrangian Form. To obtain the equations of motion in the Lagrangian form we may evidently rewrite our fundamental equation (135) in the form

$$\int_{t_1}^{t_2} \left(\frac{\partial H}{\partial \phi_1} \delta\phi_1 + \frac{\partial H}{\partial \phi_2} \delta\phi_2 + \cdots + \frac{\partial H}{\partial \dot\phi_1} \delta\dot\phi_1 + \frac{\partial H}{\partial \dot\phi_2} \delta\dot\phi_2 + \cdots \right.$$
$$\left. + \Phi_1 \delta\phi_1 + \Phi_2 \delta\phi_2 + \cdots \right) dt = 0 \tag{138}$$

We have now, however,

$$\delta\dot\phi_1 = \frac{d}{dt}(\delta\phi_1), \qquad \delta\dot\phi_2 = \frac{d}{dt}(\delta\phi_2), \qquad \text{etc.,}$$

which gives us

$$\int_{t_1}^{t_2} \frac{\partial H}{\partial \dot\phi_1} \delta\dot\phi_1 \, dt = \int_{t_1}^{t_2} \frac{\partial H}{\partial \dot\phi_1} \frac{d}{dt}(\delta\phi_1) \, dt$$
$$= \left[\frac{\partial H}{\partial \dot\phi_1} \delta\phi_1 \right]_{t_1}^{t_2} - \int_{t_1}^{t_2} \delta\phi_1 \frac{d}{dt}\left(\frac{\partial H}{\partial \dot\phi_1} \right) dt,$$

or, since $\delta\phi_1$, $\delta\phi_2$, etc., are by hypothesis zero at times t_1 and t_2, we obtain

$$\int_{t_1}^{t_2} \frac{\partial H}{\partial \dot\phi_1} \delta\dot\phi_1 = - \int_{t_1}^{t_2} \frac{d}{dt}\left(\frac{\partial H}{\partial \dot\phi_1} \right) \delta\phi_1 \, dt,$$
$$\int_{t_1}^{t_2} \frac{\partial H}{\partial \dot\phi_2} \delta\dot\phi_2 = - \int_{t_1}^{t_2} \frac{d}{dt}\left(\frac{\partial H}{\partial \dot\phi_2} \right) \delta\phi_2 \, dt,$$

etc.

On substituting these expressions in (138) we obtain

$$\int_{t_1}^{t_2} \left[\left(\frac{\partial H}{\partial \phi_1} - \frac{d}{dt}\left(\frac{\partial H}{\partial \dot{\phi}_1} \right) + \Phi_1 \right) \delta\phi_1 \right.$$
$$\left. + \left(\frac{\partial H}{\partial \phi_2} - \frac{d}{dt}\left(\frac{\partial H}{\partial \dot{\phi}_2} \right) + \Phi_2 \right) \delta\phi_2 + \cdots \right] dt = 0,$$

and since the variations of ϕ_1, ϕ_2, etc., are entirely independent and the limits of integration t_1 and t_2 are entirely at our disposal, this equation will be true only when each of the following equations is true. And these are the equations of motion in the desired Lagrangian form,

$$\frac{d}{dt}\frac{\partial H}{\partial \dot{\phi}_1} - \frac{\partial H}{\partial \phi_1} = \Phi_1,$$
$$\frac{d}{dt}\frac{\partial H}{\partial \dot{\phi}_2} - \frac{\partial H}{\partial \phi_2} = \Phi_2, \tag{139}$$

etc.

In these equations H is the kinetic potential of a system whose state is determined by the generalized coördinates ϕ_1, ϕ_2, etc., and their time derivatives $\dot{\phi}_1$, $\dot{\phi}_2$ etc., where Φ_1, Φ_2, etc., are the generalized external forces acting on the system in such a sense as to tend to *increase* the values of the corresponding generalized coördinates.

109. Introduction of the Principle of Relativity. Let us now investigate the relation between our dynamical principle and the principle of the relativity of motion. To do this we must derive an equation for transforming the kinetic potential H for a given system from one set of coördinates to another. In other words, if S and S' are two sets of reference axes, S' moving past S in the X direction with the velocity V, what will be the relation between H and H', the values for the kinetic potential of a given system as measured with reference to S and S'?

It is evident from the theory of relativity that our fundamental equation (135) must hold for the behavior of a given system using either set of coördinates S or S', so that both of the equations

$$\int_{t_1}^{t_2} (\delta H + W)\,dt = 0 \qquad \text{and} \qquad \int_{t_1'}^{t_2'} (\delta H' + W')\,dt' = 0, \qquad (140)$$

or

$$\int_{t_1}^{t_2} (\delta H + W)\,dt = \int_{t_1'}^{t_2'} (\delta H' + W')\,dt' = 0,$$

must hold for a given process, where it will be necessary, of course, to choose the limits of integration t_1 and t_2, t_1' and t_2' wide enough apart so that for both sets of coördinates the varied motion will be completed within the time interval. Since we shall find it possible now to show that in general $\int W\,dt = \int W'\,dt'$, we shall be able to obtain from the above equations a simple relation between H and H'.

110. Relation between $\int W\,dt$ and $\int W'\,dt'$. To obtain the desired proof we must call attention in the first place to the fact that all kinds of force which can act at a given point must be governed by the same transformation equations when changing from system S to system S'. This arises because when two forces of a different nature are of such a magnitude as to exactly balance each other and produce no acceleration for measurements made with one set of coördinates they must evidently do so for any set of coördinates (see Chapter IV, Section 42). Since we have already found transformation equations for the force acting at a point, in our consideration of the dynamics of a particle, we may now use these expressions in general for the evaluation $\int W'\,dt'$.

W' is the work which would be done by the external forces if at any instant t' we should displace our system from its actual configuration to the simultaneous configuration on the displaced path. Hence it is evident that $\int W'\,dt'$ will be equal to a sum of terms of the type

$$\int (F_x'\,\delta x' + F_y'\,\delta y' + F_z'\,\delta z')\,dt',$$

where F_x', F_y', F_z', is the force acting at a given point of the system and $\delta x'$, $\delta y'$, $\delta z'$ are the displacements necessary to reach the corresponding point on the displaced path, all these quantities being measured with respect to S'.

Into this expression we may substitute, however, in accordance with equations (61), (62), (63) and (13), the values

$$F_x' = F_x - \frac{\dot{y}V}{c^2}\frac{1}{1 - \dfrac{\dot{x}V}{c^2}}F_y - \frac{\dot{z}V}{c^2}\frac{1}{1 - \dfrac{\dot{x}V}{c^2}}F_z,$$

$$F_y' = \frac{F_y \kappa^{-1}}{1 - \dfrac{\dot{x}V}{c^2}},$$

$$F_z' = \frac{F_z \kappa^{-1}}{1 - \dfrac{\dot{x}V}{c^2}},$$

$$dt' = \kappa\left(1 - \frac{\dot{x}V}{c^2}\right)dt. \tag{141}$$

We may also make substitutions for $\delta x'$, $\delta y'$ and $\delta z'$ in terms of δx, δy and δz, but to obtain transformation equations for these quantities is somewhat complicated owing to the fact that positions on the actual and displaced path, which are simultaneous when measured with respect to S', will not be simultaneous with respect to S. We have denoted by t' the time in system S' when the point on the *actual* path has the position x', y', z' and simultaneously the point on the *displaced* path has the position $(x' + \delta x')$, $(y' + \delta y')$, $(z' + \delta z')$, when measured in system S', or by our fundamental transformation equations (9), (10) and (11) the positions $\kappa(x'+Vt')$, y', z' and $\kappa([x'+\delta x']+Vt')$, $(y'+\delta y')$, $(z' + \delta z')$ when measured in system S. If now we denote by t_A and t_D the corresponding times in system S we shall have, by our fundamental transformation equation (12),

$$t_A = \kappa\left(t' + \frac{Vx'}{c^2}\right),$$

$$t_D = \kappa\left(t' + \frac{V}{c^2}[x' + \delta x']\right),$$

and we see that in system S the point has reached the displaced position at a time later than that of the actual position by the amount

$$t_D - t_A = \frac{\kappa V}{c^2}\,\delta x',$$

and, since during this time-interval the displaced point would have moved, neglecting higher-order terms, the distances

$$\dot{x}\,\frac{\kappa V}{c^2}\,\delta x', \qquad \dot{y}\,\frac{\kappa V}{c^2}\,\delta x', \qquad \dot{z}\,\frac{\kappa V}{c^2}\,\delta x',$$

these quantities must be subtracted from the coördinates of the displaced point in order to obtain a position on the displaced path which will be simultaneous with t_A as measured in system S. We obtain for the simultaneous position on the displaced path

$$\kappa\big([x' + \delta x'] + Vt'\big) - \kappa\,\frac{\dot{x}V}{c^2}\,\delta x', \qquad y' + \delta y' - \kappa\,\frac{\dot{x}V}{c^2}\,x',$$

$$z' + \delta z' - \kappa\,\frac{\dot{z}V}{c^2}\,\delta x',$$

and for the corresponding position on the actual path

$$\kappa(x' + Vt'), \quad y', \quad z',$$

and obtain by subtraction

$$\delta x = \kappa\left(1 - \frac{\dot{x}V}{c^2}\right)\delta x',$$

$$\delta y = \delta y' - \kappa\frac{\dot{y}V}{c^2}\,\delta x', \tag{142}$$

$$\delta z = \delta z' - \kappa\frac{\dot{z}V}{c^2}\,\delta x'.$$

Substituting now these equations, together with the other transformation equations (141), in our expression we obtain

$$\int (F_x{}' \, \delta x' + F_y{}' \, \delta y' + F_z{}' \, \delta z') \, dt'$$

$$= \int \left(\left[F_x - \frac{\dot{y}V}{c^2} \frac{F_y}{1 - \frac{\dot{x}V}{c^2}} - \frac{\dot{z}V}{c^2} \frac{F_z}{1 - \frac{\dot{x}V}{c^2}} \right] \frac{\kappa^{-1}}{1 - \frac{\dot{x}V}{c^2}} \, \delta x \right.$$

$$+ \frac{\kappa^{-1}}{1 - \frac{\dot{x}V}{c^2}} F_y \left[\delta y + \frac{\dot{y}V/c^2}{1 - \frac{\dot{x}V}{c^2}} \, \delta x \right] \tag{143}$$

$$+ \left. \frac{\kappa^{-1}}{1 - \frac{\dot{x}V}{c^2}} F_z \left[\delta z + \frac{\dot{z}V/c^2}{1 - \frac{\dot{x}V}{c^2}} \, \delta x \right] \right) \kappa \left(1 - \frac{\dot{x}V}{c^2} \right)$$

$$= \int (F_x \, \delta x + F_y \, \delta y + F_z \, \delta z) \, dt'.$$

We thus see that we must always have the general equality

$$\int W' \, dt' = \int W \, dt. \tag{144}$$

111. Relation between H' and H. Introducing this equation into our earlier expression (140) we obtain as a general relation between H' and H

$$\int \delta H' \, dt' = \int \delta H \, dt. \tag{145}$$

Restricting ourselves to systems of such a nature that we can assign them a definite velocity $u = \dot{x}\mathbf{i} + \dot{y}\mathbf{j} + \dot{z}\mathbf{k}$, we can rewrite this expression in the following form, where by H_D and H_A we denote the values of the kinetic potential respectively on the displaced and actual paths

$$\int \delta H' \, dt' = \int H_D{}' \, dt' - \int H_A{}' \, dt' = \int H_D{}'\kappa \left(1 - \frac{(\dot{x} + \delta\dot{x})V}{c^2} \right) dt$$

$$- \int H_A{}'\kappa \left(1 - \frac{\dot{x}V}{c^2} \right) dt = \int H_D \, dt - \int H_A \, dt,$$

and hence obtain for such systems the simple expression

$$H' = \frac{H}{\kappa \left(1 - \frac{\dot{x}V}{c^2}\right)}.$$

Noting the relation between $\sqrt{1 - \frac{u'^2}{c^2}}$ and $\sqrt{1 - \frac{u^2}{c^2}}$ given in equation (17), this can be rewritten

$$\frac{H'}{\sqrt{1 - \frac{u'^2}{c^2}}} = \frac{H}{\sqrt{1 - \frac{u^2}{c^2}}}, \tag{146}$$

and this is the expression which we shall find most useful for our future development of the consequences of the theory of relativity. Expressing the requirement of the equation in words we may say that the theory of relativity requires an invariance of $\dfrac{H}{\sqrt{1 - \frac{u^2}{c^2}}}$ in the Lorentz transformation.

112. As indicated above, the use of this equation is obviously restricted to systems moving with some perfectly definite velocity $\mathbf{u}$. Systems satisfying this condition would include particles, infinitesimal portions of continuous systems, and larger systems in a steady state.

113. Our general method of procedure in different fields of investigation will now be to examine the expression for kinetic potential which is known to hold for the field in question, provided the velocities involved are low and by making slight alterations when necessary, see if this expression can be made to agree with the requirements of equation (146) without changing its value for low velocities. Thus it is well known, for example, that, in the case of low velocities, for a single particle acted on by external forces the kinetic potential may be taken as the kinetic energy $\frac{1}{2}m_0 u^2$. For relativity mechanics, as will be seen from the developments of Chapter VII, we may take for the kinetic potential, $-m_0c^2\sqrt{1 - \dfrac{u^2}{c^2}}$, an expression which, except for an additive constant, becomes identical with $\frac{1}{2}m_0u^2$ at low velocities, and which at all velocities agrees with equation (146).

CHAPTER X.

THE DYNAMICS OF ELASTIC BODIES.

We shall now treat with the help of the principle of least action the rather complicated problem of the dynamics of continuous elastic media. Our considerations will *extend* the appreciation of the intimate relation between mass and energy which we found in our treatment of the dynamics of a particle. We shall also be able to show that the dynamics of a particle may be regarded as a special case of the dynamics of a continuous elastic medium, and to apply our considerations to a number of other important problems.

114. On the Impossibility of Absolutely Rigid Bodies. In the older treatises on mechanics, after considering the dynamics of a particle it was customary to proceed to a discussion of the dynamics of rigid bodies. These rigid bodies were endowed with definite and unchangeable size and shape and hence were assigned five degrees of freedom, since it was necessary to state the values of five variables completely to specify their position in space. As pointed out by Laue, however, our newer ideas as to the velocity of light as a limiting value will no longer permit us to conceive of a continuous body as having only a finite number of degrees of freedom. This is evident since it is obvious that we could start disturbances simultaneously at an indefinite number of points in a continuous body, and as these disturbances cannot spread with infinite velocity it will be necessary to give the values of an infinite number of variables in order completely to specify the succeeding states of the system. For our newer mechanics the nearest approach to an absolutely rigid body would of course be one in which disturbances are transmitted with the velocity of light. Since, then, the theory of relativity does not permit rigid bodies we may proceed at once to the general theory of deformable bodies.

PART I. STRESS AND STRAIN.

115. Definition of Strain. In the more familiar developments of the theory of elasticity it is customary to limit the considerations to the case of strains small enough so that higher powers of the displacements can be neglected, and this introduces considerable simplification into a science which under any circumstances is necessarily one of great complication. Unfortunately for our purposes, we cannot in general introduce such a simplification if we wish to apply the theory of relativity, since in consequence of the Lorentz shortening a body which appears unstrained to one observer may appear tremendously compressed or elongated to an observer moving with a different velocity. The best that we can do will be arbitrarily to choose our state of zero deformation such that the strains will be small when measured in the particular system of coördinates S in which we are specially interested.

A theory of strains of any magnitude was first attempted by Saint-Venant and has been amplified and excellently presented by Love in his *Treatise on the Theory of Elasticity*, Appendix to Chapter I. In accordance with this theory, the strain at any point in a body is completely determined by six component strains which can be defined by the following equations, wherein (u, v, w) is the displacement of a point having the unstrained position (x, y, z):

$$\epsilon_{xx} = \frac{\partial u}{\partial x} + \tfrac{1}{2}\left\{\left(\frac{\partial u}{\partial x}\right)^2 + \left(\frac{\partial v}{\partial x}\right)^2 + \left(\frac{\partial w}{\partial x}\right)^2\right\},$$

$$\epsilon_{yy} = \frac{\partial y}{\partial v} + \tfrac{1}{2}\left\{\left(\frac{\partial u}{\partial y}\right)^2 + \left(\frac{\partial v}{\partial y}\right)^2 + \left(\frac{\partial w}{\partial y}\right)^2\right\}, \qquad (148)$$

$$\epsilon_{zz} = \frac{\partial w}{\partial z} + \tfrac{1}{2}\left\{\left(\frac{\partial u}{\partial z}\right)^2 + \left(\frac{\partial v}{\partial z}\right)^2 + \left(\frac{\partial w}{\partial z}\right)^2\right\},$$

$$\epsilon_{yz} = \frac{\partial w}{\partial y} + \frac{\partial v}{\partial z} + \frac{\partial u}{\partial y}\frac{\partial u}{\partial z} + \frac{\partial v}{\partial y}\frac{\partial v}{\partial z} + \frac{\partial w}{\partial y}\frac{\partial w}{\partial z},$$

$$\epsilon_{xz} = \frac{\partial w}{\partial x} + \frac{\partial u}{\partial z} + \frac{\partial u}{\partial x}\frac{\partial u}{\partial z} + \frac{\partial v}{\partial x}\frac{\partial v}{\partial z} + \frac{\partial w}{\partial x}\frac{\partial w}{\partial z}, \tag{148}$$

$$\epsilon_{xy} = \frac{\partial v}{\partial x} + \frac{\partial u}{\partial y} + \frac{\partial u}{\partial x}\frac{\partial u}{\partial y} + \frac{\partial v}{\partial x}\frac{\partial v}{\partial y} + \frac{\partial w}{\partial x}\frac{\partial w}{\partial y}.$$

It will be seen that these expressions for strain reduce to those familiar in the theory of small strains if such second-order quantities as $\left(\frac{\partial u}{\partial x}\right)^2$ or $\frac{\partial u}{\partial y}\frac{\partial u}{\partial z}$ can be neglected.

116. A physical significance for these strain components will be obtained if we note that it can be shown from geometrical considerations that lines which are originally parallel to the axes have, when strained, the elongations

$$e_x = \sqrt{1 + 2\epsilon_{xx}} - 1,$$

$$e_y = \sqrt{1 + 2\epsilon_{yy}} - 1, \tag{149}$$

$$e_z = \sqrt{1 + 2\epsilon_{zz}} - 1,$$

and that the angles between lines originally parallel to the axes are given in the strained condition by the expressions

$$\cos\theta_{yz} = \frac{\epsilon_{yz}}{\sqrt{1 + 2\epsilon_{yy}}\,\sqrt{1 + 2\epsilon_{zz}}},$$

$$\cos\theta_{xz} = \frac{\epsilon_{xz}}{\sqrt{1 + 2\epsilon_{xx}}\,\sqrt{1 + 2\epsilon_{zz}}}, \tag{150}$$

$$\cos\theta_{xy} = \frac{\epsilon_{xy}}{\sqrt{1 + 2\epsilon_{xx}}\,\sqrt{1 + 2\epsilon_{yy}}},$$

Geometrical considerations are also sufficient to show that in case the strain is a simple elongation of amount e the following equation will be true:

$$\frac{\epsilon_{xx}}{l^2} = \frac{\epsilon_{yy}}{m^2} = \frac{\epsilon_{zz}}{n^2} = \frac{\epsilon_{yz}}{2mn} = \frac{\epsilon_{xz}}{2ln} = \frac{\epsilon_{xy}}{2lm} = e + \tfrac{1}{2}e^2, \tag{151}$$

where l, m, n are the cosines which determine the direction of the elongation.

117. Definition of Stress. We have just considered the expressions for the strain at a given point in an elastic medium; we may now define stress in terms of the work done in changing from one state of strain to another. Considering the material contained in *unit volume when the body is unstrained*, we may write, for the work done by this material on its surroundings when a change in strain takes place,

$$\delta W = -\delta E = t_{xx}\,\delta\epsilon_{xx} + t_{yy}\,\delta\epsilon_{yy} + t_{zz}\,\delta\epsilon_{zz} \\ + t_{yz}\,\delta\epsilon_{yz} + t_{xz}\,\delta\epsilon_{xz} + t_{xy}\,\delta\epsilon_{xy}, \tag{152}$$

and this equation serves to define the stresses t_{xx}, t_{yy}, etc. In case the strain varies from point to point we must consider of course the work done *per* unit volume of the unstrained material. In case the strains are small it will be noticed that the stresses thus defined are identical with those used in the familiar theories of elasticity.

118. Transformation Equations for Strain. We must now prepare for the introduction of the theory of relativity into our considerations, by determining the way the strain at a given point P appears to observers moving with different velocities. Let the point P in question be moving with the velocity $\mathbf{u} = x\mathbf{i} + y\mathbf{j} + z\mathbf{k}$ as measured in system S. Since the state of zero deformation from which to measure strains can be chosen perfectly arbitrarily, let us for convenience take the strain as zero as measured in system S, giving us

$$\epsilon_{xx} = \epsilon_{yy} = \epsilon_{zz} = \epsilon_{yz} = \epsilon_{xz} = \epsilon_{xy} = 0. \tag{153}$$

What now will be the strains as measured by an observer moving along with the point P in question? Let us call the system of coördinates used by this observer S°. It is evident now from our considerations as to the shape of moving systems presented in Chapter V that in system S° the material in the neighborhood of the point in question will appear to have been elongated in the direction of motion in the ratio of $1 : \sqrt{1 - \dfrac{u^2}{c^2}}$. Hence in system S° the strain will be an elongation

$$e = \frac{1}{\sqrt{1 - \dfrac{u^2}{c^2}}} - 1 \tag{154}$$

in the line determined by the direction cosines

$$l = \frac{\dot{x}}{u}, \qquad m = \frac{\dot{y}}{u}, \qquad n = \frac{\dot{z}}{u}. \tag{155}$$

We may now calculate from this elongation the components of strain by using equation (151). We obtain

$$\epsilon^\circ{}_{xx} = \frac{\dot{x}^2}{2c^2}\left[\frac{1}{1 - \dfrac{u^2}{c^2}}\right], \quad \epsilon^\circ{}_{yy} = \frac{\dot{y}^2}{2c^2}\left[\frac{1}{1 - \dfrac{u^2}{c^2}}\right], \quad \epsilon^\circ{}_{zz} = \frac{\dot{z}^2}{2c^2}\left[\frac{1}{1 - \dfrac{u^2}{c^2}}\right],$$

$$\epsilon^\circ{}_{yz} = \frac{\dot{y}\dot{z}}{c^2}\left[\frac{1}{1 - \dfrac{u^2}{c^2}}\right], \quad \epsilon^\circ{}_{xz} = \frac{\dot{x}\dot{z}}{c^2}\left[\frac{1}{1 - \dfrac{u^2}{c^2}}\right], \quad \epsilon^\circ{}_{xy} = \frac{\dot{x}\dot{y}}{c^2}\left[\frac{1}{1 - \dfrac{u^2}{c^2}}\right], \tag{156}$$

and these are the desired equations for the strains at the point P, the accent $^\circ$ indicating that they are measured with reference to a system of coördinates S° moving along with the point itself.

119. Variation in the Strain. We shall be particularly interested in the variation in the strain as measured in S° when the velocity experiences a small variation $\delta\mathbf{u}$, the strains remaining zero as measured in S. For the sake of simplicity let us choose our coördinates in such a way that the X axis is parallel to the original velocity, so that our change in velocity will be from $\mathbf{u} = \dot{x}\mathbf{i}$ to

$$\mathbf{u} + \delta\mathbf{u} = (\dot{x} + \delta\dot{x})\,\mathbf{i} + \delta\dot{y}\,\mathbf{j} + \delta\dot{z}\,\mathbf{k}.$$

Taking $\delta\mathbf{u}$ small enough so that higher orders can be neglected, and noting that $\dot{y} = \dot{z} = 0$, we shall then have, from equations (156),

$$\delta\epsilon^\circ{}_{xx} = \frac{1}{\left(1 - \dfrac{u^2}{c^2}\right)^2} \frac{\dot{x}}{c^2} \delta\dot{x}, \qquad \delta\epsilon^\circ{}_{yy} = 0,$$

$$\delta\epsilon^\circ{}_{zz} = 0, \qquad\qquad\qquad \delta\epsilon^\circ{}_{yz} = 0, \qquad\qquad (157)$$

$$\delta\epsilon^\circ{}_{xz} = \frac{1}{\left(1 - \dfrac{u^2}{c^2}\right)^2} \frac{\dot{x}}{c^2} \delta\dot{z}, \qquad \delta\epsilon^\circ{}_{xy} = \frac{1}{\left(1 - \dfrac{u^2}{c^2}\right)^2} \frac{\dot{x}}{c^2} \delta\dot{y}.$$

We shall also be interested in the variation in the strain as measured in S° produced by a variation in the strain as measured in S. Considering again for simplicity that the X axis is parallel to the motion of the point, we must calculate the variation produced in $\epsilon^\circ{}_{xx}$, $\epsilon^\circ{}_{yy}$, etc., by changing the values of ϵ_{xx}, ϵ_{yy}, etc., from zero to $\delta\epsilon_{xx}$, $\delta\epsilon_{yy}$, etc.

The variation $\delta\epsilon_{xx}$ will produce a variation in $\epsilon^\circ{}_{xx}$ whose amount can be calculated as follows: By equations (149) a line which has unit length and is parallel to the X axis in the unstrained condition will have when strained the length $\sqrt{1 + 2\epsilon_{xx}}$ when measured in system S and $\sqrt{1 + 2\epsilon^\circ{}_{xx}}$ when measured in system S°. Since the strain in system S is small, the line remains sensibly parallel to the X axis, which is also the direction of motion, and these quantities will be connected in accordance with the Lorentz shortening by the equation

$$\sqrt{1 + 2\epsilon_{xx}} = \sqrt{1 - \frac{u^2}{c^2}} \sqrt{1 + 2\epsilon^\circ{}_{xx}}. \qquad (158)$$

Carrying out now our variation $\delta\epsilon_{xx}$, neglecting ϵ_{xx} in comparison with larger quantities and noting that except for second order quantities,

$$\sqrt{1 + 2\epsilon^\circ{}_{xx}} = \frac{1}{\sqrt{1 - \dfrac{u^2}{c^2}}} \qquad (159)$$

we obtain

$$\delta\epsilon^\circ{}_{xx} = \frac{\delta\epsilon_{xx}}{\left(1 - \dfrac{u^2}{c^2}\right)}. \qquad (160)$$

Since the variations $\delta\epsilon_{yy}$, $\delta\epsilon_{zz}$, $\delta\epsilon_{yz}$ affect only lines which are at right angles to the direction of motion, we may evidently write

$$\delta\epsilon^{\circ}_{yy} = \delta\epsilon_{yy}, \qquad \delta\epsilon^{\circ}_{zz} = \delta\epsilon_{zz}, \qquad \delta\epsilon^{\circ}_{yz} = \delta\epsilon_{yz}. \qquad (161)$$

To calculate $\delta\epsilon^{\circ}_{xz}$ we may note that in accordance with equations (150) we must have

$$\cos\theta_{xz} = \frac{\epsilon_{xz}}{\sqrt{1+2\epsilon_{xx}}\,\sqrt{1+2\epsilon_{zz}}},$$

$$\cos\theta^{\circ}_{xz} = \frac{\epsilon^{\circ}_{xz}}{\sqrt{1+2\epsilon^{\circ}_{xx}}\,\sqrt{1+2\epsilon^{\circ}_{zz}}},$$

where θ_{xz} is the angle between lines which in the unstrained condition are parallel to the X and Z axes respectively. In accordance with the Lorentz shortening, however, we shall have

$$\cos\theta_{xz} = \sqrt{1 - \frac{u^2}{c^2}}\,\cos\theta^{\circ}_{xz}.$$

Introducing this relation, remembering that $\epsilon_{xx} = \epsilon^{\circ}_{zz} = 0$, and noting equation (159), we obtain

$$\delta\epsilon^{\circ}_{xz} = \frac{\delta\epsilon_{xz}}{\left(1 - \dfrac{u^2}{x^2}\right)}, \qquad (162)$$

and similarly

$$\delta\epsilon^{\circ}_{xy} = \frac{\delta\epsilon_{xy}}{\left(1 - \dfrac{u^2}{x^2}\right)}. \qquad (163)$$

We may now combine these equations (160), (161), (162) and (163) with those for the variation in strain with velocity and obtain the final set which we desire:

$$\delta\epsilon^\circ{}_{xx} = \frac{1}{\left(1 - \dfrac{u^2}{c^2}\right)^2} \frac{\dot{x}}{c^2}\,\delta\dot{x} + \frac{1}{\left(1 - \dfrac{u^2}{c^2}\right)}\,\delta\epsilon_{xx},$$

$$\delta\epsilon^\circ{}_{yy} = \delta\epsilon_{yy},$$

$$\delta\epsilon^\circ{}_{zz} = \delta\epsilon_{zz},$$

$$\delta\epsilon^\circ{}_{yz} = \delta\epsilon_{yz}, \tag{164}$$

$$\delta\epsilon^\circ{}_{xz} = \frac{1}{\left(1 - \dfrac{u^2}{c^2}\right)^2} \frac{\dot{x}}{c^2}\,\delta\dot{z} + \frac{1}{\left(1 - \dfrac{u^2}{c^2}\right)}\,\delta\epsilon_{xz},$$

$$\delta\epsilon^\circ{}_{xy} = \frac{1}{\left(1 - \dfrac{u^2}{c^2}\right)^2} \frac{\dot{x}}{c^2}\,\delta\dot{y} + \frac{1}{\left(1 - \dfrac{u^2}{c^2}\right)}\,\delta\epsilon_{xy}.$$

These equations give the variation in the strain measured in system S° at a point P moving in the X direction with velocity u, provided the strains are negligibly small as measured in S.

PART II. INTRODUCTION OF THE PRINCIPLE OF LEAST ACTION.

120. The Kinetic Potential for an Elastic Body. We are now in a position to develop the mechanics of an elastic body with the help of the principle of least action. In Newtonian mechanics, as is well known, the kinetic potential for unit volume of material at a given point P in an elastic body may be put equal to the density of kinetic energy minus the density of potential energy, and it is obvious that our choice for kinetic potential must reduce to that value at low velocities. Our choice of an expression for kinetic potential is furthermore limited by the fundamental transformation equation for kinetic potential which we found in the last chapter

$$\frac{H}{\sqrt{1 - \dfrac{u^2}{c^2}}} = \frac{H'}{\sqrt{1 - \dfrac{u'^2}{c^2}}}. \tag{146}$$

Taking these requirements into consideration, we may write for the kinetic potential per unit volume of the material at a point P moving with the velocity $\mathbf{u}$ the expression

$$H = -E^\circ \sqrt{1 - \frac{u^2}{c^2}},$$

where E° is the energy as measured in system S° of the amount of material which in the unstrained condition (*i.e.*, as measured in system S) is contained in unit volume.

The above expression obviously satisfies our fundamental transformation equation (146) and at low velocities reduces in accordance with the requirements of Newtonian mechanics to

$$H = \tfrac{1}{2} m^\circ u^2 - E^\circ,$$

provided we introduce the substitution made familiar by our previous work, $m^\circ = \dfrac{E^\circ}{c^2}$.

121. Lagrange's Equations. Making use of this expression for the kinetic potential in an elastic body, we may now obtain the equations of motion and stress for an elastic body by substituting into Lagrange's equations (139) Chapter IX.

Considering the material at the point P contained in unit volume in the unstrained condition, we may choose as our generalized coördinates the six component strains ϵ_{xx}, ϵ_{yy}, etc., with the corresponding stresses $-t_{xx}$, $-t_{yy}$, etc., as generalized forces, and the three coördinates x, y, z which give the position of the point with the corresponding forces F_x, F_y and F_z.

It is evident that the kinetic potential will be independent of the time derivatives of the strains, and if we consider cases in which E° is independent of position, the kinetic potential will also be independent of the absolute magnitudes of the coördinates x, y and z. Substituting in Lagrange's equations (139), we then obtain

$$
\left.
\begin{aligned}
-\frac{\partial}{\partial \epsilon_{xx}}\left(-E^\circ\sqrt{1-\frac{u^2}{c^2}}\right) &= -t_{xx}, \\[2mm]
-\frac{\partial}{\partial \epsilon_{yy}}\left(-E^\circ\sqrt{1-\frac{u^2}{c^2}}\right) &= -t_{yy}, \\[2mm]
-\frac{\partial}{\partial \epsilon_{zz}}\left(-E^\circ\sqrt{1-\frac{u^2}{c^2}}\right) &= -t_{zz}, \\[2mm]
-\frac{\partial}{\partial \epsilon_{yz}}\left(-E^\circ\sqrt{1-\frac{u^2}{c^2}}\right) &= -t_{yz}, \\[2mm]
-\frac{\partial}{\partial \epsilon_{xz}}\left(-E^\circ\sqrt{1-\frac{u^2}{c^2}}\right) &= -t_{xz}, \\[2mm]
-\frac{\partial}{\partial \epsilon_{xy}}\left(-E^\circ\sqrt{1-\frac{u^2}{c^2}}\right) &= -t_{xy},
\end{aligned}
\right\}
\tag{165}
$$

$$
\left.
\begin{aligned}
\frac{d}{dt}\frac{\partial}{\partial \dot{x}}\left(-E^\circ\sqrt{1-\frac{u^2}{c^2}}\right) &= F_x, \\[2mm]
\frac{d}{dt}\frac{\partial}{\partial \dot{y}}\left(-E^\circ\sqrt{1-\frac{u^2}{c^2}}\right) &= F_y, \\[2mm]
\frac{d}{dt}\frac{\partial}{\partial \dot{z}}\left(-E^\circ\sqrt{1-\frac{u^2}{c^2}}\right) &= F_z.
\end{aligned}
\right\}
\tag{166}
$$

We may simplify these equations, however; by performing the indicated differentiations and making suitable substitutions, we have

$$
\frac{\partial E^\circ{}_{xx}}{\partial \epsilon_{xx}} = \frac{\partial E^\circ{}_{xx}}{\partial \epsilon^\circ{}_{xx}}\frac{\partial \epsilon^\circ{}_{xx}}{\partial \epsilon_{xx}}.
$$

But in accordance with equation (152) we may write

$$\frac{\partial E^{\circ}{}_{xx}}{\partial \epsilon^{\circ}{}_{xx}} = -t^{\circ}{}_{xx}$$

and from equations (164) we may put

$$\frac{\partial \epsilon^{\circ}{}_{xx}}{\partial \epsilon_{xx}} = \frac{1}{1 - \dfrac{u^2}{c^2}}.$$

Making the substitutions in the first of the Lagrangian equations we obtain

$$t_{xx} = -\frac{\partial}{\partial \epsilon_{xx}}\left(E^{\circ}\sqrt{1 - \frac{u^2}{c^2}}\right) = t^{\circ}{}_{xx}\frac{1}{1 - \dfrac{u^2}{c^2}}\sqrt{1 - \frac{u^2}{c^2}} = \frac{t^{\circ}{}_{xx}}{\sqrt{1 - \dfrac{u^2}{c^2}}}.$$

122. Transformation Equations for Stress. Similar substitutions can be made in all the equations of stress, and we obtain as our set of transformation equations

$$t_{xx} = \frac{t^{\circ}{}_{xx}}{\sqrt{1 - \dfrac{u^2}{c^2}}}, \qquad t_{yy} = \sqrt{1 - \frac{u^2}{c^2}}\, t^{\circ}{}_{yy}, \qquad t_{zz} = \sqrt{1 - \frac{u^2}{c^2}}\, t^{\circ}{}_{zz},$$

$$t_{yx} = \sqrt{1 - \frac{u^2}{c^2}}\, t^{\circ}{}_{yx}, \qquad t_{xz} = \frac{t^{\circ}{}_{xz}}{\sqrt{1 - \dfrac{u^2}{c^2}}}, \qquad t_{xy} = \frac{t^{\circ}{}_{xy}}{\sqrt{1 - \dfrac{u^2}{c^2}}}.$$

$$(167)$$

123. Value of E°. With the help of these transformation equations for stress we may calculate the value of E°, the energy content, as measured in system S°, of material which in the unstrained condition is contained in unit volume.

Consider unit volume of the material in the unstrained condition and call its energy content $w^{\circ\circ}$. Give it now the velocity $u = \dot{x}$, keeping its state of strain unchanged in system S. Since the *strain* is not changing in system S, the stresses t_{xx}, etc., will also be constant in system S. In system S°, however, the component strain will change in accordance with equations (156) from zero to

$$\epsilon^\circ{}_{xx} = \frac{\dot{x}^2}{2c^2} \frac{1}{\left(1 - \dfrac{u^2}{c^2}\right)},$$

and the corresponding stress will be given at any instant by the expression just derived,

$$t^\circ{}_{xx} = t_{xx}\sqrt{1 - \frac{u^2}{c^2}},$$

t_{xx} being, as we have just seen, a constant. We may then write for E° the expression

$$E^\circ = w^{\circ\circ} - t_{xx} \int_0^w \sqrt{1 - \frac{u^2}{c^2}}\, d\left[\frac{1}{\left(1 - \dfrac{u^2}{c^2}\right)} \frac{\dot{x}}{2c^2}\right].$$

Noting that $u = \dot{x}$ we obtain on integration,

$$E^\circ = w^{\circ\circ} + t_{xx} - \frac{t_{xx}}{\sqrt{1 - \dfrac{u^2}{c^2}}} \tag{168}$$

as the desired expression for the energy as measured in system S° contained in the material which in system S is unstrained and has unit volume.

124. The Equations of Motion in the Lagrangian Form. We are now in a position to simplify the three Lagrangian equations (166) for F_x, F_y and F_z. Carrying out the indicated differentiation we have

$$F_x = \frac{d}{dt}\frac{\partial}{\partial \dot{x}}\left(-E^\circ\sqrt{1 - \frac{u^2}{c^2}}\right) = \frac{d}{dt}\left[\frac{E^\circ}{\sqrt{1 - \dfrac{u^2}{c^2}}}\frac{\dot{x}}{c^2} - \sqrt{1 - \frac{u^2}{c^2}}\frac{\partial E^\circ}{\partial \dot{x}}\right],$$

and introducing the value of E° given by equation (168) we obtain

$$F_x = \frac{d}{dt}\left[\frac{w^{\circ\circ} + t_{xx}}{\sqrt{1 - \dfrac{u^2}{c^2}}}\,\frac{\dot{x}}{c^2}\right].\tag{169}$$

Simple calculations will also give us values for F_y and F_z. We have from (166)

$$F_y = \frac{d}{dt}\frac{\partial}{\partial\dot{y}}\left(-E^\circ\sqrt{1 - \frac{u^2}{c^2}}\right) = \frac{d}{dt}\left[\frac{E^\circ}{\sqrt{1 - \dfrac{u^2}{c^2}}}\,\frac{\dot{y}}{c^2} - \sqrt{1 - \frac{u^2}{c^2}}\,\frac{\partial E^\circ}{\partial\dot{y}}\right].$$

But since we have adapted our considerations to cases in which the direction of motion is along the X axis, we have $\dot{y} = 0$; furthermore we may substitute, in accordance with equations (152), (157) and (167),

$$\frac{\partial E^\circ}{\partial\dot{y}} = \frac{\partial E^\circ}{\partial\epsilon^\circ{}_{xy}}\frac{\partial\epsilon^\circ{}_{xy}}{\partial\dot{y}} = -t^\circ{}_{xy}\frac{1}{\left(1 - \dfrac{u^2}{c^2}\right)}\frac{\dot{x}}{c^2} = \frac{-t_{xy}}{\sqrt{1 - \dfrac{u^2}{c^2}}}\,\frac{\dot{x}}{c^2}.$$

We thus obtain as our three equations of motion

$$F_x = \frac{d}{dt}\left[\frac{w^{\circ\circ} + t_{xx}}{\sqrt{1 - \dfrac{u^2}{c^2}}}\,\frac{\dot{x}}{c^2}\right],$$

$$F_y = \frac{d}{dt}\left(t_{xy}\,\frac{\dot{x}}{c^2}\right),\tag{170}$$

$$F_z = \frac{d}{dt}\left(t_{xz}\,\frac{\dot{x}}{c^2}\right).$$

In these equations the quantities F_x, F_y and F_z are the components of force acting on a particular system, namely that quantity of material which at the instant in question has unit volume. Since the volume of this material will in general be changing, F_x, F_y and F_z do not give us the force per unit volume as usually defined. If we represent, however, by f_x, f_y and f_z the components of force per unit volume, we may rewrite these equations in the form

$$F_x \, \delta V = \frac{d}{dt} \left[\frac{w^{\circ\circ} + t_{xx}}{\sqrt{1 - \dfrac{u^2}{c^2}}} \frac{\dot{x}}{c^2} \, \delta V \right],$$

$$F_y \, \delta V = \frac{d}{dt} \left(t_{xy} \frac{\dot{x}}{c^2} \, \delta V \right),$$

$$F_z \, \delta V = \frac{d}{dt} \left(t_{xz} \frac{\dot{x}}{c^2} \, \delta V \right),$$

$$(171)$$

where by δV we mean a small element of volume at the point in question.

125. Density of Momentum. Since we customarily define force as equal to the time rate of change of momentum, we may now write for the density of momentum **g** at a point in an elastic body which is moving in the X direction with the velocity $u = \dot{x}$

$$\mathbf{g}_x = \frac{w^{\circ\circ} + t_{xx}}{\sqrt{1 - \dfrac{u^2}{c^2}}} \frac{\dot{x}}{c^2}, \qquad \mathbf{g}_y = t_{xy} \frac{\dot{x}}{c^2}, \qquad \mathbf{g}_y = t_{xy} \frac{\dot{x}}{c^2}. \qquad (172)$$

It is interesting to point out that there are components of momentum in the Y and Z directions in spite of the fact that the material at the point in question is moving in the X direction. We shall later see the important significance of this discovery.

126. Density of Energy. It will be remembered that the forces whose equations we have just obtained are those acting on unit volume of the material as measured in system S, and hence we are now in a position to calculate the energy density of our material. Let us start out with unit volume of our material at rest, with the energy content $w^{\circ\circ}$ and determine the work necessary to give it the velocity $u = \dot{x}$ without change in stress or strain. Since the only component of force which suffers displacement is F_x, we have

$$w = w^{\circ\circ} + \int_0^u \frac{d}{dt}\left[\frac{w^{\circ\circ} + t_{xx}}{\sqrt{1 - \dfrac{u^2}{c^2}}}\,\frac{\dot{x}}{c^2}\right]\dot{x}\,dt,$$

$$= w^{\circ\circ} + (w^{\circ\circ} + t_{xx})\int_0^u \dot{x}\,d\left[\frac{1}{\sqrt{1 - \dfrac{u^2}{c^2}}}\,\frac{\dot{x}}{c^2}\right], \qquad (173)$$

$$= \left\{\frac{w^{\circ\circ} + t_{xx}}{\sqrt{1 - \dfrac{u^2}{c^2}}} - t_{xx}\right\}$$

as an expression for the energy density of the elastic material.

127. Summary of Results Obtained from the Principle of Least Action. We may now tabulate for future reference the results obtained from the principle of least action.

At a given point in an elastic medium which is moving in the X direction with the velocity $u = \dot{x}$, we have for the components of stress

$$t_{xx} = \frac{t^{\circ}_{xx}}{\sqrt{1 - \dfrac{u^2}{c^2}}}, \qquad t_{yy} = \sqrt{1 - \frac{u^2}{c^2}}\,t^{\circ}_{yy}, \qquad t_{zz} = \sqrt{1 - \frac{u^2}{c^2}}\,t^{\circ}_{zz},$$

$$t_{yz} = \sqrt{1 - \frac{u^2}{c^2}}\,t^{\circ}_{yz}, \qquad t_{xz} = \frac{t^{\circ}_{xz}}{\sqrt{1 - \dfrac{u^2}{c^2}}}, \qquad t_{xy} = \frac{t^{\circ}_{xz}}{\sqrt{1 - \dfrac{u^2}{c^2}}}, \qquad (167)$$

For the density of energy at the point in question we have

$$w = \frac{w^{\circ\circ} + t_{xx}}{\sqrt{1 - \dfrac{u^2}{c^2}}} - t_{xx}. \qquad (173)$$

For the density of momentum we have

$$\mathbf{g}_x = \frac{w^{\circ\circ} + t_{xx}}{\sqrt{1 - \dfrac{u^2}{c^2}}}\,\frac{\dot{x}}{c^2}, \qquad \mathbf{g}_y = t_{xy}\,\frac{\dot{x}}{c^2}, \qquad \mathbf{g}_z = t_{xz}\,\frac{\dot{x}}{c^2}. \tag{172}$$

PART III. SOME MATHEMATICAL RELATIONS.

Before proceeding to the applications of these results which we have obtained from the principle of least action, we shall find it desirable to present a number of mathematical relations which will later prove useful.

128. The Unsymmetrical Stress Tensor t. We have defined the components of stress acting at a point by equation (152)

$$\delta W = t_{xx}\,\delta\epsilon_{xx} + t_{yy}\,\delta\epsilon_{yy} + t_{zz}\,\delta\epsilon_{zz} + t_{yz}\,\delta\epsilon_{yz} + t_{xz}\,\delta\epsilon_{xz} + t_{xy}\,\delta\epsilon_{xy},$$

where δW is the work which accompanies a change in strain and is performed on the surroundings by the amount of material which was contained in unit volume in the unstrained state. Since for convenience we have taken as our state of zero strain the condition of the body as measured in system S, it is evident that the components t_{xx}, t_{yy}, etc., may be taken as the forces acting on the faces of a unit cube of material at the point in question, the first letter of the subscript indicating the direction of the force and the second subscript the direction of the normal to the face in question.

Interpreting the components of stress in this fashion, we may now add three further components and obtain a complete tensor

$$\mathbf{t} = \begin{cases} t_{xx} & t_{xy} & t_{xz} \\ t_{yx} & t_{yy} & t_{yz} \\ t_{zx} & t_{zy} & t_{zz} \end{cases} \tag{174}$$

The three new components t_{yx}, t_{zx}, t_{zy} are forces acting on the unit cube, in the directions and on the faces indicated by the subscripts. A knowledge of their value was not necessary for our developments of the consequences of the principle of least action, since it was possible to obtain an expression for the work accompanying a change in strain without their introduction. We shall find them quite important for our later considerations, however, and may proceed to determine their value.

t_{yz} is the force acting in the Y direction tangentially to a face of the cube perpendicular to the X axis, and measured with a system of coördinates S. Using a system of coördinates S° which is stationary with respect to the point in question, we should obtain, for the measurement of this force,

$$t^{\circ}{}_{yx} = \frac{t_{yx}}{\sqrt{1 - \dfrac{u^2}{c^2}}}$$

in accordance with our transformation equation for force (62), Chapter VI. Similarly we shall have the relation

$$t^{\circ}{}_{xy} = t_{xy}.$$

In accordance with the elementary theory of elasticity, however, the forces $t^{\circ}{}_{yx}$ and $t^{\circ}{}_{xy}$ which are measured by an observer moving with the body will be connected by the relation

$$t^{\circ}{}_{xy} = \frac{t^{\circ}{}_{yx}}{\sqrt{1 - \dfrac{u^2}{c^2}}},$$

$t^{\circ}{}_{xy}$ being larger than $t^{\circ}{}_{yx}$ in the ratio of the areas of face upon which they act. Combining these three equations, and using similar methods for the other quantities, we can obtain the desired relations

$$t_{yx} = \left(1 - \frac{u^2}{c^2}\right) t_{xy}, \qquad t_{zx} = \left(1 - \frac{u^2}{c^2}\right) t_{xz}, \qquad t_{zy} = t_{yz}. \qquad (175)$$

We see that $\mathbf{t}$ is an unsymmetrical tensor.

129. The Symmetrical Tensor p. Besides this unsymmetrical tensor $\mathbf{t}$ we shall find it desirable to define a further tensor $\mathbf{p}$ by the equation

$$\mathbf{p} = \mathbf{t} + \mathbf{gu}. \tag{176}$$

We shall call $\mathbf{gu}$ the tensor product of $\mathbf{g}$ and $\mathbf{u}$ and may indicate tensor products in general by a simple juxtaposition of vectors. $\mathbf{gu}$ is itself a tensor with components as indicated below:

$$\mathbf{gu} = \begin{cases} g_x u_x & g_x u_y & g_x u_z, \\ g_y u_x & g_y u_y & g_y u_z, \\ g_z u_x & g_z u_y & g_z u_z. \end{cases} \tag{177}$$

Unlike $\mathbf{t}$, $\mathbf{p}$ will be a symmetrical tensor, since we may show, by substitution of the values for $\mathbf{g}$ and $\mathbf{u}$ already obtained, that

$$p_{yx} = p_{xy}, \qquad p_{zx} = p_{xz}, \qquad p_{zy} = p_{yz}. \tag{178}$$

Consider for example the value of p_{yx}; we have from our definition

$$p_{yx} = t_{yx} + g_y u_x,$$

and by equations (175) and (172) we have

$$t_{xy} = \left(1 - \frac{u^2}{c^2}\right) t_{xy}, \qquad g_y = t_{xy} \frac{u_x}{c^2},$$

and hence by substitution obtain

$$p_{yx} = t_{xy}.$$

We also have, however, by definition

$$p_{xy} = t_{xy} + g_x u_y,$$

and since for the case we are considering $u_y = 0$, we arrive at the equality

$$p_{xy} = p_{yx}.$$

The other equalities may be shown in a similar way.

130. Relation between $\operatorname{div} \mathbf{t}$ **and** $\mathbf{t}_n$**.** At a given point P in our elastic body we shall define the divergence of the tensor $\mathbf{t}$ by the equation

$$\begin{aligned}
\operatorname{div} \mathbf{t} = {} & \left(\frac{\partial t_{xx}}{\partial x} + \frac{\partial t_{xy}}{\partial y} + \frac{\partial t_{xz}}{\partial z} \right) \mathbf{i} \\
& + \left(\frac{\partial t_{yx}}{\partial x} + \frac{\partial t_{yy}}{\partial y} + \frac{\partial t_{yz}}{\partial z} \right) \mathbf{j} \\
& + \left(\frac{\partial t_{zx}}{\partial x} + \frac{\partial t_{zy}}{\partial y} + \frac{\partial t_{zz}}{\partial z} \right) \mathbf{k},
\end{aligned} \tag{179}$$

where $\mathbf{i}$, $\mathbf{j}$ and $\mathbf{k}$ are unit vectors parallel to the axes, $\operatorname{div} \mathbf{t}$ thus being an ordinary vector. It will be seen that $\operatorname{div} \mathbf{t}$ is the elastic force acting per unit volume of material at the point P.

Considering an element of surface dS, we shall define a further vector $\mathbf{t}_n$ by the equation

$$\begin{aligned}
\mathbf{t}_n = {} & (t_{xx} \cos \alpha + t_{xy} \cos \beta + t_{xz} \cos \gamma)\, \mathbf{i} \\
& + (t_{yx} \cos \alpha + t_{yy} \cos \beta + t_{yz} \cos \gamma)\, \mathbf{j} \\
& + (t_{zx} \cos \alpha + t_{zy} \cos \beta + t_{zz} \cos \gamma)\, \mathbf{k},
\end{aligned} \tag{180}$$

where $\cos \alpha$, $\cos \beta$ and $\cos \gamma$ are the direction cosines of the inward-pointing normal to the element of surface dS.

Considering now a definite volume V enclosed by the surface S it is evident that $\operatorname{div} \mathbf{t}$ and $\mathbf{t}_n$ will be connected by the relation

$$- \int \operatorname{div} \mathbf{t}\, dV = \int_0 \mathbf{t}_n\, dS, \tag{181}$$

where the symbol 0 indicates that the integration is to be taken over the whole surface which encloses the volume V. This equation is of course merely a direct application of Gauss's formula, which states in general the equality

$$-\int\left(\frac{\partial P}{\partial x}+\frac{\partial Q}{\partial y}+\frac{\partial R}{\partial z}\right)dV = \int_0 (P\cos\alpha + Q\cos\beta + R\cos\gamma)\,dS, \quad (182)$$

where P, Q and R may be any functions of x, y and z.

We shall also find use for a further relation between $\operatorname{div}\mathbf{t}$ and $\mathbf{t}_n$. Consider a given point of reference O, and let $\mathbf{r}$ be the radius vector to any point P in the elastic body; we can then show with the help of Gauss's Formula (182) that

$$-\int(\mathbf{r}\times\operatorname{div}\mathbf{t})\,dV = \int_0(\mathbf{r}\times\mathbf{t}_n)\,dS$$
$$-\int\left[(t_{yz}-t_{zy})\mathbf{jk}+(t_{xz}-t_{zx})\mathbf{ik}+(t_{xy}-t_{yx})\mathbf{ij}\right]dV,$$

where $\times$ signifies as usual the outer product. Taking account of equations (172) and (175) this can be rewritten

$$-\int(\mathbf{r}\times\operatorname{div}\mathbf{t})\,dV = \int_0(\mathbf{r}\times\mathbf{t}_n)\,dS - \int(\mathbf{u}\times\mathbf{g})\,dV. \quad (183)$$

131. The Equations of Motion in the Eulerian Form. We saw in Sections 124 and 125 that the equations of motion in the Lagrangian form might be written

$$\mathbf{f}\,\delta V = \frac{d}{dt}(\mathbf{g}\,\delta V),$$

where $\mathbf{f}$ is the density of force acting at any point and $\mathbf{g}$ is the density of momentum.

Provided that there are no external forces acting and $\mathbf{f}$ is produced solely by the elastic forces, our definition of the divergence of a tensor will now permit us to put

$$\mathbf{f} = -\operatorname{div}\mathbf{t},$$

and write for our equation of motion

$$(-\operatorname{div}\mathbf{t})\,\delta V = \frac{d}{dt}(\mathbf{g}\,\delta V) = \delta V\,\frac{d\mathbf{g}}{dt} + \mathbf{g}\,\frac{d(\delta V)}{dt}.$$

Expressing $\dfrac{d\mathbf{g}}{dt}$ in terms of partial differentials, and putting

$$\frac{d(\delta V)}{dt} = \delta V\,\operatorname{div}\mathbf{u}$$

we obtain

$$-\operatorname{div}\mathbf{t} = \left(\frac{\partial\mathbf{g}}{\partial t} + u_x\,\frac{\partial\mathbf{g}}{\partial x} + u_y\,\frac{\partial\mathbf{g}}{\partial y} + u_z\,\frac{\partial\mathbf{g}}{\partial z}\right) + \mathbf{g}\,\operatorname{div}\mathbf{u}.$$

Our symmetrical tensor $\mathbf{p}$, however, was defined by the equation (176)

$$\mathbf{p} = \mathbf{t} + \mathbf{gu},$$

and hence we may now write our equations of motion in the very beautiful Eulerian form

$$-\operatorname{div}\mathbf{p} = \frac{\partial\mathbf{g}}{\partial t}. \tag{184}$$

We shall find this simple form for the equations of motion very interesting in connection with our considerations in the last chapter.

PART IV. APPLICATIONS OF THE RESULTS.

We may now use the results which we have obtained from the principle of least action to elucidate various problems concerning the behavior of elastic bodies.

132. Relation between Energy and Momentum. In our work on the dynamics of a particle we found that the mass of a particle was equal to its energy divided by the square of the velocity of light, and hence have come to expect in general a necessary relation between the existence of momentum in any particular direction and the transfer of energy in that same direction. We find, however, in the case of elastically stressed bodies a somewhat more complicated state of affairs than in the case of particles, since besides the energy which is transported bodily by the motion of the medium an additional quantity of energy may be transferred through the medium by the action of the forces which hold it in its state of strain. Thus, for example, in the case of a longitudinally compressed rod moving parallel to its length, the forces holding it in its state of longitudinal compression will be doing work at the rear end of the rod and delivering an equal quantity of energy at the front end, and this additional transfer of energy must be included in the calculation of the momentum of the bar.

As a matter of fact, an examination of the expressions for momentum which we obtained from the principle of least action will show the justice of these considerations. For the density of momentum in the X direction we obtained the expression

$$g_x = (w + t_{xx}) \frac{\dot{x}}{c^2},$$

and we see that in order to calculate the momentum in the X direction we must consider not merely the energy w which is being bodily carried along in that direction with the velocity $\dot{x}$, but also must take into account the additional flow of energy which arises from the stress t_{xx}. As we have already seen in Section 128, this stress t_{xx} can be thought of as resulting from forces which act on the front and rear faces of a centimeter cube of our material. Since the cube is moving with the velocity $\dot{x}$, the force on the rear face will do the work $t_{xx}\dot{x}$ per second and this will be given up at the forward face. We thus have an additional density of energy-flow in the X direction of the magnitude $t_{xx}\dot{x}$ and hence a corresponding density of momentum $\dfrac{t_{xx}\dot{x}}{c^2}$.

Similar considerations explain the interesting occurrence of components of momentum in the Y and Z directions,

$$g_y = t_{xy}\,\frac{\dot{x}}{c^2}, \qquad g_z = t_{xz}\,\frac{\dot{x}}{c^2},$$

in spite of the fact that the material involved is moving in the X direction. The stress t_{xy}, for example, can be thought of as resulting from forces which act tangentially in the X direction on the pair of faces of our unit cube which are perpendicular to the Y axis. Since the cube is moving in the X direction with the velocity $\dot{x}$, we shall have the work $t_{xy}\dot{x}$, done at one surface per second and transferred to the other, and the resulting flow of energy in the X direction is accompanied by the corresponding momentum $\dfrac{t_{xy}\dot{x}}{c^2}$.

133. The Conservation of Momentum. It is evident from our previous discussions that we may write the equation of motion for an elastic medium in the form

$$\mathbf{f}\,\delta V = \frac{d(\mathbf{g}\,\delta V)}{dt},$$

where $\mathbf{g}$ is the density of momentum at any given point and $\mathbf{f}$ is the force acting per unit volume of material. We have already obtained, from the principle of least action, expressions (172) which permit the calculation of $\mathbf{g}$ in terms of the energy density, stress and velocity at the point in question, and our present problem is to discuss somewhat further the nature of the force $\mathbf{f}$.

We shall find it convenient to analyze the total force per unit volume of material $\mathbf{f}$ into those external forces $\mathbf{f}_{\text{ext.}}$ like gravity, which are produced by agencies outside of the elastic body and the internal force $\mathbf{f}_{\text{int.}}$ which arises from the elastic interaction of the parts of the strained body itself. It is evident from the way in which we have defined the divergence of a tensor (179) that for this latter we may write

$$\mathbf{f}_{\text{int.}} = -\operatorname{div}\mathbf{t}. \tag{185}$$

Our equation of motion then becomes

$$(\mathbf{f}_{\text{ext.}} - \operatorname{div}\mathbf{t})\,\delta V = \frac{d(\mathbf{g}\,\delta V)}{dt}, \tag{186}$$

or, integrating over the total volume of the elastic body,

$$\int \mathbf{f}_{\text{ext.}}\,dV - \int \operatorname{div}\mathbf{t}\,dV = \frac{d}{dt}\int \mathbf{g}\,dV = \frac{d\mathbf{G}}{dt}, \tag{187}$$

where $\mathbf{G}$ is the total momentum of the body. With the help of the purely analytical relation (181) we may transform the above equation into

$$\int \mathbf{f}_{\text{ext.}}\,dV + \int \mathbf{t}_n\,dS = \frac{d\mathbf{G}}{dt}, \tag{188}$$

where $\mathbf{t}_n$ is defined in accordance with (180) so that the integral $\displaystyle\int_0 \mathbf{t}_n\,dS$ becomes the force exerted by the surroundings on the surface of the elastic body.

In the case of an isolated system both $\mathbf{f}_{\text{ext.}}$ and $\mathbf{t}_n$ would evidently be equal to zero and we have the principle of the conservation of momentum.

134. The Conservation of Angular Momentum. Consider the radius vector $\mathbf{r}$ from a point of reference O to any point P in an elastic body; then the angular momentum of the body about O will be

$$\mathbf{M} = \int (\mathbf{r}\times\mathbf{g})\,dV,$$

and its rate of change will be

$$\frac{d\mathbf{M}}{dt} = \int \left(\mathbf{r}\times\frac{d\mathbf{g}}{dt}\right)dV + \int \left(\frac{d\mathbf{r}}{dt}\times\mathbf{g}\right)dV. \tag{189}$$

Substituting equation (186), this may be written

$$\frac{d\mathbf{M}}{dt} = \int (\mathbf{r}\times\mathbf{f}_{\text{ext.}})\,dV - \int (\mathbf{r}\times\operatorname{div}\mathbf{t})\,dV + \int (\mathbf{u}\times\mathbf{g})\,dV,$$

or, introducing the purely mathematical relation (183) we have,

$$\frac{d\mathbf{M}}{dt} = \int (\mathbf{r} \times \mathbf{f}_{\text{ext.}}) \, dV + \int_0 (\mathbf{r} \times \mathbf{t}_n) \, dS. \tag{190}$$

We see from this equation that the rate of change of the angular momentum of an elastic body is equal to the moment of the external forces acting on the body plus the moment of the surface forces.

In the case of an isolated system this reduces to the important principle of the conservation of angular momentum.

135. Relation between Angular Momentum and the Unsymmetrical Stress Tensor. The fact that at a point in a strained elastic medium there may be components of momentum at right angles to the motion of the point itself, leads to the interesting conclusion that even in a state of steady motion the angular momentum of a strained body will in general be changing.

This is evident from equation (189), in the preceding section, which may be written

$$\frac{d\mathbf{M}}{dt} = \int \left(\mathbf{r} \times \frac{d\mathbf{g}}{dt} \right) dV + \int (\mathbf{u} \times \mathbf{g}) \, dV. \tag{191}$$

In the older mechanics velocity $\mathbf{u}$ and momentum $\mathbf{g}$ were always in the same direction so that the last term of this equation became zero. In our newer mechanics, however, we have found (172) components of momentum at right angles to the velocity and *hence even for a body moving in a straight line with unchanging stresses and velocity we find that the angular momentum is increasing at the rate*

$$\frac{d\mathbf{M}}{dt} = \int (\mathbf{u} \times \mathbf{g}) \, dV, \tag{192}$$

and in order to maintain the body in its state of uniform motion we must apply external forces with a turning moment of this same amount.

The presence of this increasing angular momentum in a strained body arises from the unsymmetrical nature of the stress tensor; the integral $\int (\mathbf{u} \times \mathbf{g})\, dV$ being as a matter of fact exactly equal to the integral over the same volume of the turning moments of the unsymmetrical components of the stress. Thus, for example, if we have a body moving in the X direction with the velocity $\mathbf{u} = \dot{x}\mathbf{i}$ we can easily see from equations (172) and (175) the truth of the equality

$$(\mathbf{u} \times \mathbf{g}) = \left[(t_{yz} - t_{zy})\,\mathbf{jk} + (t_{xz} - t_{zx})\,\mathbf{ik} + (t_{xy} - t_{yx})\,\mathbf{ij} \right].$$

136. The Right-Angled Lever. An interesting example of the principle that in general a turning moment is needed for the uniform translatory motion of a strained body is seen in the apparently paradoxical case of the right-angled lever.

Consider the right-angled lever shown in Fig. 14. This lever is stationary with respect to a system of coördinates S°. Referred to S° the two lever arms are equal in length:

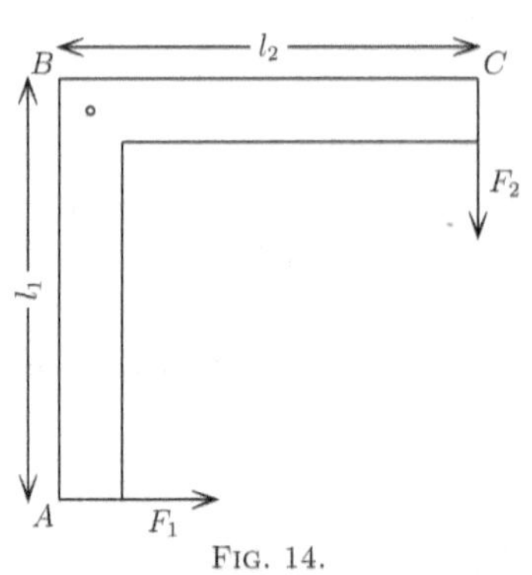

FIG. 14.

$$l_1{}^{\circ} = l_2{}^{\circ},$$

and the lever is in equilibrium under the action of the equal forces

$$F_1{}^{\circ} = F_2{}^{\circ}.$$

Let us now consider the equilibrium as it appears, using a system of coördinates S with reference to which the lever is moving in X direction with the velocity V. Referred to this new system of coördinates the length l_1 of the arm which lies in the Y direction will be the same as in system S°, giving us

$$l_1 = l_1{}^{\circ}.$$

But for the other arm which lies in the direction of motion we shall have, in accordance with the Lorentz shortening,

$$l_2 = l_2{}^{\circ}\sqrt{1 - \frac{V^2}{c^2}}.$$

For the forces F_1 and F_2 we shall have, in accordance with our equations for the transformation of force (61) and (62),

$$F_1 = F_1°,$$

$$F_2 = F_2°\sqrt{1 - \frac{V^2}{c^2}}.$$

We thus obtain for the moment of the forces around the pivot B

$$F_1 l_1 - F_2 l_2 = F_1°l_1° - F_2°l_2°\left(1 - \frac{V^2}{c^2}\right) = F_1°l_1°\frac{V^2}{c^2}, = F_1 l_1 \frac{V^2}{c^2},$$

and are led to the remarkable conclusion that such a moving lever will be in equilibrium only if the external forces have a definite turning moment of the magnitude given above.

The explanation of this apparent paradox is obvious, however, in the light of our previous discussion. In spite of the fact that the lever is in uniform motion in a straight line, its angular momentum is continually increasing owing to the fact that it is elastically strained, and it can be shown by carrying out the integration indicated in equation (192) that the rate of change of angular momentum is as a matter of fact just equal to the turning moment $F_1 l_1 \dfrac{V^2}{c^2}$.

This necessity for a turning moment $F_1 l_1 \dfrac{V^2}{c^2}$ can also be shown directly from a consideration of the energy flow in the lever. Since the force F_1 is doing the work $F_1 V$ per second at the point A, a stream of energy of this amount is continually flowing through the lever from A to the pivot B. In accordance with our ideas as to the relation between energy and mass, this new energy which enters at A each second has the mass $\dfrac{F_1 V}{c^2}$, and hence each second the angular momentum of the system around the point B is increased by the amount

$$\frac{F_1 V}{c^2} V l_1 = F_1 l_1 \frac{V^2}{c^2}.$$

We have already found, however, exactly this same expression for the moment of the forces around the pivot B and hence see that they are of just the magnitude necessary to keep the lever from turning, thus solving completely our apparent paradox.

137. Isolated Systems in a Steady State. Our considerations have shown that the density of momentum is equal to the density of energy flow divided by the square of the velocity of light. If we have a system which is in a steady internal state, and is either isolated or merely subjected to an external pressure with no components of force tangential to the bounding surface, it is evident that the resultant flow of energy for the whole body must be in the direction of motion, and hence for these systems momentum and velocity will be in the same direction without the complications introduced by a transverse energy flow.

Thus for an *isolated* system in a steady *internal* state we may write,

$$\mathbf{G} = \frac{E}{c^2}\,\mathbf{u} = \frac{\dfrac{E^\circ}{c^2}}{\sqrt{1 - \dfrac{u^2}{c^2}}}\,\mathbf{u}. \tag{193}$$

138. The Dynamics of a Particle. It is important to note that particles are interesting examples of systems in which there will obviously be no transverse component of energy flow since their infinitesimal size precludes the action of tangential surface forces. We thus see that the dynamics of a particle may be regarded as a special case of the more general dynamics which we have developed in this chapter, the equation of motion for a particle being

$$\mathbf{F} = \frac{d}{dt}\left[\frac{\dfrac{E^\circ}{c^2}}{\sqrt{1 - \dfrac{u^2}{c^2}}}\,\mathbf{u}\right] = \frac{d}{dt}\left[\frac{m^\circ}{\sqrt{1 - \dfrac{u^2}{c^2}}}\,\mathbf{u}\right],$$

in agreement with the work of Chapter VI.

139. Conclusion. We may now point out in conclusion the chief results of this chapter. With the help of Einstein's equations for spatial and temporal considerations, we have developed a set of transformation equations for the strain in an elastic body. Using the components of strain and velocity as generalized coördinates, we then introduced the principle of least action, choosing a form of function for kinetic potential which agrees at low velocities with the choice made in the older theories of elasticity and at all velocities agrees with the requirements of the principle of relativity. Using the Lagrangian equations, we were then able to develop all that is necessary for a complete theory of elasticity.

The most important consequence of these considerations is an extension in our ideas as to the relation between momentum and energy. We find that the density of momentum in any direction must be placed equal to the total density of energy flow in that same direction divided by the square of the velocity of light; and we find that we must include in our density of energy flow that transferred through the elastic body by the forces which hold it in its state of strain and suffer displacement as the body moves. This involves in general a flow of energy and hence momentum at right angles to the motion of the body itself.

At present we have no experiments of sufficient accuracy so that we can investigate the differences between this new theory of elasticity and the older ones, and hence of course have found no experimental contradiction to the new theory. It will be seen, however, from the expressions for momentum that even at low velocities the consequences of this new theory will become important as soon as we run across elastic systems in which very large stresses are involved. It is also important to show that a theory of elasticity can be developed which agrees with the requirements of the theory of relativity. In fairness, it must, however, be pointed out in conclusion that since our expression for kinetic potential was not absolutely uniquely determined there may also be other theories of elasticity which will agree with the principle of relativity and with all the facts as now known.

CHAPTER XI.

THE DYNAMICS OF A THERMODYNAMIC SYSTEM.

We may now use our conclusions as to the relation between the principle of least action and the theory of relativity to obtain information as to the behavior of thermodynamic systems in motion.

140. The Generalized Coördinates and Forces. Let us consider a thermodynamic system whose state is defined by the *generalized coördinates* volume v, entropy S and the values of x, y and z which determine its position. Corresponding to these coördinates we shall have the generalized external forces, the negative of the pressure, $-p$, temperature, T, and the components of force, F_x, F_y and F_z. These generalized coördinates and forces are related to the energy change δE accompanying a small displacement δ, in accordance with the equation

$$\delta E = -\delta W = -p\,\delta v + T\,\delta S + F_x\,\delta x + F_y\,\delta y + F_z\,\delta z. \qquad (194)$$

141. Transformation Equation for Volume. Before we can apply the principle of least action we shall need to have transformation equations for the generalized coördinates, volume and entropy.

In accordance with the Lorentz shortening, we may write the following expression for the volume v of the system in terms of v° as measured with a set of axes S° with respect to which the system is stationary:

$$v = v^\circ \sqrt{1 - \frac{u^2}{c^2}} = v^\circ \sqrt{1 - \frac{\dot{x}^2 + \dot{y}^2 + \dot{z}^2}{c^2}},$$

where u is the velocity of the system.

By differentiation we may obtain expressions which we shall find useful,

$$\frac{\partial v^\circ}{\partial v} = \frac{1}{\sqrt{1 - \frac{u^2}{c^2}}}, \qquad (195)$$

$$\frac{\partial v^\circ}{\partial \dot{x}} = \frac{v}{\left(1 - \dfrac{u^2}{c^2}\right)^{\frac{3}{2}}} \frac{\dot{x}}{c^2} = \frac{v^\circ}{\left(1 - \dfrac{u^2}{c^2}\right)} \frac{\dot{x}}{c^2}. \tag{196}$$

142. Transformation Equation for Entropy. As for the entropy of a thermodynamic system, this is a quantity which must appear the same to all observers regardless of their motion. This invariance of entropy is a direct consequence of the close relation between the entropy of a system in a given state and the probability of that state. Let us write, in accordance with the Boltzmann-Planck ideas as to the interdependence of these quantities,

$$S = k \log W,$$

where S is the entropy of the system in the state in question, k is a universal constant, and W the probability of having a microscopic arrangement of molecules or other elementary constituent parts which corresponds to the desired thermodynamic state. Since this probability is evidently independent of the relative motion of the observer and the system we see that the entropy of a system S must be an invariant and may write

$$S = S^\circ. \tag{197}$$

143. Introduction of the Principle of Least Action. The Kinetic Potential. We are now in a position to introduce the principle of least action into our considerations by choosing a form of function for the kinetic potential which will agree at low velocities with the familiar principles of thermodynamics and will agree at all velocities with the requirements of the theory of relativity.

If we use volume and entropy as our generalized coördinates, these conditions are met by taking for kinetic potential the expression

$$H = -E^\circ \sqrt{1 - \frac{u^2}{c^2}}. \tag{198}$$

This expression agrees with the requirements of the theory of relativity that $\dfrac{H}{\sqrt{1 - \dfrac{u^2}{c^2}}}$ shall be an invariant (see Section 111) and at low velocities reduces to $H = -E$, which with our choice of coördinates is the familiar form for the kinetic potential of a thermodynamic system.

It should be noted that this expression for the kinetic potential of a thermodynamic system applies of course only provided we pick out volume v and entropy S as generalized coördinates. If, following Helmholtz, we should think it more rational to take v as one coördinate and a quantity θ whose time derivative is equal to temperature, $\dot{\theta} = T$, as the other coördinate, we should obtain of course a different expression for the kinetic potential; in fact should have under those circumstances

$$H = (E^\circ - T^\circ S^\circ)\sqrt{1 - \frac{u^2}{c^2}}.$$

Using this value of kinetic potential, however, with the corresponding coördinates we should obtain results exactly the same as those which we are now going to work out with the help of the other set of coördinates.

144. The Lagrangian Equations. Having chosen a form for the kinetic potential we may now substitute into the Lagrangian equations (139) and obtain the desired information with regard to the behavior of thermodynamic systems.

Since we shall consider cases in which the energy of the system is independent of the position in space, the kinetic potential will be independent of the coördinates x, y and z, depending only on their time derivatives. Noting also that the kinetic potential is independent of the time derivatives of volume and entropy, we shall obtain the Lagrangian equations in the simple form

$$-\frac{\partial}{\partial v}\left(-E^{\circ}\sqrt{1-\frac{u^2}{c^2}}\right) = -p,$$

$$-\frac{\partial}{\partial S}\left(-E^{\circ}\sqrt{1-\frac{u^2}{c^2}}\right) = T,$$

$$\frac{d}{dt}\frac{\partial}{\partial \dot{x}}\left(-E^{\circ}\sqrt{1-\frac{u^2}{c^2}}\right) = F_x,$$

$$\frac{d}{dt}\frac{\partial}{\partial \dot{y}}\left(-E^{\circ}\sqrt{1-\frac{u^2}{c^2}}\right) = F_y,$$

$$\frac{d}{dt}\frac{\partial}{\partial \dot{z}}\left(-E^{\circ}\sqrt{1-\frac{u^2}{c^2}}\right) = F_z. \tag{199}$$

145. Transformation Equation for Pressure. We may use the first of these equations to show that the pressure is a quantity which appears the same to all observers regardless of their relative motion. We have

$$p = \frac{\partial}{\partial v}\left(-E^{\circ}\sqrt{1-\frac{u^2}{c^2}}\right) = -\sqrt{1-\frac{u^2}{c^2}}\frac{\partial E^{\circ}}{\partial v} = -\sqrt{1-\frac{u^2}{c^2}}\frac{\partial E^{\circ}}{\partial v^{\circ}}\frac{\partial v^{\circ}}{\partial v}.$$

But, in accordance with equation (194), $p^{\circ} = -\dfrac{\partial E^{\circ}}{\partial v^{\circ}}$, and in accordance with equation (195),

$$\frac{\partial v^{\circ}}{\partial v} = \frac{1}{\sqrt{1-\frac{u^2}{c^2}}},$$

which gives us the desired relation

$$p = p^{\circ}. \tag{200}$$

Defining pressure as force per unit area, this result will be seen to be identical with that which is obtained from the transformation equations for force and area which result from our earliest considerations.

146. Transformation Equation for Temperature. The second of the Lagrangian equations (199) will provide us information as to measurements of temperature made by observers moving with different velocities. We have

$$T = \frac{\partial}{\partial S}\left(E^\circ \sqrt{1 - \frac{u^2}{c^2}} \right) = \sqrt{1 - \frac{u^2}{c^2}}\, \frac{\partial E^\circ}{\partial S^\circ}\, \frac{\partial S^\circ}{\partial S}.$$

But, in accordance with equation (194), $\dfrac{\partial E^\circ}{\partial S^\circ} = T^\circ$ and in accordance with (197) $\dfrac{\partial S^\circ}{\partial S} = 1$. We obtain as our transformation equation,

$$T = T^\circ \sqrt{1 - \frac{u^2}{c^2}}, \tag{201}$$

and see that the quantity $\dfrac{T}{\sqrt{1 - \dfrac{u^2}{c^2}}}$ is an invariant for the Lorentz transformation.

147. The Equations of Motion for Quasistationary Adiabatic Acceleration. Let us now turn our attention to the last three of the Lagrangian equations. These are the equations for the motion of a thermodynamic system under the action of external force. It is evident, however, that these equations will necessarily apply only to cases of quasistationary acceleration, since our development of the principle of least action gave us an equation for kinetic potential which was true only for systems of infinitesimal extent or large systems in a steady internal state. It is also evident that we must confine our considerations to cases of adiabatic acceleration, since otherwise the value of E° which occurs in the expression for kinetic potential might be varying in a perfectly unknown manner.

The Lagrangian equations for force may be advantageously transformed. We have

$$F_x = \frac{d}{dt}\frac{\partial}{\partial \dot{x}}\left(-E^\circ\sqrt{1-\frac{u^2}{c^2}}\right) = \frac{d}{dt}\left[\frac{E^\circ}{\sqrt{1-\frac{u^2}{c^2}}}\frac{\dot{x}}{c^2} - \sqrt{1-\frac{u^2}{c^2}}\frac{\partial E^\circ}{\partial \dot{x}}\right]$$

$$= \frac{d}{dt}\left\{\frac{E^\circ}{\sqrt{1-\frac{u^2}{c^2}}}\frac{\dot{x}}{c^2} - \sqrt{1-\frac{u^2}{c^2}}\left(\frac{\partial E^\circ}{\partial v^\circ}\frac{\partial v^\circ}{\partial \dot{x}} + \frac{\partial E^\circ}{\partial S^\circ}\frac{\partial S^\circ}{\partial \dot{x}}\right)\right\}.$$

But by equations (194), (196) and (197) we have

$$\frac{\partial E^\circ}{\partial v^\circ} = -p^\circ, \qquad \frac{\partial v^\circ}{\partial \dot{x}} = \frac{v^\circ}{\left(1-\frac{u^2}{c^2}\right)}\frac{\dot{x}}{c^2}, \qquad \text{and} \qquad \frac{\partial S^\circ}{\partial \dot{x}} = 0.$$

We obtain

$$F_x = \frac{d}{dt}\left\{\frac{E^\circ + p^\circ v^\circ}{\sqrt{1-\frac{u^2}{c^2}}}\frac{\dot{x}}{c^2}\right\}. \tag{202}$$

Similar equations may be obtained for the components of force in the Y and Z directions and these combined to give the vector equation

$$\mathbf{F} = \frac{d}{dt}\left\{\frac{E^\circ + p^\circ v^\circ}{\sqrt{1-\frac{u^2}{c^2}}}\frac{\mathbf{u}}{c^2}\right\}. \tag{203}$$

This is the fundamental equation of motion for the dynamics of a thermodynamic system.

148. The Energy of a Moving Thermodynamic System. We may use this equation to obtain an expression for the energy of a moving thermodynamic system. If we adiabatically accelerate a thermodynamic system in the direction of its motion, its energy will increase both because of the work done by the force

$$\mathbf{F} = \frac{d}{dt}\left\{\frac{E^\circ + p^\circ v^\circ}{\sqrt{1 - \dfrac{u^2}{c^2}}}\,\frac{\mathbf{u}}{c^2}\right\}$$

which produces the acceleration and because of the work done by the pressure $p = p^\circ$ which acts on a volume which is continually diminishing as the velocity u increases, in accordance with the expression $v = v^\circ\sqrt{1 - \dfrac{u^2}{c^2}}$. Hence we may write for the total energy

$$E = E^\circ + \int_0^u \frac{d}{dt}\left\{\frac{E^\circ + p^\circ v^\circ}{\sqrt{1 - \dfrac{u^2}{c^2}}}\,\frac{\mathbf{u}}{c^2}\right\}\mathbf{u}\,dt + p^\circ v^\circ\left(1 - \sqrt{1 - \frac{u^2}{c^2}}\right),$$

$$E = \frac{E^\circ + p^\circ v^\circ}{\sqrt{1 - \dfrac{u^2}{c^2}}} - p^\circ v^\circ\sqrt{1 - \frac{u^2}{c^2}} = \frac{E^\circ + p^\circ v^\circ}{\sqrt{1 - \dfrac{u^2}{c^2}}} - pv. \tag{204}$$

149. The Momentum of a Moving Thermodynamic System. We may compare this expression for the energy of a thermodynamic system with the following expression for momentum which is evident from the equation (203) for force:

$$\mathbf{G} = \frac{E^\circ + p^\circ v^\circ}{\sqrt{1 - \dfrac{u^2}{c^2}}}\,\frac{\mathbf{u}}{c^2}. \tag{205}$$

We find again, as in our treatment of elastic bodies presented in the last chapter, that the momentum of a moving system may be calculated by taking the *total* flow of energy in the desired direction and dividing by c^2. Thus, comparing equations (204) and (205), we have

$$\mathbf{G} = \frac{E}{c^2}\mathbf{u} + \frac{pv}{c^2}\mathbf{u}, \tag{206}$$

where the term $\dfrac{E}{c^2}\,\mathbf{u}$ takes care of the energy transported bodily along by the system and the term $\dfrac{pv}{c^2}\,\mathbf{u}$ takes care of the energy transferred in the $\mathbf{u}$ direction by the action of the external pressure on the rear and front end of the moving system.

150. The Dynamics of a Hohlraum. As an application of our considerations we may consider the dynamics of a hohlraum, since a hohlraum in thermodynamic equilibrium is of course merely a special example of the general dynamics which we have just developed. The simplicity of the hohlraum and its importance from a theoretical point of view make it interesting to obtain by the present method the same expression for momentum that can be obtained directly but with less ease of calculation from electromagnetic considerations.

As is well known from the work of Stefan and Boltzmann, the energy content E° and pressure p° of a hohlraum at rest and in thermodynamic equilibrium are completely determined by the temperature T° and volume v° in accordance with the equations

$$E^\circ = av^\circ T^{\circ 4},$$

$$p^\circ = \frac{a}{3}\,T^{\circ 4},$$

where a is the so-called Stefan's constant.

Substituting these values of E° and p° in the equation for the motion of a thermodynamic system (203), we obtain

$$\mathbf{F} = \frac{d}{dt}\left[\frac{4}{3}\,\frac{av^\circ T^{\circ 4}}{\sqrt{1 - \dfrac{u^2}{c^2}}}\,\frac{\mathbf{u}}{c^2}\right] = \frac{d}{dt}\left[\frac{4}{3}\,\frac{avT^4}{\left(1 - \dfrac{u^2}{c^2}\right)^3}\,\frac{\mathbf{u}}{c^2}\right] \tag{207}$$

as the equation for the quasistationary adiabatic acceleration of a hohlraum. In view of this equation we may write for the momentum of a hohlraum the expression

$$G = \frac{4}{3} \frac{av^\circ T^{\circ 4}}{\sqrt{1 - \frac{u^2}{c^2}}} \frac{u}{c^2}. \tag{208}$$

It is a fact of significance that our dynamics leads to a result for the momentum of a hohlraum which had been adopted on the ground of electromagnetic considerations even without the express introduction of relativity theory.

CHAPTER XII.

ELECTROMAGNETIC THEORY.

The Einstein theory of relativity proves to be of the greatest significance for electromagnetics. On the one hand, the new electromagnetic theory based on the first postulate of relativity obviously accounts in a direct and straightforward manner for the results of the Michelson-Morley experiment and other unsuccessful attempts to detect an ether drift, and on the other hand also accounts just as simply for the phenomena of moving dielectrics as did the older theory of a stationary ether. Furthermore, the theory of relativity provides considerably simplified methods for deriving a great many theorems which were already known on the basis of the ether theory, and gives us in general a clarified insight into the nature of electromagnetic action.

151. The Form of the Kinetic Potential. In Chapter IX we investigated the general relation between the principle of least action and the theory of the relativity of motion. We saw that the development of any branch of dynamics would agree with the requirements of relativity provided only that the kinetic potential H has such a form that the quantity $\dfrac{H}{\sqrt{1 - \dfrac{u^2}{c^2}}}$ is an invariant for the Lorentz transformation. Making use of this discovery we have seen the possibility of developing the dynamics of a particle, the dynamics of an elastic body, and the dynamics of a thermodynamic system, all of them in forms which agree with the theory of relativity by merely introducing slight modifications into the older expressions for kinetic potential in such a way as to obtain the necessary invariance for $\dfrac{H}{\sqrt{1 - \dfrac{u^2}{c^2}}}$. In the case of electrodynamics, however, on account of the closely interwoven historical development of the theories of electricity and relativity, we shall not find it necessary to introduce any modification in the form of the kinetic potential, but may take for H the following expression, which is known to lead to the familiar equations of the Lorentz electron theory

$$H = \int dV \left\{ \frac{\mathbf{e}^2}{2} + \frac{(\operatorname{curl} \boldsymbol{\phi})^2}{2} - \boldsymbol{\phi} \cdot \left(\frac{\dot{\mathbf{e}}}{c} + \rho \frac{\mathbf{u}}{c} \right) \right\}, \qquad (209)$$

where the integration is to extend over the whole volume of the system V, $\mathbf{e}$ is the intensity of the electric field at the point in question, $\boldsymbol{\phi}$ is the value of the vector potential, ρ the density of charge and $\mathbf{u}$ its velocity.*

Let us now show that the expression which we have chosen for kinetic potential does lead to the familiar equations of the electron theory.

152. The Principle of Least Action. If now we denote by $\mathbf{f}$ the force per unit volume of material exerted by the electromagnetic action it is evident that we may write in accordance with the principle of least action (135)

$$\int dt \, dV \left[\delta \left\{ \frac{\mathbf{e}^2}{2} + \frac{(\operatorname{curl} \boldsymbol{\phi})^2}{2} - \boldsymbol{\phi} \cdot \left(\frac{\dot{\mathbf{e}}}{c} + \rho \frac{\mathbf{u}}{c} \right) \right\} + \mathbf{f} \cdot \delta \mathbf{r} \right] = 0, \quad (210)$$

where $\delta \mathbf{r}$ is the variation in the radius vector to the particle under consideration, and where the integration is to be taken over the whole volume occupied by the system and between two instants of time t_1 and t_2 at which the actual and displaced configurations of the system coincide.

153. The Partial Integrations. In order to simplify this equation, we shall need to make use of two results which can be obtained by partial integrations with respect to time and space respectively.

---

*Strictly speaking this expression for kinetic potential is not quite correct, since kinetic potential must have the dimensions of energy. To complete the equation and give all the terms their correct dimensions, we could multiply the first term by the dielectric inductivity of free space ϵ, and the last two terms by the magnetic permeability μ. Since, however, ϵ and μ have the numerical value unity with the usual choice of units, we shall not be led into error in our particular considerations if we omit these factors.

Thus we may write

$$\int_{t_1}^{t_2} dt\,(a\,\dot{\delta b}) = \int_{t_1}^{t_2} a\,d(\delta b) = [a\,\delta b]_{t_1}^{t_2} - \int_{t_1}^{t_2} dt\left(\frac{da}{dt}\,\delta b\right),$$

or, since the displaced and actual motions coincide at t_1 and t_2,

$$\int dt\,(a\,\dot{\delta b}) = -\int dt\left(\frac{da}{dt}\,\delta b\right). \tag{211}$$

We may also write

$$\int dV\left(a\,\frac{db}{dx}\right) = \int dy\,dz\,(a\,db) = \int dy\,dz\,[ab]_{x=-\infty}^{x=+\infty} - \int dV\left(b\,\frac{da}{dx}\right),$$

or, since we are to carry out our integrations over the whole volume occupied by the system, we shall take our functions as zero at the limits of integration and may write

$$\int dV\left(a\,\frac{db}{dx}\right) = -\int dV\left(b\,\frac{da}{dx}\right). \tag{212}$$

Since similar considerations apply to derivatives with respect to the other variables y and z, we can also obtain

$$\int dV\,a\,\operatorname{div}\mathbf{b} = -\int dV\,\mathbf{b}\cdot\operatorname{grad} a, \tag{213}$$

$$\int dV\,\mathbf{a}\cdot\operatorname{curl}\mathbf{b} = \int dV\,\mathbf{b}\cdot\operatorname{curl}\mathbf{a}. \tag{214}$$

154. Derivation of the Fundamental Equations of Electromagnetic Theory. Making use of these purely mathematical relationships we are now in a position to develop our fundamental equation (210). Carrying out the indicated variation, noting that

$\delta \mathbf{u} = \dfrac{d(\delta \mathbf{r})}{dt}$ and making use of (211) and (214) we easily obtain

$$\int dt\, dV \left[\left\{ \mathbf{e} + \frac{1}{c} \frac{\partial \phi}{\partial t} \right\} \cdot \delta \mathbf{e} + \left\{ \operatorname{curl} \operatorname{curl} \phi - \left(\frac{\dot{\mathbf{e}}}{c} + \rho \frac{\mathbf{u}}{c} \right) \right\} \cdot \delta \phi \right.$$
$$\left. - \frac{\phi}{c} \cdot \delta(\rho \mathbf{u}) + \mathbf{f} \cdot \delta \mathbf{r} \right] = 0. \tag{215}$$

In developing the consequences of this equation, it should be noted, however, that the variations are not all of them independent; thus, since we shall define the density of charge by the equation

$$\rho = \operatorname{div} \mathbf{e}, \tag{216}$$

it is evident that it will be necessary to preserve the truth of this equation in any variation that we carry out. This can evidently be done if we add to our equation (215) the expression

$$\int dt\, dV\, \psi[\delta \rho - \operatorname{div} \delta \mathbf{e}] = 0,$$

where ψ is an undetermined scalar multiplier. We then obtain with the help of (213)

$$\int dt\, dV \left[\left\{ \mathbf{e} + \frac{1}{c} \frac{\partial \phi}{\partial t} + \operatorname{grad} \psi \right\} \cdot \delta \mathbf{e} \right.$$
$$\left. + \left\{ \operatorname{curl} \operatorname{curl} \phi - \left(\frac{\dot{\mathbf{e}}}{c} + \rho \frac{\mathbf{u}}{c} \right) \right\} \cdot \delta \phi - \frac{\phi}{c} \cdot \delta(\rho \mathbf{u}) + \psi\, \delta \rho + \mathbf{f} \cdot \delta \mathbf{r} \right] = 0, \tag{217}$$

and may now treat the variations $\delta \mathbf{e}$ and $\delta \phi$ as entirely independent of the others; we must then have the following equations true

$$\mathbf{e} = -\frac{1}{c} \frac{\partial \phi}{\partial t} - \operatorname{grad} \psi, \tag{218}$$

$$\operatorname{curl} \operatorname{curl} \phi = \frac{\dot{\mathbf{e}}}{c} + \frac{\rho \mathbf{u}}{c}, \tag{219}$$

and have thus derived from the principle of least action the fundamental equations of modern electron theory. We may put these in their familiar form by defining the magnetic field strength $\mathbf{h}$ by the equation

$$\mathbf{h} = \operatorname{curl} \boldsymbol{\phi}. \tag{220}$$

We then obtain from (219)

$$\operatorname{curl} \mathbf{h} = \frac{1}{c}\frac{\partial \mathbf{e}}{\partial t} + \rho\,\frac{\mathbf{u}}{c}, \tag{221}$$

and, noting the mathematical identity $\operatorname{curl} \operatorname{grad} \psi = 0$, we obtain from (218)

$$\operatorname{curl} \mathbf{e} = -\frac{1}{c}\frac{\partial \mathbf{h}}{\partial t}. \tag{222}$$

We have furthermore by definition (216)

$$\operatorname{div} \mathbf{e} = \rho, \tag{223}$$

and noting equation (220) may write the mathematical identity

$$\operatorname{div} \mathbf{h} = 0. \tag{224}$$

These four equations (221)–(224) are the familiar expressions which have been made the foundation of modern electron theory. They differ from Maxwell's original four field equations only by the introduction in (221) and (223) of terms which arise from the density of charge ρ of the electrons, and reduce to Maxwell's set in free space.

155. We have not yet made use of the last three terms in the fundamental equation (217) which results from the principle of least action. As a matter of fact, it can be shown that these terms can be transformed into the expression

$$\int dt\,dV \left[\frac{\rho}{c}\frac{\partial \boldsymbol{\phi}}{\partial t} - \frac{\rho}{c}[\mathbf{u} \times \operatorname{curl} \boldsymbol{\phi}]^{*} + \rho\,\operatorname{grad}\psi + \mathbf{f} \right] \cdot \delta\mathbf{r}, \tag{225}$$

and hence lead to the familiar fifth fundamental equation of modern electron theory,

$$\mathbf{f} = \rho \left\{ -\frac{\partial \phi}{c\partial t} - \operatorname{grad} \psi + \left[\frac{\mathbf{u}}{c} \times \operatorname{curl} \mathbf{\Phi} \right]^* \right\},$$

$$\mathbf{f} = \rho \left\{ \mathbf{e} + \left[\frac{\mathbf{u}}{c} \times \mathbf{h} \right]^* \right\}. \tag{226}$$

The transformation of the last three terms of (217) into the form given above (225) is a complicated one and it has not seemed necessary to present it here since in a later paragraph we shall show the possibility of deriving the fifth fundamental equation of the electron theory (226) by combining the four field equations (221)–(224) with the transformation equations for force already obtained from the principle of relativity. The reader may carry out the transformation himself, however, if he makes use of the partial integrations which we have already obtained, notes that in accordance with the principle of the conservation of electricity we must have $\delta\rho = -\operatorname{div}\rho\,\delta\mathbf{r}$ and notes that $\delta\mathbf{u} = \dfrac{d(\delta\mathbf{r})}{dt}$, where the differentiation $\dfrac{d}{dt}$ indicates that we are following some particular particle in its motion, while the differentiation $\dfrac{\partial}{\partial t}$ occurring in $\dfrac{\partial\phi}{\partial t}$ indicates that we intend the rate of change at some particular stationary point.

156. The Transformation Equations for e, h and ρ. We have thus shown the possibility of deriving the fundamental equations of modern electron theory from the principle of least action. We now wish to introduce the theory of relativity into our discussions by presenting a set of equations for transforming measurements of $\mathbf{e}$, $\mathbf{h}$ and ρ from one set of space-time coördinates S to another set S' moving past S in the X direction with the velocity V. This set of equations is as follows:

$$e_x' = e_x, \qquad e_y' = \kappa\left(e_y - \frac{V}{c}h_z\right), \qquad e_z' = \kappa\left(e_z + \frac{V}{c}h_y\right), \tag{227}$$

$$h_x' = h_x, \qquad h_y' = \kappa\left(h_y + \frac{V}{c}e_z\right), \qquad h_z' = \kappa\left(h_z - \frac{V}{c}e_y\right), \tag{228}$$

$$\rho' = \rho\kappa\left(1 - \frac{u_z V}{c^2}\right),\qquad(229)$$

where κ has its customary significance $\dfrac{1}{\sqrt{1 - \dfrac{V^2}{c^2}}}$.

As a matter of fact, this set of transformation equations fulfills all the requirements imposed by the theory of relativity. Thus, in the first place, it will be seen, on development, that these equations are themselves perfectly symmetrical with respect to the primed and unprimed quantities except for the necessary change from $+V$ to $-V$. In the second place, it will be found that the substitution of these equations into our five fundamental equations for electromagnetic theory (221), (222), (223), (224), (226) will successfully transform them into an entirely similar set with primed quantities replacing the unprimed ones. And finally it can be shown that these equations agree with the general requirement derived in Chapter IX that the quantity $\dfrac{H}{\sqrt{1 - \dfrac{u^2}{c^2}}}$ shall be an invariant for the Lorentz transformation.

To demonstrate this important invariance of $\dfrac{H}{\sqrt{1 - \dfrac{u^2}{c^2}}}$ we may point out that by introducing equations (220), (221) and (214), our original expression for kinetic potential

$$H = \int dV\left\{\frac{\mathbf{e}^2}{2} + \frac{(\operatorname{curl}\boldsymbol{\phi})^2}{2} - \boldsymbol{\phi}\cdot\left(\frac{\dot{\mathbf{e}}}{c} + \rho\frac{\mathbf{u}}{c}\right)\right\}$$

can easily be shown equal to

$$\int dV\left(\frac{\mathbf{e}^2}{2} - \frac{\mathbf{h}^2}{2}\right),\qquad(230)$$

and, noting that our fundamental equations for space and time provide us with the relation

$$\frac{dV}{\sqrt{1 - \frac{u^2}{c^2}}} = \frac{dV'}{\sqrt{1 - \frac{u'^2}{c^2}}},$$

we can easily show that our transformation equations for $\mathbf{e}$ and $\mathbf{h}$ do lead to the equality

$$\frac{H}{\sqrt{1 - \frac{u^2}{c^2}}} = \frac{H'}{\sqrt{1 - \frac{u'^2}{c^2}}}.$$

We thus know that our development of the fundamental equations for electromagnetic theory from the principle of least action is indeed in complete accordance with the theory of relativity, since it conforms with the general requirement which was found in Chapter IX to be imposed by the theory of relativity on all dynamical considerations.

157. The Invariance of Electric Charge. As to the significance of the transformation equations which we have presented for $\mathbf{e}$, $\mathbf{h}$ and ρ, we may first show, in accordance with the last of these equations, that a given electric charge will appear the same to all observers no matter what their relative motion.

To demonstrate this we merely have to point out that, by introducing equation (17), we may write our transformation equation for ρ (229) in the form

$$\frac{\rho'}{\rho} = \frac{\sqrt{1 - \frac{u^2}{c^2}}}{\sqrt{1 - \frac{u'^2}{c^2}}},$$

which shows at once that the two measurements of density of charge made by O and O' are in exactly the same ratio as the corresponding measurements for the Lorentz shortening of the charged body, so that the total charge will evidently measure the same for the two observers.

We might express this invariance of electric charge by writing the equation

$$Q' = Q. \tag{231}$$

It should be noted in passing that this result is in entire accord with the whole modern development of electrical theory, which lays increasing stress on the fundamentality and indivisibility of the electron as the natural unit quantity of electricity. On this basis the most direct method of determining the charge on an electrified body would be to count the number of electrons present and this number must obviously appear the same both to observer O and observer O'.*

158. The Relativity of Magnetic and Electric Fields. As to the significance of equations (227) and (228) for transforming the values of the electric and magnetic field strengths from one system to another, we see that at a given point in space we may distinguish between the electric vector $\mathbf{e} = e_x\mathbf{i} + e_y\mathbf{j} + e_z\mathbf{k}$ as measured by our original observer O and the vector $\mathbf{e}' = e_x'\mathbf{i} + e_y'\mathbf{j} + e_z'\mathbf{k}$ as measured in units of his own system by an observer O' who is moving past O with the velocity V in the X direction. Thus if O finds in an unvarying electromagnetic field that $Q\mathbf{e}$ is the force on a small test charge Q which is stationary with respect to his system, O' will find experimentally for a similar test charge that moves along with him a value for the force $Q\mathbf{e}'$, where $\mathbf{e}'$ can be calculated from with the help of these equations (227). Similar remarks would apply to the forces which would act on magnetic poles.

These considerations show us that we should now use caution in speaking of a pure electrostatic or pure magnetic field, since the description of an electromagnetic field is determined by the particular choice of coördinates with reference to which the field is measured.

159. Nature of Electromotive Force. We also see that the "electromotive" force which acts on a charge moving through a magnetic

---

*A similar invariance of electric charge has been made fundamental in the author's development of the theory of similitude (*i.e.*, the theory of the relativity of size). See for example *Phys. Rev.*, vol. 3, p. 244 (1914).

field finds its interpretation as an "electric" force provided we make use of a system of coördinates which are themselves stationary with respect to the charge. Such considerations throw light on such questions, for example, as to the seat of the "electromotive" forces in "homopolar" electric dynamos where there is relative motion of a conductor and a magnetic field.

Derivation of the Fifth Fundamental Equation.

160. We may now make use of this fact that the forces acting on a moving charge of electricity may be treated as purely electrostatic, by using a set of coördinates which are themselves moving along with the charge, to derive the fifth fundamental equation of electromagnetic theory.

Consider an electromagnetic field having the values $\mathbf{e}$ and $\mathbf{h}$ for the electric and magnetic field strengths at some particular point. What will be the value of the electromagnetic force $\mathbf{f}$ acting per unit volume on a charge of density ρ which is passing through the point in question with the velocity $\mathbf{u}$?

To solve the problem take a system of coördinates S' which itself moves with the same velocity as the charge, for convenience letting the X axis coincide with the direction of the motion of the charge. Since the charge of electricity is stationary with respect to this system, the force acting on it as measured in units of this system will be by definition equal to the product of the charge by the strength of the electric field as it appears to an observer in this system, so that we may write

$$\mathbf{F} = Q'\mathbf{e}',$$

or

$$F_x' = Q'e_x', \qquad F_y' = Q'e_y', \qquad F_z' = Q'e_z'.$$

For the components of the electrical field e_x', e_y', e_z', we have just obtained the transformation equations (227), while in our earlier dynamical considerations in Chapter VI we obtained transformation equations

(61), (62), and (63) for the components of force. Substituting above and bearing in mind that $u_x = V$, $u_y = u_z = 0$, and that $Q' = Q$, we obtain on simplification

$$F_x = Qe_x,$$
$$F_y = Q\left(e_y - \frac{u_x}{c}h_z\right),$$
$$F_z = Q\left(e_z - \frac{u_x}{c}h_y\right),$$

which in vectorial form gives us the equation

$$\mathbf{F} = Q\left(\mathbf{e} - \frac{1}{c}[\mathbf{u} \times \mathbf{h}]^*\right)$$

or for the force per unit volume

$$\mathbf{f} = \rho\left(\mathbf{e} + \frac{1}{c}[\mathbf{u} \times \mathbf{h}]^*\right). \tag{226}$$

This is the well-known fifth fundamental equation of the Maxwell-Lorentz theory of electromagnetism. We have already indicated the method by which it could be derived from the principle of least action. This derivation, however, from the transformation equations, provided by the theory of relativity, is particularly simple and attractive.

Difference between the Ether and the Relativity Theories of Electromagnetism.

161. In spite of the fact that we have now found five equations which can be used as a basis for electromagnetic theory which agree with the requirements of relativity and also have exactly the same form as the five fundamental equations used by Lorentz in building up the stationary ether theory, it must not be supposed that the relativity and ether theories of electromagnetism are identical. Although the older equations have exactly the same form as the ones which we shall henceforth use, they have a different interpretation, since our equations are true for measurements made with the help of any non-accelerated set of coördinates, while the equations of Lorentz were, in the first instance, supposed to be true only for measurements which were referred to a set of coördinates which were stationary with respect to the assumed luminiferous ether. Suppose, for example, we desire to calculate with the help of equation (226),

$$\mathbf{t} = \rho \left(\mathbf{e} + \frac{1}{\mathbf{c}} \left[\mathbf{u} \times \mathbf{h} \right]^* \right),$$

the force acting on a charged body which is moving with the velocity $\mathbf{u}$; we must note that for the stationary ether theory, $\mathbf{u}$ must be the velocity of the charged body through the ether, while for us $\mathbf{u}$ may be taken as the velocity past any set of unaccelerated coördinates, provided $\mathbf{e}$ and $\mathbf{h}$ are measured with reference to the same set of coördinates. It will be readily seen that such an extension in the meaning of the fundamental equations is an important simplification.

162. A word about the development from the theory of a stationary ether to our present theory will not be out of place. When it was found that the theory of a stationary ether led to incorrect conclusions in the case of the Michelson-Morley experiment, the hypothesis was advanced by Lorentz and Fitzgerald that the failure of that experiment to show any motion through the ether was due to a contraction of the apparatus in the direction of its motion through the ether in the ratio $1 : \sqrt{1 - \dfrac{u^2}{c^2}}$. Lorentz then showed that if all systems should be thus contracted in the line of their motion through the ether, and observers moving with such system make use of suitably contracted meter sticks and clocks adjusted to give what Lorentz called the "local time," their measurements of electromagnetic phenomena could be described by a set of equations which have nearly the same form as the original four field equations which would be used by a stationary observer. It will be seen that Lorentz was thus making important progress towards our present idea of the complete relativity of motion. The final step could not be taken, however, without abandoning our older ideas of space and time and giving up the Galilean transformation equations as the basis of kinematics. It was Einstein who, with clearness and boldness of vision, pointed out that the failure of the Michelson-Morley experiment, and all other attempts to detect motion through the ether, is not due to a fortuitous compensation of effects but is the expression of an important general principle, and the new transformation equations for kinematics to which he was led have not only provided the basis for an *exact* transformation of the field equations but have so completely revolutionized our ideas of space and time that hardly a branch of science remains unaffected.

163. With regard to the present status of the ether in scientific theory, it must be definitely stated that this concept has certainly lost both its fundamentality and the greater part of its usefulness, and this has been brought about by a gradual process which has only found its culmination in the work of Einstein. Since the earliest days of the luminiferous ether, the attempts of science to increase the substantiality of this medium have met with little success. Thus we have had solid elastic ethers of most extreme tenuity, and ethers with a density of a thousand tons per cubic millimeter; we have had quasi-material tubes of force and lines of force; we have had vibratory gyrostatic ethers and perfect gases of zero atomic weight; but after every debauch of model-making, science has recognized anew that a correct mathematical description of the actual phenomena of light propagation is superior to any of these sublimated material media. Already for Lorentz the ether had been reduced to the bare function of providing a stationary system of reference for the measurement of positions and velocities, and now even this function has been taken from it by the work of Einstein, which has shown that any unaccelerated system of reference is just as good as any other.

To give up the notion of an ether will be very hard for many physicists, in particular since the phenomena of the interference and polarization of light are so easily correlated with familiar experience with wave motions in material elastic media. Consideration will show us, however, that by giving up the ether we have done nothing to destroy the periodic or polarizable nature of a light disturbance. When a plane polarized beam of light is passing through a given point in space we merely find that the electric and magnetic fields at that point lie on perpendiculars to the direction of propagation and undergo regular periodic changes in magnitude. There is no need of going beyond these actual experimental facts and introducing any hypothetical medium. It is just as simple, indeed simpler, to say that the electric or magnetic field has a certain intensity at a given point in space as to speak of a complicated sort of strain at a given point in an assumed ether.

Applications to Electromagnetic Theory.

164. The significant fact that the fundamental equations of the new electromagnetic theory have the same form as those of Lorentz makes it of course possible to retain in the structure of modern electrical theory nearly all the results of his important researches, care being taken to give his mathematical equations an interpretation in accordance with the fundamental ideas of the theory of relativity. It is, however, entirely beyond our present scope to make any presentation of electromagnetic theory as a whole, and in the following paragraphs we shall confine ourselves to the proof of a few theorems which can be handled with special ease and directness by the methods introduced by the theory of relativity.

165. The Electric and Magnetic Fields around a Moving Charge. Our transformation equations for the electromagnetic field make it very easy to derive expressions for the field around a point charge in uniform motion. Consider a point charge Q moving with the velocity V. For convenience consider a system of reference S such that Q is moving along the X axis and at the instant in question, $t = 0$, let the charge coincide with the origin of coördinates O. We desire now to calculate the values of electric field **e** and the magnetic field **h** at any point in space x, y, z.

Consider another system of reference, S', which moves along with the same velocity as the charge Q, the origin of coördinates O' and the charge always coinciding in position. Since the charge is stationary with respect to their new system of reference, we shall have the electric field at any point x', y', z' in this system given by the equations

$$e_x' = \frac{Qx'}{(x'^2 + y'^2 + z'^2)^{3/2}},$$

$$e_y' = \frac{Qy'}{(x'^2 + y'^2 + z'^2)^{3/2}},$$

$$e_z' = \frac{Qz'}{(x'^2 + y'^2 + z'^2)^{3/2}},$$

while the magnetic field will obviously be zero for measurements made in system S', giving us

$$h_x' = 0, \qquad h_y' = 0, \qquad h_z' = 0.$$

Introducing our transformation equations (9), (10) and (11) for x', y' and z' and our transformation equations (227) and (228) for the electric and magnetic fields and substituting $t = 0$, we obtain for the values of **e** and **h** in system S at the instant when the charge passes through the point O,

$$e_x = \frac{Q\kappa x}{(\kappa^2 x^2 + y^2 + z^2)^{3/2}} = \frac{Q\left(1 - \frac{V^2}{c^2}\right)x}{\left[x^2 + \left(1 - \frac{V^2}{c^2}\right)(y^2 + z^2)\right]^{3/2}},$$

$$e_y = \frac{Q\kappa y}{(\kappa^2 x^2 + y^2 + z^2)^{3/2}} = \frac{Q\left(1 - \frac{V^2}{c^2}\right)y}{\left[x^2 + \left(1 - \frac{V^2}{c^2}\right)(y^2 + z^2)\right]^{3/2}},$$

$$e_z = \frac{Q\kappa z}{(\kappa^2 x^2 + y^2 + z^2)^{3/2}} = \frac{Q\left(1 - \frac{V^2}{c^2}\right)z}{\left[x^2 + \left(1 - \frac{V^2}{c^2}\right)(y^2 + z^2)\right]^{3/2}},$$

$$h_x = 0,$$

$$h_y = -\frac{V}{c}\,e_z,$$

$$h_z = \frac{V}{c}\,e_y,$$

or, putting s for the important quantity $\sqrt{x^2 + \left(1 - \frac{V^2}{c^2}\right)(y^2 + z^2)}$ and writing the equations in the vectorial form where we put

$$\mathbf{r} = (x\,\mathbf{i} + y\,\mathbf{j} + z\,\mathbf{k}),$$

we obtain the familiar equations for the field around a point charge in uniform motion with the velocity $u = V$ in the X direction

$$\mathbf{e} = Q\,\frac{\left(1 - \frac{u^2}{c^2}\right)\mathbf{r}}{s^3}, \tag{232}$$

$$\mathbf{h} = \frac{1}{c}\,[\mathbf{u} \times \mathbf{e}]^*. \tag{233}$$

166. The Energy of a Moving Electromagnetic System. Our transformation equations will permit us to obtain a very important expression for the energy of an isolated electromagnetic system in terms of the velocity of the system and the energy of the same system as it appears to an observer who is moving along with it.

Consider a physical system surrounded by a shell which is impermeable to electromagnetic radiation. This system is to be thought of as consisting of the various mechanical parts, electric charges and electromagnetic fields which are inside of the impermeable shell. The system is free in space, except that it may be acted on by external electromagnetic fields, and its energy content thus be changed.

Let us now equate the increase in the energy of the system to the work done by the action of the external field on the electric charges in the system. Since the force which a magnetic field exerts on a charge is at right angles to the motion of the charge it does no work and we need to consider only the work done by the external electric field and may write for the increase in the energy of the system

$$\Delta E = \iiiint \rho(e_x u_x + e_y u_y + e_z u_z)\, dx\, dy\, dz\, dt, \qquad (234)$$

where the integration is to be taken over the total volume of the system and over any time interval in which we may be interested.

Let us now transform this expression with the help of our transformation equations for the electric field (227) for electric charge (229), and for velocities (14), (15), (16). Noting that our fundamental equations for kinematic quantities give us $dx\, dy\, dz\, dt = dx'\, dy'\, dz'\, dt'$, we obtain

$$\Delta E = \kappa \iiiint \rho'(e_x{}' u_x{}' + e_y{}' u_y{}' + e_z{}' u_z{}')\, dx'\, dy'\, dz'\, dt'$$

$$+ \kappa V \iiiint \rho' \left(e_x{}' + \frac{u_y{}'}{c} h_z{}' - \frac{u_z{}'}{c} h_y{}' \right) dx'\, dy'\, dz'\, dt'.$$

Consider now a system which *both at the beginning and end of our time interval is free from the action of external forces*; we may then rewrite the above equation for this special case in the form

$$\Delta E = \kappa \Delta E' + \kappa V \int \sum F_x{}'\, dt',$$

where, in accordance with our earlier equation (234), $\Delta E'$ is the increase in the energy of the system as it appears to observer O' and $\sum F_x{}'$ is the total force acting on the system in X direction as measured by O'.

The restriction that the system shall be unacted on by external forces both at the beginning and end of our time interval is necessary because it is only under those circumstances that an integration between two values of t can be considered as an integration between two definite values of t', simultaneity in different parts of the system not being the same for observers O and O'.

We may now apply this equation to a specially interesting case. Let the system be of such a nature that we can speak of it as being at rest with respect to S', meaning thereby that all the mechanical parts have low velocities with respect to S' and that their center of gravity moves permanently along with S'. Under these circumstances we may evidently put $\int \sum F_x' \, dt' = 0$ and may write the above equation in the form

$$\Delta E = \frac{\Delta E_0}{\sqrt{1 - \dfrac{u^2}{c^2}}},$$

or

$$\frac{\partial \Delta E}{\partial E_0} = \frac{1}{\sqrt{1 - \dfrac{u^2}{c^2}}},$$

where u is the velocity of the system, and E° is its energy as measured by an observer moving along with it. The energy of a system which is *unacted on by external forces* is thus a function of two variables, its energy E_0 as measured by an observer moving along with the system and its velocity u.

We may now write

$$E = \frac{1}{\sqrt{1 - \dfrac{u^2}{c^2}}} E_0 + \phi(u) + \text{const.},$$

where $\phi(u)$ represents the energy of the system which depends solely on the velocity of the system and not on the changes in its E_0 values.

$\phi(u)$ will thus evidently be the kinetic energy of the mechanical masses in the system which we have already found (82) to have the value

$$\frac{m_0 c^2}{\sqrt{1 - \dfrac{u^2}{c^2}}} - m_0 c^2$$

where m_0 is to be taken as the total mass of the mechanical part of our system when at rest. We may now write

$$E = \frac{1}{\sqrt{1 - \dfrac{u^2}{c^2}}} \, (m_0 c^2 + E_0) - m_0 c^2 + \text{const.}$$

Or, assuming as before that the constant is equal to $m_0 c^2$, which will be equivalent to making a system which has zero energy also have zero mass, we obtain

$$E = \frac{1}{\sqrt{1 - \dfrac{u^2}{c^2}}} \, (m_0 c^2 + E_0), \qquad (235)$$

which is the desired expression for the energy of an isolated system which may contain both electrical and mechanical parts.

167. Relation between Mass and Energy. This expression for the energy of a system that contains electrical parts permits us to show that the same relation which we found between mass and energy for mechanical systems also holds in the case of electromagnetic energy. Consider a system containing electromagnetic energy and enclosed by a shell which is impermeable to radiation. Let us apply a force $\mathbf{F}$ to the system in such a way as to change the velocity of the system without changing its E_0 value. We can then equate the work done per second by the force to the rate of increase of the energy of the system. We have

$$\mathbf{F} \cdot \mathbf{u} = \frac{dE}{dt}.$$

But from equation (235) we can obtain a value for the rate of increase of energy $\dfrac{dE}{dt}$, giving us

$$\mathbf{F} \cdot \mathbf{u} = F_x u_x + F_y u_y + F_z u_z = \left(m_0 + \frac{E_0}{c^2} \right) \frac{u \dfrac{du}{dt}}{\left(1 - \dfrac{u^2}{c^2} \right)^{\frac{3}{2}}},$$

and solving this equation for $\mathbf{F}$ we obtain

$$\mathbf{F} = \frac{d}{dt} \left[\frac{\left(m_0 + \dfrac{E_0}{c^2} \right)}{\sqrt{1 - \dfrac{u^2}{c^2}}} \, \mathbf{u} \right], \tag{236}$$

which for low velocities assumes the form

$$\mathbf{F} = \frac{d}{dt} \left[\left(m_0 + \frac{E_0}{c^2} \right) \mathbf{u} \right]. \tag{237}$$

Examination of these expressions shows that our system which contains electromagnetic energy behaves like an ordinary mechanical system with the mass $\left(m_0 + \dfrac{E_0}{c^2} \right)$ at low velocities or $\dfrac{m_0 + \dfrac{E_0}{c^2}}{\sqrt{1 - \dfrac{u^2}{c^2}}}$ at any desired velocity u. To the energy of the system E_0, part of which is electromagnetic, we must ascribe the mass $\dfrac{E_0}{c^2}$ just as we found in the case of mechanical energy. We realize again that matter and energy are but different names for the same fundamental entity, 10^{21} ergs of energy having the mass 1 gram.

The Theory of Moving Dielectrics.

168. The principle of relativity proves to be very useful for the development of the theory of moving dielectrics.

It was first shown by Maxwell that a theory of electromagnetic phenomena in material media can be based on a set of field equations similar in form to those for free space, provided we introduce besides the electric and magnetic field strengths, **E** and **F**, two new field vectors, the dielectric displacement **D** and the magnetic induction **B**, and also the density of electric current in the medium **i**. These quantities are found to be connected by the four following equations similar in form to the four field equations for free space:

$$\operatorname{curl} \mathbf{H} = \frac{1}{c}\left(\frac{\partial \mathbf{D}}{\partial t} + \mathbf{i}\right), \tag{238}$$

$$\operatorname{curl} \mathbf{E} = -\frac{1}{c}\frac{\partial \mathbf{B}}{\partial t}, \tag{239}$$

$$\operatorname{div} \mathbf{D} = \rho, \tag{240}$$

$$\operatorname{div} \mathbf{B} = 0. \tag{241}$$

For *stationary homogeneous* media, the dielectric displacement, magnetic induction and electric current are connected with the electric and magnetic field strengths by the following equations:

$$\mathbf{D} = \epsilon \mathbf{E}, \tag{242}$$

$$\mathbf{B} = \mu \mathbf{H}, \tag{243}$$

$$\mathbf{i} = \sigma \mathbf{E}, \tag{244}$$

where ϵ is the dielectric constant, μ the magnetic permeability and σ the electrical conductivity of the medium in question.

169. Relation between Field Equations for Material Media and Electron Theory. It must not be supposed that the four field equations (238)–(241) for electromagnetic phenomena in *material media* are in any sense contradictory to the four equations (221)–(224) for free space which we took as the fundamental basis for our development of electromagnetic theory. As a matter of fact, one of the main achievements of modern electron theory has been to show that the electromagnetic behavior of material media can be explained in terms of the behavior of the individual electrons and ions which they contain, these electrons and ions acting in accordance with the four fundamental field equations for free space. Thus our new equations for material media merely express from a *macroscopic* point of view the statistical result of the behavior of the individual electrons in the material in question. $\mathbf{E}$ and $\mathbf{H}$ in these new equations are to be looked upon as the average values of $\mathbf{e}$ and $\mathbf{h}$ which arise from the action of the individual electrons in the material, the process of averaging being so carried out that the results give the values which a *macroscopic* observer would actually find for the electric and magnetic forces acting respectively on a unit charge and a unit pole at the point in question. These average values, $\mathbf{E}$ and $\mathbf{H}$, will thus pay no attention to the rapid fluctuations of $\mathbf{e}$ and $\mathbf{h}$ which arise from the action and motion of the individual electrons, the macroscopic observer using in fact differentials for time, dt, and space, dx, which would be large from a microscopic or molecular viewpoint.

Since from a microscopic point of view $\mathbf{E}$ and $\mathbf{H}$ are not really the instantaneous values of the field strength at an actual point in space, it has been found necessary to introduce two new vectors, electric displacement, $\mathbf{D}$, and magnetic induction, $\mathbf{B}$, whose time rate of change will determine the curl of $\mathbf{E}$ and $\mathbf{H}$ respectively. It will evidently be possible, however, to relate $\mathbf{D}$ and $\mathbf{B}$ to the actual electric and magnetic fields $\mathbf{e}$ and $\mathbf{h}$ produced by the individual electrons, and this relation has been one of the problems solved by modern electron theory, and the field equations (238)–(241) for material media have thus been shown to stand in complete agreement with the most modern views as to the structure of matter and electricity. For the purposes of the rest of our discussion we shall merely take these equations as expressing the experimental facts in stationary or in moving media.

170. Transformation Equations for Moving Media. Since equations (238) to (241) are assumed to give a correct description of electromagnetic phenomena in media whether stationary or moving with respect to our reference system S, it is evident that the equations must be unchanged in form if we refer our measurements to a new system of coördinates S' moving past S, say, with the velocity V in the X direction.

As a matter of fact, equations (238) to (241) can be transformed into an entirely similar set

$$\operatorname{curl}\mathbf{H}' = \frac{1}{c}\left(\frac{\partial\mathbf{D}'}{\partial t'} + \mathbf{i}'\right),$$

$$\operatorname{curl}\mathbf{E}' = -\frac{1}{c}\frac{\partial\mathbf{B}'}{\partial t'},$$

$$\operatorname{div}\mathbf{D}' = \rho',$$

$$\operatorname{div}\mathbf{B}' = 0,$$

provided we substitute for x, y, z and t the values of x', y', z' and t' given by the fundamental transformation equations for space and time (9) to (12), and substitute for the other quantities in question the relations

$$E_x' = E_x, \quad E_y' = \kappa\left(E_y - \frac{V}{c}B_z\right), \quad E_z' = \kappa\left(E_z + \frac{V}{c}B_y\right),$$
$$D_x' = D_x, \quad D_y' = \kappa\left(D_y - \frac{V}{c}H_z\right), \quad D_z' = \kappa\left(D_z + \frac{V}{c}H_y\right), \tag{245}$$

$$H_x' = H_x, \quad H_y' = \kappa\left(H_y + \frac{V}{c}D_z\right), \quad H_z' = \kappa\left(H_z - \frac{V}{c}D_y\right),$$
$$B_x' = B_x, \quad B_y' = \kappa\left(B_y + \frac{V}{c}E_z\right), \quad B_z' = \kappa\left(B_z - \frac{V}{c}E_y\right), \tag{246}$$

$$\rho' = \kappa\left(\rho - \frac{V}{c^2}i_x\right), \qquad i_x' = \kappa(i_x - V\rho), \qquad i_y' = i_y, \qquad i_z' = i_z. \tag{247}$$

It will be noted that for free space these equations will reduce to the same form as our earlier transformation equations (227) to (229) since we shall have the simplifications $\mathbf{D} = \mathbf{E}$, $\mathbf{B} = \mathbf{H}$ and $\mathbf{i} = \rho\mathbf{u}$.

We may also call attention at this point to the fact that our funda-mental equations for electromagnetic phenomena (238)–(241) in dielec-tric media might have been derived from the principle of least action, making use of an expression for kinetic potential which could be shown equal to $H = \int dV \left(\dfrac{\mathbf{E} \cdot \mathbf{D}}{2} - \dfrac{\mathbf{H} \cdot \mathbf{B}}{2} \right)$, and it will be noticed that our transformation equations for these quantities are such as to preserve that necessary invariance for $\dfrac{H}{\sqrt{1 - \dfrac{u^2}{c^2}}}$ which we found in Chapter IX to be the general requirement for any dynamical development which agrees with the theory of relativity.

171. We are now in a position to handle the theory of moving me-dia. Consider a homogeneous medium moving past a system of coör-dinates S in the X direction with the velocity V; our problem is to discover relations between the various electric and magnetic vectors in this medium. To do this, consider a new system of coördinates S' also moving past our original system with the velocity V. Since the medium is stationary with respect to this new system S' we may write for mea-surements referred to S' in accordance with equations (242) to (244) the relations

$$\mathbf{D}' = \epsilon \mathbf{E}',$$
$$\mathbf{B}' = \mu \mathbf{H}',$$
$$\mathbf{i}' = \sigma \mathbf{E}',$$

which, as we have already pointed out, are known experimentally to be true in the case of *stationary, homogeneous* media. ϵ, μ and σ are evi-dently the values of dielectric constant, permeability and conductivity of the material in question, which would be found by an experimenter with respect to whom the medium is stationary.

Making use of our transformation equations (245) to (247) we can obtain by obvious substitutions the following set of relations for measurements made with respect to the original system of coördinates S:

$$D_x = \epsilon E_x,$$

$$D_y - \frac{V}{c}H_z = \epsilon\left(E_y - \frac{V}{c}B_z\right),$$

$$D_z + \frac{V}{c}H_y = \epsilon\left(E_z + \frac{V}{c}B_y\right), \qquad (248)$$

$$B_x = \mu H_x,$$

$$B_y + \frac{V}{c}E_z = \mu\left(H_y + \frac{V}{c}D_z\right),$$

$$B_z - \frac{V}{c}E_y = \mu\left(H_z - \frac{V}{c}D_y\right), \qquad (249)$$

$$\kappa(i_x - V_\rho) = \sigma E_x,$$

$$i_y = \sigma\kappa\left(E_y - \frac{V}{c}B_z\right),$$

$$i_z = \sigma\kappa\left(E_z + \frac{V}{c}B_y\right). \qquad (250)$$

172. Theory of the Wilson Experiment. The equations which we have just developed for moving media are, as a matter of fact, in complete accord with the celebrated experiment of H. A. Wilson on moving dielectrics and indeed all other experiments that have been performed on moving media.

Wilson's experiment consisted in the rotation of a hollow cylinder of dielectric, in a magnetic field which was parallel to the axis of the cylinder. The inner and outer surfaces of the cylinder were covered with a thin metal coating, and arrangements made with the help of wire brushes so that electrical contact could be made from these coatings to the pairs of quadrants of an electrometer. By reversing the magnetic field while the apparatus was in rotation it was possible to measure with the electrometer the charge produced by the electrical displacement in the dielectric. We may make use of our equations to compute the quantitative size of the effect.

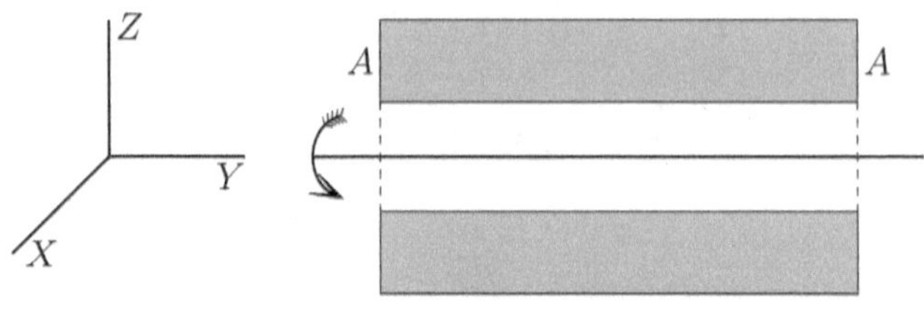

$$\textsc{Fig. 15.}$$

Let Fig. 15 represent a cross-section of the rotating cylinder. Consider a section of the dielectric AA which is moving perpendicularly to the plane of the paper in the X direction with the velocity V. Let the magnetic field be in the Y direction parallel to the axis of rotation. The problem is to calculate dielectric displacement D_z in the Z direction.

Referring to equations (248) we have

$$D_z + \frac{V}{c} H_y = \epsilon \left(E_z + \frac{V}{c} B_y \right),$$

and, substituting the value of B_y given by equations (249),

$$B_y + \frac{V}{c} E_z = \mu \left(H_y + \frac{V}{c} D_z \right)$$

we obtain

$$\left(1 - \epsilon\mu \frac{V^2}{c^2} \right) D_z = \epsilon \left(1 - \frac{V^2}{c^2} \right) E_z + \frac{V}{c} \left(\epsilon\mu - 1 \right) H_y,$$

or, neglecting terms of orders higher than $\dfrac{V}{c}$, we have

$$D_z = \epsilon E_z + \frac{V}{c} \left(\epsilon\mu - 1 \right) H_y. \tag{251}$$

For a substance whose permeability is practically unity such as Wilson actually used the equation reduces to

$$D_z = \epsilon E_z + \frac{V}{c}\left(\epsilon - 1\right) H_y,$$

and this was found to fit the experimental facts, since measurements with the electrometer show the surface charge actually to have the magnitude D_z per square centimeter in accordance with our equation $\operatorname{div} D = \rho$.

It would be a matter of great interest to repeat the Wilson experiment with a dielectric of high permeability so that we could test the complete equation (251). This is of some importance since the original Lorentz theory led to a different equation,

$$D_z = \epsilon E_z + \frac{V}{c}\left(\epsilon - 1\right) \mu H_y.$$

CHAPTER XIII.

FOUR-DIMENSIONAL ANALYSIS.

173. In the present chapter we shall present a four-dimensional method of expressing the results of the Einstein theory of relativity, a method which was first introduced by Minkowski, and in the form which we shall use, principally developed by Wilson and Lewis. The point of view adopted consists essentially in considering the properties of an assumed four-dimensional space in which intervals of time are thought of as plotted along an axis perpendicular to the three Cartesian axes of ordinary space, the science of kinematics thus becoming the geometry of this new four-dimensional space.

The method often has very great advantages not only because it sometimes leads to considerable simplification of the mathematical form in which the results of the theory of relativity are expressed, but also because the analogies between ordinary geometry and the geometry of this imaginary space often suggest valuable modes of attack. On the other hand, in order to carry out actual numerical calculations and often in order to appreciate the physical significance of the conclusions arrived at, it is necessary to retranslate the results obtained by this four-dimensional method into the language of ordinary kinematics. It must further be noted, moreover, that many important results of the theory of relativity can be more easily obtained if we do not try to employ this four-dimensional geometry. The reader should also be on his guard against the fallacy of thinking that extension in time is of the same nature as extension in space merely because intervals of space and time can both be represented by plotting along axes drawn on the same piece of paper.

174. Idea of a Time Axis. In order to grasp the method let us consider a particle constrained to move along a single axis, say OX, and let us consider a time axis OT perpendicular to OX. Then the *position* of the particle at any *instant* of time can be represented by a point in the XT plane, and its motion as time progresses by a line in the plane.

If, for example, the particle were stationary, its behavior in time and space could be represented by a line parallel to the time axis OT as shown for example by the line ab in Fig. 16. A particle moving with

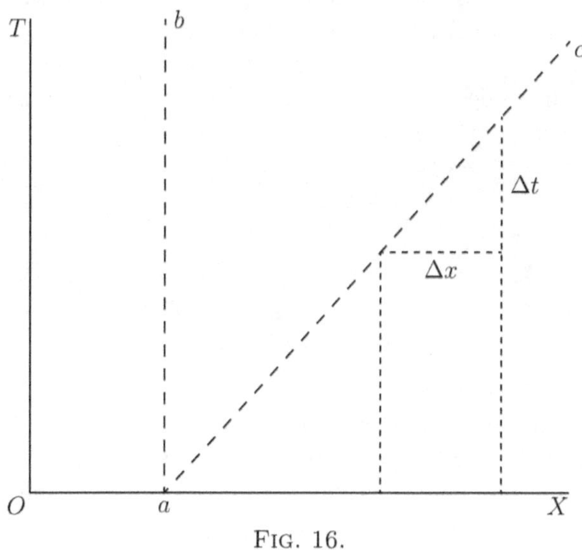

Fig. 16.

the uniform velocity $u = \dfrac{dx}{dt}$ could be represented by a straight line ac making an angle with the time axes, and the kinematical behavior of an accelerated particle could be represented by a curved line.

By conceiving of a *four*-dimensional space we can extend this method which we have just outlined to include motion parallel to all three space axes, and in accordance with the nomenclature of Minkowski might call such a geometrical representation of the space-time manifold "the world," and speak of the points and lines which represent the instantaneous positions and the motions of particles as "world-points" and "world-lines."

175. Non-Euclidean Character of the Space. It will be at once evident that the graphical method of representing kinematical events which is shown by Fig. 16 still leaves something to be desired. One of the most important conclusions drawn from the theory of relativity was the fact that it is impossible for a particle to move with a velocity greater than that of light, and it is evident that there is nothing in our plot to indicate that fact, since we could draw a line making any desired angle with the time axis, up to perpendicularity, and thus represent particles moving with any velocity up to infinity,

$$u = \frac{\Delta x}{\Delta t} = \infty.$$

It is also evident that there is nothing in our plot to correspond to that invariance in the velocity of light which is a cornerstone of the theory of relativity. Suppose, for example, the line OC, in Fig. 17, represents the trajectory of a beam of light with the velocity $\frac{\Delta x}{\Delta t} = c$; there is then nothing so far introduced into our method of plotting to indicate the fact that we could not equally well make use of another set of axes $OX'T'$, inclined to the first and thus giving quite a different value, $\frac{\Delta x'}{\Delta t'}$, to the velocity of the beam of light.

There are a number of methods of meeting this difficulty and obtaining the invariance for the four-dimensional expression $x^2 + y^2 + z^2 - c^2 t^2$ (see Chapter IV) which must characterize our system of kinematics. One of these is to conceive of a four-dimensional Euclidean space with an imaginary time axis, such that instead of plotting real instants in time along this axis we should plot the quantity $l = ict$ where $i = \sqrt{-1}$. In this way we should obtain invariance for the quantity $x^2 + y^2 + z^2 + l^2 = x^2 + y^2 + z^2 - c^2 t^2$, since it may be regarded as the square of the magnitude of an imaginary four-dimensional radius vector. This method of treatment has been especially developed by Minkowski, Laue, and Sommerfeld. Another method of attack, which has been developed by Wilson and Lewis and is the one which we shall adopt in this chapter, is to use a real time axis, for plotting the real

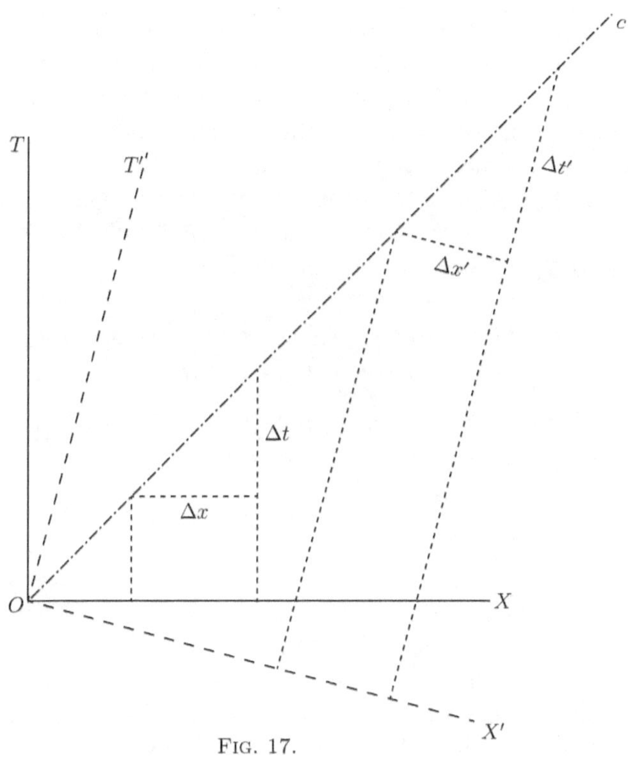

Fig. 17.

quantity ct, but to make use of a non-Euclidean four-dimensional space in which the quantity $(x^2 + y^2 + z^2 - c^2t^2)$ is itself taken as the square of the magnitude of a radius vector. This latter method has of course the disadvantages that come from using a non-Euclidean space; we shall find, however, that these reduce largely to the introduction of certain rules as to signs. The method has the considerable advantage of retaining a real time axis which is of some importance, if we wish to visualize the methods of attack and to represent them graphically.

We may now proceed to develop an analysis for this non-Euclidean space. We shall find this to be quite a lengthy process but at its completion we shall have a very valuable instrument for expressing in condensed language the results of the theory of relativity. Our method of treatment will be almost wholly analytical, and the geometrical analogies may be regarded merely as furnishing convenient names for useful analytical expressions. A more geometrical method of attack will be found in the original work of Wilson and Lewis.

PART I. VECTOR ANALYSIS OF THE NON-EUCLIDEAN
FOUR-DIMENSIONAL MANIFOLD.

176. Consider a four-dimensional manifold in which the position of a point is determined by a radius vector

$$\mathbf{r} = (x_1\mathbf{k}_1 + x_2\mathbf{k}_2 + x_3\mathbf{k}_3 + x_4\mathbf{k}_4),$$

where $\mathbf{k}_1$, $\mathbf{k}_2$, $\mathbf{k}_3$ and $\mathbf{k}_4$ may be regarded as unit vectors along four mutually perpendicular axes and x_1, x_2, x_3, and x_4 as the magnitudes of the four components of $\mathbf{r}$ along these four axes. We may identify x_1, x_2, and x_3 with the three spatial coördinates of a point x, y and z with reference to an ordinary set of space axes and consider x_4 as a coördinate which specifies the time (multiplied by the velocity of light) when the occurrence in question takes place at the point xyz. We have

$$x_1 = x, \qquad x_2 = y, \qquad x_3 = z, \qquad x_4 = ct, \tag{252}$$

and from time to time we shall make these substitutions when we wish to interpret our results in the language of ordinary kinematics. We shall retain the symbols x_1, x_2, x_3, and x_4 throughout our development, however, for the sake of symmetry.

177. Space, Time and Singular Vectors. Our space will differ in an important way from Euclidean space since we shall consider three classes of one-vector, space, time and singular vectors. Considering the coördinates x_1, x_2, x_3, and x_4 which determine the end of a radius vector,

Space or γ-vectors will have components such that

$$(x_1{}^2 + x_2{}^2 + x_3{}^2) > x_4{}^2,$$

and we shall put for their magnitude

$$s = \sqrt{x_1{}^2 + x_2{}^2 + x_3{}^2 - x_4{}^2}. \tag{253}$$

Time or δ-vectors will have components such that

$$x_4{}^2 > (x_1{}^2 + x_2{}^2 + x_3{}^2),$$

and we shall put for their magnitude

$$s = \sqrt{x_4{}^2 - x_1{}^2 - x_2{}^2 - x_3{}^2}. \tag{254}$$

Singular or α-vectors will have components such that

$$(x_1{}^2 + x_2{}^2 + x_3{}^2) = x_4{}^2,$$

and their magnitude will be zero.

178. Invariance of $x^2 + y^2 + z^2 - c^2t^2$. Since we shall naturally consider the magnitude of a vector to be independent of any particular choice of axes we have obtained at once by our definition of magnitude for any rotation of axes that invariance for the expression

$$(x_1{}^2 + x_2{}^2 + x_3{}^2 - x_4{}^2) = (x^2 + y^2 + z^2 - c^2t^2),$$

which is characteristic of the Lorentz transformation, and have thus evidently set up an imaginary space which will be suitable for plotting kinematical events in accordance with the requirements of the theory of the relativity of motion.

179. Inner Product of One-Vectors. We shall define the inner product of two one-vectors with the help of the following rules for the multiplication of unit vectors along the axes

$$\mathbf{k}_1 \cdot \mathbf{k}_1 = \mathbf{k}_2 \cdot \mathbf{k}_2 = \mathbf{k}_3 \cdot \mathbf{k}_3 = 1, \qquad \mathbf{k}_4 \cdot \mathbf{k}_4 = -1, \qquad \mathbf{k}_n \cdot \mathbf{k}_m = 0. \quad (255)$$

It should be noted, of course, that there is no particular significance in picking out the product $\mathbf{k}_4 \cdot \mathbf{k}_4$ as the one which is negative; it would be equally possible to develop a system in which the products $\mathbf{k}_1 \cdot \mathbf{k}_1, \mathbf{k}_2 \cdot \mathbf{k}_2$ and $\mathbf{k}_3 \cdot \mathbf{k}_3$ should be negative and $\mathbf{k}_4 \cdot \mathbf{k}_4$ positive.

The above rules for unit vectors are sufficient to define completely the inner product provided we include the further requirements that this product shall obey the *associative law* for a scalar factor and the *distributive* and *commutative* laws, namely

$$(n\mathbf{a}) \cdot \mathbf{b} = n(\mathbf{a} \cdot \mathbf{b}) = (\mathbf{a} \cdot \mathbf{b})(n),$$
$$\mathbf{a} \cdot (\mathbf{b} + \mathbf{c}) = \mathbf{a} \cdot \mathbf{b} + \mathbf{a} \cdot \mathbf{c}, \qquad (256)$$
$$\mathbf{a} \cdot \mathbf{b} = \mathbf{b} \cdot \mathbf{a}.$$

For the inner product of a one-vector by itself we shall have, in accordance with these rules,

$$\mathbf{r} \cdot \mathbf{r} = (x_1\mathbf{k}_1 + x_2\mathbf{k}_2 + x_3\mathbf{k}_3 + x_4\mathbf{k}_4) \cdot (x_1\mathbf{k}_1 + x_2\mathbf{k}_2 + x_3\mathbf{k}_3 + x_4\mathbf{k}_4)$$
$$= (x_1^2 + x_2^2 + x_3^2 - x_4^2) \quad (257)$$

and hence may use the following expressions for the magnitudes of vectors in terms of inner product

$$s = \sqrt{\mathbf{r} \cdot \mathbf{r}} \text{ for } \gamma\text{-vectors}, \qquad s = \sqrt{-\mathbf{r} \cdot \mathbf{r}} \text{ for } \delta\text{-vectors}. \quad (258)$$

For curved lines we shall define interval along the curve by the equations

$$\int ds = \int \sqrt{dr \cdot dr} \text{ for } \gamma\text{-curves},$$
$$\int ds = \int \sqrt{-dr \cdot dr} \text{ for } \delta\text{-curves}. \qquad (259)$$

Our rules further show us that we may obtain the space components of any one vector by taking its inner product with a unit vector along the desired axis and may obtain the time component by taking the negative of the corresponding product. Thus

$$\begin{aligned}
\mathbf{r} \cdot \mathbf{k}_1 &= (x_1\mathbf{k}_1 + x_2\mathbf{k}_2 + x_3\mathbf{k}_3 + x_4\mathbf{k}_4) \cdot \mathbf{k}_1 = x_1, \\
\mathbf{r} \cdot \mathbf{k}_2 &= (x_1\mathbf{k}_1 + x_2\mathbf{k}_2 + x_3\mathbf{k}_3 + x_4\mathbf{k}_4) \cdot \mathbf{k}_2 = x_2, \\
\mathbf{r} \cdot \mathbf{k}_3 &= (x_1\mathbf{k}_1 + x_2\mathbf{k}_2 + x_3\mathbf{k}_3 + x_4\mathbf{k}_4) \cdot \mathbf{k}_3 = x_3, \\
\mathbf{r} \cdot \mathbf{k}_4 &= (x_1\mathbf{k}_1 + x_2\mathbf{k}_2 + x_3\mathbf{k}_3 + x_4\mathbf{k}_4) \cdot \mathbf{k}_4 = -x_4.
\end{aligned} \tag{260}$$

We see finally moreover in general that the inner product of any pair of vectors will be numerically equal to the product of the magnitude of either by the projection of the other upon it, the sign depending on the nature of the vectors involved.

180. Non-Euclidean Angle. We shall define the non-Euclidean angle θ between two vectors $\mathbf{r}_1$ and $\mathbf{r}_2$ in terms of their magnitudes s_1 and s_2 by the expressions

$$\pm \mathbf{r}_1 \cdot \mathbf{r}_2 = (s_1 \times \text{projection } s_2) = s_1 s_2 \cosh \theta, \tag{261}$$

the sign depending on the nature of the vectors in the way indicated in the preceding section. We note the analogy between this equation and those familiar in Euclidean vector-analysis, the hyperbolic trigonometric functions taking the place of the circular functions used in the more familiar analysis.

For the angle between unit vectors $\mathbf{k}$ and $\mathbf{k}'$ we shall have

$$\cosh \theta = \pm \mathbf{k} \cdot \mathbf{k}', \tag{262}$$

where the sign must be chosen so as to make $\cosh \theta$ positive, the plus sign holding if both are γ-vectors and the minus sign if both are δ-vectors.

181. Kinematical Interpretation of Angle in Terms of Velocity. At this point we may temporarily interrupt the development of our four-dimensional analysis to consider a kinematical interpretation of non-Euclidean angles in terms of velocity. It will be evident from our introduction that the behavior of a moving particle can be represented in our four-dimensional space by a δ-curve,* each point on this curve denoting the position of the particle at a given instant of time, and it is evident that the velocity of the particle will be determined by the angle which this curve makes with the axes.

Let **r** be the radius vector to a given point on the curve and consider the derivative of **r** with respect to the interval s along the curve; we have

$$\mathbf{w} = \frac{d\mathbf{r}}{ds} = \frac{dx_1}{ds}\,\mathbf{k}_1 + \frac{dx_2}{ds}\,\mathbf{k}_2 + \frac{dx_3}{ds}\,\mathbf{k}_3 + \frac{dx_4}{ds}\,\mathbf{k}_4, \qquad (263)$$

and this may be regarded as a unit vector tangent to the curve at the point in question.

If ϕ is the angle between the $\mathbf{k}_4$ axis and the tangent to the curve at the point in question, we have by equation (262)

$$\cosh \phi = -\mathbf{w} \cdot \mathbf{k}_4 = \frac{dx_4}{ds};$$

making the substitutions for x_1, x_2, x_3, and x_4, in terms of x, y, z and t we may write, however,

$$ds = \sqrt{dx_4^2 - dx_1^2 - dx_2^2 - dx_3^2} = \sqrt{1 - \frac{u^2}{c^2}}\,c\,dt, \qquad (264)$$

which gives us

$$\cosh \phi = \frac{1}{\sqrt{1 - \dfrac{u^2}{c^2}}} \qquad (265)$$

---

*It is to be noted that the actual trajectories of particles are all of them represented by δ-curves since as we shall see γ-curves would correspond to velocities greater than that of light.

and by the principles of hyperbolic trigonometry we may write the further relations

$$\sinh \phi = \frac{\dfrac{u}{c}}{\sqrt{1 - \dfrac{u^2}{c^2}}}, \tag{266}$$

$$\tanh \phi = \frac{u}{c}. \tag{267}$$

Vectors of Higher Dimensions

182. Outer Products. We shall define the outer product of two one-vectors so that it obeys the *associative law* for a scalar factor, the *distributive law* and the *anti-commutative law*, namely,

$$(n\mathbf{a}) \times \mathbf{b} = n(\mathbf{a} \times \mathbf{b}) = \mathbf{a} \times (n\mathbf{b}),$$
$$\mathbf{a} \times (\mathbf{b} + \mathbf{c}) = \mathbf{a} \times \mathbf{b} + \mathbf{a} \times \mathbf{c}, \quad (\mathbf{a} + \mathbf{b}) \times \mathbf{c} = \mathbf{a} \times \mathbf{c} + \mathbf{b} \times \mathbf{c}, \tag{268}$$
$$\mathbf{a} \times \mathbf{b} = -\mathbf{b} \times \mathbf{a}.$$

From a geometrical point of view, we shall consider the outer product of two one-vectors to be itself a *two-vector*, namely the parallelogram, or more generally, the area which they determine. The sign of the two-vector may be taken to indicate the direction of progression clockwise or anti-clockwise around the periphery. In order to accord with the requirement that the area of a parallelogram determined by two lines becomes zero when they are rotated into the same direction, we may complete our definition of outer product by adding the requirement that the outer product of a vector by itself shall be zero.

$$\mathbf{a} \times \mathbf{a} = 0. \tag{269}$$

We may represent the outer products of unit vectors along the chosen axes as follows:

$$\mathbf{k}_1 \times \mathbf{k}_1 = \mathbf{k}_2 \times \mathbf{k}_2 = \mathbf{k}_3 \times \mathbf{k}_3 = \mathbf{k}_4 \times \mathbf{k}_4 = 0,$$
$$\mathbf{k}_1 \times \mathbf{k}_2 = -\mathbf{k}_2 \times \mathbf{k}_1 = \mathbf{k}_{12} = -\mathbf{k}_{21}, \tag{270}$$
$$\mathbf{k}_1 \times \mathbf{k}_3 = -\mathbf{k}_3 \times \mathbf{k}_1 = \mathbf{k}_{13} = -\mathbf{k}_{31}, \quad \text{etc.,}$$

where we may regard $\mathbf{k}_{12}$, for example, as a unit parallelogram in the plane $X_1 O X_2$.

We shall continue to use small letters in Clarendon type for one-vectors and shall use capital letters in Clarendon type for two-vectors. The components of a two-vector along the six mutually perpendicular planes $X_1 O X_2$, $X_1 O X_3$, etc., may be obtained by expressing the one-vectors involved in terms of their components along the axes and carrying out the indicated multiplication, thus:

$$\begin{aligned} \mathbf{A} = \mathbf{a} \times \mathbf{b} &= (a_1\mathbf{k}_1 + a_2\mathbf{k}_2 + a_3\mathbf{k}_3 + a_4\mathbf{k}_4) \\ &\quad \times (b_1\mathbf{k}_1 + b_2\mathbf{k}_2 + b_3\mathbf{k}_3 + b_4\mathbf{k}_4) \\ &= (a_1b_2 - a_2b_1)\mathbf{k}_{12} + (a_1b_3 - a_3b_1)\mathbf{k}_{13} + (a_1b_4 - a_4b_1)\mathbf{k}_{14} \\ &\quad + (a_2b_3 - a_3b_2)\mathbf{k}_{23} + (a_2b_4 - a_4b_2)\mathbf{k}_{24} + (a_3b_4 - a_4b_3)\mathbf{k}_{34}, \end{aligned} \tag{271}$$

or, calling the quantities $(a_1b_2 - a_2b_1)$, etc., the component magnitudes of $\mathbf{A}$, A_{12}, etc., we may write

$$\mathbf{A} = A_{12}\mathbf{k}_{12} + A_{13}\mathbf{k}_{13} + A_{14}\mathbf{k}_{14} + A_{23}\mathbf{k}_{23} + A_{24}\mathbf{k}_{24} + A_{34}\mathbf{k}_{34}. \tag{272}$$

The concept of outer product may be extended to include the idea of vectors of higher number of dimensions than two. Thus the outer product of three one-vectors, or of a one-vector and a two-vector will be a three-vector which may be regarded as a *directed* parallelopiped in our four-dimensional space. The outer product of four one-vectors will lead to a four-dimensional solid which would have direction only in a space of more than four dimensions and hence in our case will be called a pseudo-scalar. The outer product of vectors the sum of whose dimensions is greater than that of the space considered will vanish.

The results which may be obtained from different types of outer multiplication are tabulated below, where one-vectors are denoted by small Clarendon type, two-vectors by capital Clarendon type, three-vectors by Tudor black capitals, and pseudo-scalars by bold face Greek letters.

$$\mathbf{A} = \mathbf{a} \times \mathbf{b} = -\mathbf{b} \times \mathbf{a}$$
$$= (a_1 b_2 - a_2 b_1)\mathbf{k}_{12} + (a_1 b_4 - a_3 b_1)\mathbf{k}_{13} + (a_1 b_4 - a_4 b_1)\mathbf{k}_{14}$$
$$+ (a_2 b_3 - a_3 b_2)\mathbf{k}_{23} + (a_2 b_4 - a_4 b_2)\mathbf{k}_{21} + (a_3 b_4 - a_4 b_3)\mathbf{k}_{34},$$

$$\mathcal{A} = \mathbf{c} \times \mathbf{A}$$
$$= (c_1 A_{23} - c_2 A_{13} + c_3 A_{12})\mathbf{k}_{123} + (c_1 A_{24} - c_2 A_{14} + c_4 A_{12})\mathbf{k}_{124} \qquad (273)$$
$$+ (c_1 A_{34} - c_2 A_{14} + c_4 A_{15})\mathbf{k}_{134} + (c_2 A_{34} - c_3 A_{24} + c_4 A_{23})\mathbf{k}_{234}$$

$$\alpha = \mathbf{d} \times \mathcal{A} = -\mathcal{A} \times \mathbf{d}$$
$$= (d_1 \mathcal{A}_{234} - d_2 \mathcal{A}_{134} + d_3 \mathcal{A}_{124} - d_4 \mathcal{A}_{123})\mathbf{k}_{1234},$$
$$\alpha = \mathbf{A} \times \mathbf{B}$$
$$= (A_{12}B_{34} - A_{13}B_{24} + A_{14}B_{23} + A_{23}B_{14} - A_{24}B_{13} + A_{34}B_{12})\mathbf{k}_{1234}.$$

The signs in these expressions are determined by the general rule that the sign of any unit vector $\bar{\mathbf{k}}_{nmo}$ *will be reversed by each transposition of the order of a pair of adjacent subscripts, thus:*

$$k_{abcd} = -k_{bacd} = k_{bcad}, \qquad \text{etc.,} \quad \cdots. \qquad (274)$$

183. Inner Product of Vectors in General. We have previously defined the inner product for the special case of a pair of one-vectors, in order to bring out some of the important characteristics of our non-Euclidean space. We may now give a general rule for the inner product of vectors of any number of dimensions.

The inner product of any pair of vectors follows the *associative* law for scalar factors, and follows the *distributive* and *commutative* laws.

Since we can express any vector in terms of its components, the above rules will completely determine the inner product of any pair of vectors provided that we also have a rule for obtaining the inner products of the unit vectors determined by the mutually perpendicular axes. This rule is as follows: Transpose the subscripts of the unit vectors involved so that the common subscripts occur at the end and in the same order and cancel these common subscripts. If both the unit vectors still have subscripts the product is zero; if neither vector has subscripts the product is unity, and if one of the vectors still has subscripts that itself will be the product. The sign is to be taken as that resulting from the transposition of the subscripts (see equation (274)), unless the subscript 4 has been cancelled, when the sign will be changed.

For example:

$$\mathbf{k}_{124} \cdot \mathbf{k}_{34} = \mathbf{k}_{12} \cdot \mathbf{k}_3 = 0,$$
$$\mathbf{k}_{132} \cdot \mathbf{k}_{123} = -\mathbf{k}_{123} \cdot \mathbf{k}_{123} = -1, \tag{275}$$
$$\mathbf{k}_{124} \cdot \mathbf{k}_{42} = -\mathbf{k}_{124} \cdot \mathbf{k}_{24} = \mathbf{k}_1.$$

It is evident from these rules that we may obtain the magnitude of any desired component of a vector by taking the inner product of the vector by the corresponding unit vector, it being noticed, of course, that when the unit vector involved contains the subscript 4 we obtain the negative of the desired component. For example, we may obtain the k_{12} component of a two-vector as follows:

$$A_{12} = \mathbf{A} \cdot \mathbf{k}_{12} = (A_{12}\mathbf{k}_{12} + A_{13}\mathbf{k}_{13} + A_{14}\mathbf{k}_{14} \\ + A_{23}\mathbf{k}_{23} + A_{24}\mathbf{k}_{24} + A_{34}\mathbf{k}_{34}) \cdot \mathbf{k}_{12}. \tag{276}$$

184. The Complement of a Vector. In an n-dimensional space any m-dimensional vector will uniquely determine a new vector of dimensions $(n - m)$ which may be called the complement of the original vector. The complement of a vector may be exactly defined as the inner product of the original vector with the unit pseudo-scalar $\mathbf{k}_{123\cdots n}$. In general, we may denote the complement of a vector by placing an asterisk $*$ after the symbol. As an example we may write as the complement of a two-vector $\mathbf{A}$ in our non-Euclidean four-dimensional space:

$$\mathbf{A}^* = \mathbf{A} \cdot \mathbf{k}_{1234} = (A_{12}\mathbf{k}_{12} + A_{13}\mathbf{k}_{13} + A_{14}\mathbf{k}_{14} \\ + A_{23}\mathbf{k}_{23} + A_{24}\mathbf{k}_{24} + A_{34}\mathbf{k}_{34}) \cdot \mathbf{k}_{1234} \tag{277}$$
$$= (A_{12}\mathbf{k}_{34} - A_{13}\mathbf{k}_{24} - A_{14}\mathbf{k}_{23} + A_{23}\mathbf{k}_{14} + A_{24}\mathbf{k}_{13} - A_{34}\mathbf{k}_{12}).$$

185. The Vector Operator, $\Diamond$ or Quad. Analogous to the familiar three-dimensional vector-operator del,

$$\nabla = \mathbf{k}_1 \frac{\partial}{\partial x_1} + \mathbf{k}_2 \frac{\partial}{\partial x_2} + \mathbf{k}_3 \frac{\partial}{\partial x_3}, \tag{278}$$

we may define the four-dimensional vector-operator quad,

$$\Diamond = \mathbf{k}_1 \frac{\partial}{\partial x_1} + \mathbf{k}_2 \frac{\partial}{\partial x_2} + \mathbf{k}_3 \frac{\partial}{\partial x_3} - \mathbf{k}_4 \frac{\partial}{\partial x_4}. \tag{279}$$

If we have a scalar or a vector field we may apply these operators by regarding them formally as one-vectors and applying the rules for inner and outer multiplication which we have already given.

Thus if we have a scalar function F which varies continuously from point to point we can obtain a one-vector which we may call the four-dimensional gradient of F at the point in question by simple multiplication; we have

$$\operatorname{grad} F = \Diamond F = \mathbf{k}_1 \frac{\partial F}{\partial x_1} + \mathbf{k}_2 \frac{\partial F}{\partial x_2} + \mathbf{k}_3 \frac{\partial F}{\partial x_3} - \mathbf{k}_4 \frac{\partial F}{\partial x_4}. \tag{280}$$

If we have a one-vector field, with a vector $\mathbf{f}$ whose value varies from point to point we may obtain by inner multiplication a scalar quantity which we may call the four-dimensional divergence of $\mathbf{f}$. We have

$$\operatorname{div} \mathbf{f} = \Diamond \cdot \mathbf{f} = \frac{\partial f_1}{\partial x_1} + \frac{\partial f_2}{\partial x_2} + \frac{\partial f_3}{\partial x_3} + \frac{\partial f_4}{\partial x_4}. \tag{280}$$

Taking the outer product with quad we may obtain a two-vector, the four-dimensional curl of $\mathbf{f}$,

$$\begin{aligned}
\operatorname{curl} \mathbf{f} = \Diamond \times \mathbf{f} = {}& \left(\frac{\partial f_2}{\partial x_1} - \frac{\partial f_1}{\partial x_2} \right) \mathbf{k}_{12} + \left(\frac{\partial f_3}{\partial x_1} - \frac{\partial f_1}{\partial x_3} \right) \mathbf{k}_{13} \\
& + \left(\frac{\partial f_4}{\partial x_1} + \frac{\partial f_1}{\partial x_4} \right) \mathbf{k}_{14} + \left(\frac{\partial f_3}{\partial x_2} - \frac{\partial f_2}{\partial x_3} \right) \mathbf{k}_{23} \\
& + \left(\frac{\partial f_4}{\partial x_2} + \frac{\partial f_2}{\partial x_4} \right) \mathbf{k}_{24} + \left(\frac{\partial f_4}{\partial x_3} + \frac{\partial f_3}{\partial x_4} \right) \mathbf{k}_{34}.
\end{aligned} \tag{282}$$

By similar methods we could apply quad to a two-vector function $\mathbf{F}$ and obtain the one-vector function $\Diamond \cdot \mathbf{F}$ and the three-vector function $\Diamond \times \mathbf{F}$.

186. Still regarding $\Diamond$ as a one-vector we may obtain a number of important expressions containing $\Diamond$ more than once; we have:

$$\Diamond \times (\Diamond F) = 0, \quad (283) \qquad \Diamond \times (\Diamond \times \mathbf{f}) = 0, \quad (286)$$

$$\Diamond \cdot (\Diamond \cdot \mathbf{F}) = 0, \quad (284) \qquad \Diamond \times (\Diamond \times \mathbf{F}) = 0, \quad (287)$$

$$\Diamond \cdot (\Diamond \cdot \mathfrak{F}) = 0, \quad (285)$$

$$\Diamond \cdot (\Diamond \times \mathbf{f}) = \Diamond(\Diamond \cdot \mathbf{f}) - (\Diamond \cdot \Diamond)\mathbf{f}, \tag{288}$$

$$\Diamond \cdot (\Diamond \times \mathbf{F}) = \Diamond \times (\Diamond \cdot \mathbf{F}) + (\Diamond \cdot \Diamond)\mathbf{F}, \tag{289}$$

$$\Diamond \cdot (\Diamond \times \mathfrak{F}) = \Diamond \times (\Diamond \cdot \mathfrak{F}) - (\Diamond \cdot \Diamond)\mathfrak{F}. \tag{290}$$

The operator $\Diamond \cdot \Diamond$ or $\Diamond^2$ has long been known under the name of the D'Alembertian,

$$\Diamond^2 = \frac{\partial^2}{\partial x_1{}^2} + \frac{\partial^2}{\partial x_2{}^2} + \frac{\partial^2}{\partial x_3{}^2} - \frac{\partial^2}{\partial x_4{}^2} = \Delta^2 - \frac{\partial^2}{c^2\,\partial t^2}. \tag{291}$$

From the definition of the complement of a vector given in the previous section it may be shown by carrying out the proper expansions that

$$(\Diamond \times \phi)^* = \Diamond \cdot \phi^*, \tag{292}$$

where ϕ is a vector of any number of dimensions.

187. Tensors. In analogy to three-dimensional tensors we may define a four-dimensional tensor as a quantity with sixteen components as given in the following table:

$$T = \begin{cases} T_{11} \ \ T_{12} \ \ T_{13} \ \ T_{14}, \\[4pt] T_{21} \ \ T_{22} \ \ T_{23} \ \ T_{24}, \\[4pt] T_{31} \ \ T_{32} \ \ T_{33} \ \ T_{34}, \\[4pt] T_{41} \ \ T_{42} \ \ T_{43} \ \ T_{44}, \end{cases} \tag{293}$$

with the additional requirement that the divergence of the tensor, defined as follows, shall itself be a one-vector.

$$\operatorname{div} T = \left\{ \frac{\partial T_{11}}{\partial x_1} + \frac{\partial T_{12}}{\partial x_2} + \frac{\partial T_{13}}{\partial x_3} + \frac{\partial T_{14}}{\partial x_4} \right\} \mathbf{k}_1$$
$$+ \left\{ \frac{\partial T_{21}}{\partial x_1} + \cdots \right\} \mathbf{k}_2$$
$$+ \left\{ \frac{\partial T_{31}}{\partial x_1} + \cdots \right\} \mathbf{k}_3 \tag{294}$$
$$+ \left\{ \frac{\partial T_{41}}{\partial x_1} + \cdots \right\} \mathbf{k}_4$$

188. The Rotation of Axes. Before proceeding to the application of our four-dimensional analysis to the actual problems of relativity theory we may finally consider the changes in the components of a vector which would be produced by a rotation of the axes. We have already pointed out that the quantity $(x_1{}^2 + x_2{}^2 + x_3{}^2 - x_4{}^2)$ is an invariant in our space for any set of rectangular coördinates having the same origin since it is the square of the magnitude of a radius vector, and have noted that in this way we have obtained for the quantity $(x^2 + y^2 + z^2 - c^2 t^2)$ the desired invariance which is characteristic of the Lorentz transformation. In fact we may look upon the Lorentz transformation as a rotation from a given set of axes to a new set, with a corresponding re-expression of quantities in terms of the new components. The particular form of Lorentz transformation, familiar in preceding chapters, in which the new set of spatial axes has a velocity component relative to the original set, in the X direction alone, will be found to correspond to a rotation of the axes in which only the directions of the X_1 and X_4 axes are changed, the X_2 and X_3 axes remaining unchanged in direction.

Let us consider a one-vector

$$\mathbf{a} = (a_1 \mathbf{k}_1 + a_2 \mathbf{k}_2 + a_3 \mathbf{k}_3 + a_4 \mathbf{k}_4) = (a_1{}' \mathbf{k_1}' + a_2{}' \mathbf{k_2}' + a_3{}' \mathbf{k_3}' + a_4{}' \mathbf{k_4}'),$$

where a_1, a_2, a_3 and a_4 are the component magnitudes, using a set of axes which have $\mathbf{k}_1$, $\mathbf{k}_2$, $\mathbf{k}_3$ and $\mathbf{k}_4$ as unit vectors and a_1', a_2', a_3' and a_4' the corresponding magnitudes using another set of mutually perpendicular axes with the unit vectors $\mathbf{k}_1'$, $\mathbf{k}_2'$, $\mathbf{k}_3'$ and $\mathbf{k}_4'$. Our problem, now, is to find relations between the magnitudes a_1, a_2, a_3 and a_4 and a_1', a_2', a_3' and a_4'.

We have already seen, Sections 179 and 183, that we may obtain any desired component magnitude of a vector by taking its inner product with a unit vector in the desired direction, reversing the sign if the subscript 4 is involved. We may obtain in this way an expression for a_1 in terms of a_1', a_2', a_3' and a_4'. We have

$$a_1 = \mathbf{a} \cdot \mathbf{k}_1 = (a_1'\mathbf{k}_1' + a_2'\mathbf{k}_2' + a_3'\mathbf{k}_3' + a_4'\mathbf{k}_4') \cdot \mathbf{k}_1$$
$$= a_1'\mathbf{k}_1' \cdot \mathbf{k}_1 + a_2'\mathbf{k}_2' \cdot \mathbf{k}_1 + a_3'\mathbf{k}_3' \cdot \mathbf{k}_1 + a_4'\mathbf{k}_4' \cdot \mathbf{k}_1. \quad (295)$$

By similar multiplications with $\mathbf{k}_2$, $\mathbf{k}_3$ and $\mathbf{k}_4$ we may obtain expressions for a_2, a_3 and $-a_4$. The results can be tabulated in the convenient form

	a_1'	a_2'	a_3'	a_4'
a_1	$\mathbf{k}_1' \cdot \mathbf{k}_1$	$\mathbf{k}_2' \cdot \mathbf{k}_1$	$\mathbf{k}_3' \cdot \mathbf{k}_1$	$\mathbf{k}_4' \cdot \mathbf{k}_1$
a_2	$\mathbf{k}_1' \cdot \mathbf{k}_2$	$\mathbf{k}_2' \cdot \mathbf{k}_2$	$\mathbf{k}_3' \cdot \mathbf{k}_2$	$\mathbf{k}_4' \cdot \mathbf{k}_2$
a_3	$\mathbf{k}_1' \cdot \mathbf{k}_3$	$\mathbf{k}_2' \cdot \mathbf{k}_3$	$\mathbf{k}_3' \cdot \mathbf{k}_3$	$\mathbf{k}_4' \cdot \mathbf{k}_3$
a_4	$-\mathbf{k}_1' \cdot \mathbf{k}_4$	$-\mathbf{k}_2' \cdot \mathbf{k}_4$	$-\mathbf{k}_3' \cdot \mathbf{k}_4$	$-\mathbf{k}_4' \cdot \mathbf{k}_4$

$$(296)$$

Since the square of the magnitude of the vector, $(a_1{}^2 + a_2{}^2 + a_3{}^2 - a_4{}^2)$, is a quantity which is to be independent of the choice of axes, we shall have certain relations holding between the quantities $\mathbf{k}_1' \cdot \mathbf{k}_1$, $\mathbf{k}_1' \cdot \mathbf{k}_2$, etc. These relations, which are analogous to the familiar conditions of orthogonality in Euclidean space, can easily be shown to be

$$
\begin{aligned}
(\mathbf{k_1'} \cdot \mathbf{k_1})^2 + (\mathbf{k_1'} \cdot \mathbf{k_2})^2 + (\mathbf{k_1'} \cdot \mathbf{k_3})^2 - (\mathbf{k_1'} \cdot \mathbf{k_4})^2 &= 1, \\
(\mathbf{k_2'} \cdot \mathbf{k_1})^2 + (\mathbf{k_2'} \cdot \mathbf{k_2})^2 + (\mathbf{k_2'} \cdot \mathbf{k_3})^2 - (\mathbf{k_2'} \cdot \mathbf{k_4})^2 &= 1, \\
(\mathbf{k_3'} \cdot \mathbf{k_1})^2 + (\mathbf{k_3'} \cdot \mathbf{k_2})^2 + (\mathbf{k_3'} \cdot \mathbf{k_3})^2 - (\mathbf{k_3'} \cdot \mathbf{k_4})^2 &= 1, \\
(\mathbf{k_4'} \cdot \mathbf{k_1})^2 + (\mathbf{k_4'} \cdot \mathbf{k_2})^2 + (\mathbf{k_4'} \cdot \mathbf{k_3})^2 - (\mathbf{k_4'} \cdot \mathbf{k_4})^2 &= -1,
\end{aligned}
\tag{297}
$$

and

$$
\begin{aligned}
(\mathbf{k_1'} \cdot \mathbf{k_1})(\mathbf{k_2'} \cdot \mathbf{k_1}) &+ (\mathbf{k_1'} \cdot \mathbf{k_2})(\mathbf{k_2'} \cdot \mathbf{k_2}) \\
&+ (\mathbf{k_1'} \cdot \mathbf{k_3})(\mathbf{k_2'} \cdot \mathbf{k_3}) - (\mathbf{k_1'} \cdot \mathbf{k_4})(\mathbf{k_2'} \cdot \mathbf{k_4}) = 0,
\end{aligned}
$$

etc., for each of the six pairs of vertical columns in table (296).

Since we shall often be interested in a simple rotation in which the directions of the X_2 and X_3 axes are not changed, we shall be able to simplify this table for that particular case by writing

$$
\mathbf{k_2'} = \mathbf{k_2}, \qquad \mathbf{k_3'} = \mathbf{k_3},
$$

and noting the simplifications thus introduced in the products of the unit vectors, we shall obtain

	a_1'	a_2'	a_3'	a_4'
a_1	$\mathbf{k_1'} \cdot \mathbf{k_1}$	0	0	$\mathbf{k_4'} \cdot \mathbf{k_1}$
a_2	0	1	0	0
a_3	0	0	1	0
a_4	$-\mathbf{k_1'} \cdot \mathbf{k_4}$	0	0	$-\mathbf{k_4'} \cdot \mathbf{k_4}$

$$\tag{298}$$

If now we call ϕ the angle of rotation between the two time axes OX_4' and OX_4, we may write, in accordance with equation (262),

$$
-\mathbf{k_4'} \cdot \mathbf{k_4} = \cosh \phi.
$$

Since we must preserve the orthogonal relations (297) and may also make use of the well-known expression of hyperbolic trigonometry

$$\cosh^2 \phi - \sinh^2 \phi = 1,$$

we may now rewrite our transformation table in the form

	$a_1{}'$	$a_2{}'$	$a_3{}'$	$a_4{}'$
a_1	$\cosh \phi$	0	0	$\sinh \phi$
a_2	0	1	0	0
a_3	0	0	1	0
a_4	$\sinh \phi$	0	0	$\cosh \phi$

$$(299)$$

By a similar process we may obtain transformation tables for the components of a two-vector $\mathbf{A}$. Expressing $\mathbf{A}$ in terms of the unit vectors $\mathbf{k}_{12}{}'$, $\mathbf{k}_{13}{}'$, $\mathbf{k}_{14}{}'$, etc., and taking successive inner products with the unit vectors $\mathbf{k}_{12}$, $\mathbf{k}_{13}$, $\mathbf{k}_{14}$, etc., we may obtain transformation equations which can be expressed by the tabulation (300) shown on the following page.

For the particular case of a rotation in which the direction of the X_2 and X_3 axes are not changed we shall have

$$\mathbf{k}_2{}' = \mathbf{k}_2, \qquad \mathbf{k}_3{}' = \mathbf{k}_3,$$

and very considerable simplification will be introduced. We shall have, for example,

$$\mathbf{k}_{12}{}' \cdot \mathbf{k}_{12} = (\mathbf{k}_1{}' \times \mathbf{k}_2{}') \cdot (\mathbf{k}_1 \times \mathbf{k}_2) = (\mathbf{k}_1{}' \times \mathbf{k}_2) \cdot (\mathbf{k}_1 \times \mathbf{k}_2) = \mathbf{k}_1{}' \cdot \mathbf{k}_1,$$

$$\mathbf{k}_{13}{}' \cdot \mathbf{k}_{12} = (\mathbf{k}_1{}' \times \mathbf{k}_3{}') \cdot (\mathbf{k}_1 \times \mathbf{k}_2) = (\mathbf{k}_1{}' \times \mathbf{k}_3) \cdot (\mathbf{k}_1 \times \mathbf{k}_2) = 0,$$

etc.

Making these and similar substitutions and introducing, as before, the relation $-\mathbf{k}_4{}' \cdot \mathbf{k}_4 = \cosh \phi$ where ϕ is the non-Euclidean angle between

$$(300)$$

	A_{12}'	A_{13}'	A_{14}'	A_{23}'	A_{24}'	A_{34}'
A_{12}	$\mathbf{k}_{12}' \cdot \mathbf{k}_{12}$	$\mathbf{k}_{13}' \cdot \mathbf{k}_{12}$	$\mathbf{k}_{14}' \cdot \mathbf{k}_{12}$	$\mathbf{k}_{23}' \cdot \mathbf{k}_{12}$	$\mathbf{k}_{24}' \cdot \mathbf{k}_{12}$	$\mathbf{k}_{34}' \cdot \mathbf{k}_{12}$
A_{13}	$\mathbf{k}_{12}' \cdot \mathbf{k}_{13}$	$\mathbf{k}_{13}' \cdot \mathbf{k}_{13}$	$\mathbf{k}_{14}' \cdot \mathbf{k}_{13}$	$\mathbf{k}_{23}' \cdot \mathbf{k}_{13}$	$\mathbf{k}_{24}' \cdot \mathbf{k}_{13}$	$\mathbf{k}_{34}' \cdot \mathbf{k}_{13}$
A_{14}	$-\mathbf{k}_{12}' \cdot \mathbf{k}_{14}$	$-\mathbf{k}_{13}' \cdot \mathbf{k}_{14}$	$-\mathbf{k}_{14}' \cdot \mathbf{k}_{14}$	$-\mathbf{k}_{23}' \cdot \mathbf{k}_{14}$	$-\mathbf{k}_{24}' \cdot \mathbf{k}_{14}$	$-\mathbf{k}_{34}' \cdot \mathbf{k}_{14}$
A_{23}	$\mathbf{k}_{12}' \cdot \mathbf{k}_{23}$	$\mathbf{k}_{13}' \cdot \mathbf{k}_{23}$	$\mathbf{k}_{14}' \cdot \mathbf{k}_{23}$	$\mathbf{k}_{23}' \cdot \mathbf{k}_{23}$	$\mathbf{k}_{24}' \cdot \mathbf{k}_{23}$	$\mathbf{k}_{34}' \cdot \mathbf{k}_{23}$
A_{24}	$-\mathbf{k}_{12}' \cdot \mathbf{k}_{24}$	$-\mathbf{k}_{13}' \cdot \mathbf{k}_{24}$	$-\mathbf{k}_{14}' \cdot \mathbf{k}_{24}$	$-\mathbf{k}_{23}' \cdot \mathbf{k}_{24}$	$-\mathbf{k}_{24}' \cdot \mathbf{k}_{24}$	$-\mathbf{k}_{34}' \cdot \mathbf{k}_{24}$
A_{34}	$-\mathbf{k}_{12}' \cdot \mathbf{k}_{34}$	$-\mathbf{k}_{13}' \cdot \mathbf{k}_{34}$	$-\mathbf{k}_{14}' \cdot \mathbf{k}_{34}$	$-\mathbf{k}_{23}' \cdot \mathbf{k}_{34}$	$-\mathbf{k}_{24}' \cdot \mathbf{k}_{34}$	$-\mathbf{k}_{34}' \cdot \mathbf{k}_{34}$

the two time axes, we may write our transformation table in the form

	A_{12}'	A_{13}'	A_{14}'	A_{23}'	A_{24}'	A_{34}'
A_{12}	$\cosh\phi$	0	0	0	$\sinh\phi$	0
A_{13}	0	$\cosh\phi$	0	0	0	$\sinh\phi$
A_{14}	0	0	1	0	0	0
A_{23}	0	0	0	1	0	0
A_{24}	$-\sinh\phi$	0	0	0	$\cosh\phi$	0
A_{34}	0	$-\sinh\phi$	0	0	0	$\cosh\phi$

$$(301)$$

189. Interpretation of the Lorentz Transformation as a Rotation of Axes. We may now show that the Lorentz transformation may be looked upon as a change from a given set of axes to a rotated set.

Since the angle ϕ which occurs in our transformation tables is that between the $\mathbf{k}_4$ axis and the new $\mathbf{k}_4'$ axis, we may write, in accordance with equations (265) and (266),

$$\cosh\phi = \frac{1}{\sqrt{1 - \dfrac{V^2}{c^2}}}, \qquad \sinh\phi = \frac{\dfrac{V}{c}}{\sqrt{1 - \dfrac{V^2}{c^2}}},$$

where V is the velocity between the two sets of space axes which correspond to the original and the rotated set of four-dimensional axes. This will permit us to rewrite our transformation table for the components of a one-vector in the forms

	a_1'	a_2'	a_3'	a_4'
a_1	$\dfrac{1}{\sqrt{1-\dfrac{V^2}{c^2}}}$	0	0	$\dfrac{V/c}{\sqrt{1-\dfrac{V^2}{c^2}}}$
a_2	0	1	0	0
a_3	0	0	1	0
a_4	$\dfrac{V/c}{\sqrt{1-\dfrac{V^2}{c^2}}}$	0	0	$\dfrac{1}{\sqrt{1-\dfrac{V^2}{c^2}}}$

$$(302)$$

	a_1	a_2	a_3	a_4
a_1'	$\dfrac{1}{\sqrt{1-\dfrac{V^2}{c^2}}}$	0	0	$\dfrac{-V/c}{\sqrt{1-\dfrac{V^2}{c^2}}}$
a_2'	0	1	0	0
a_3'	0	0	1	0
a_4'	$\dfrac{-V/c}{\sqrt{1-\dfrac{V^2}{c^2}}}$	0	0	$\dfrac{1}{\sqrt{1-\dfrac{V^2}{c^2}}}$

Consider now any point $P(x_1, x_2, x_3, x_4)$. The radius vector from the origin to this point will be $\mathbf{r} = (x_1\mathbf{k}_1 + x_2\mathbf{k}_2 + x_3\mathbf{k}_3 + x_4\mathbf{k}_4)$, or, making use of the relations between x_1, x_2, x_3, x_4 and x, y, z, t given by equations (252), we may write

$$\mathbf{r} = (x\mathbf{k}_1 + y\mathbf{k}_2 + z\mathbf{k}_3 + ct\mathbf{k}_4).$$

Applying our transformation table to the components of this one-vector, we obtain the familiar equations for the Lorentz transformation

$$x' = \frac{x - Vt}{\sqrt{1 - \dfrac{V^2}{c^2}}},$$

$$y' = y,$$
$$z' = z,$$

$$t' = \frac{1}{\sqrt{1 - \dfrac{V^2}{c^2}}} \left(t - \frac{V}{c^2}\, x \right).$$

We thus see that the Lorentz transformation is to be interpreted in our four-dimensional analysis as a rotation of axes.

190. Graphical Representation. Although we have purposely restricted ourselves in the foregoing treatment to methods of attack which are almost purely analytical rather than geometrical in nature, the importance of a graphical representation of our four-dimensional manifold should not be neglected. The difficulty of representing all four axes on a single piece of two-dimensional paper is not essentially different from that encountered in the graphical representation of the facts of ordinary three-dimensional solid geometry, and these difficulties can often be solved by considering only one pair of axes at a time, say OX_1 and OX_4, and plotting the occurrences in the X_1OX_4 plane. The fact that the geometry of this plane is a non-Euclidean one presents a more serious complication since the figures that we draw on our sheet of paper will obviously be Euclidean in nature, but this difficulty also can be met if we make certain conventions as to the significance of the lines we draw, conventions which are fundamentally not so very unlike the conventions by which we interpret as solid, a figure drawn in ordinary perspective.

Consider for example the diagram shown in Fig. 18, where we have drawn a pair of perpendicular axes, OX_1, and OX_4 and the two unit hyperbolæ given by the equations

$$x_1{}^2 - x_4{}^2 = 1,$$
$$x_1{}^2 - x_4{}^2 = -1, \tag{303}$$

together with their asymptotes, OA and OB, given by the equation

$$x_1{}^2 - x_4{}^2 = 0. \tag{304}$$

This purely Euclidean figure permits, as a matter of fact, a fairly satisfactory representation of the non-Euclidean properties of the manifold with which we have been dealing.

OX_1 and OX_4 may be considered as perpendicular axes in the non-Euclidean X_1OX_4 plane. Radius vectors lying in the quadrant AOB will have a greater component along the X_4 than along the X_1 axis and hence will be δ-vectors with the magnitude $s = \sqrt{x_4{}^2 - x_1{}^2}$, where x_1 and x_4 are the coördinates of the terminal of the vector. γ-radius-vectors will lie in the quadrant BOC and will have the magnitude $s = \sqrt{x_1{}^2 - x_4{}^2}$. Radius vectors lying along the asymptotes OA and OB will have zero magnitudes $(s = \sqrt{x_1{}^2 - x_4{}^2} = 0)$ and hence will be singular vectors.

Since the two hyperbolæ have the equations $x_1{}^2 - x_4{}^2 = 1$ and $x_1{}^2 - x_4{}^2 = -1$, rays such as Oa, Oa', Ob, etc., starting from the origin and terminating on the hyperbolæ, will all have unit magnitude. Hence we may consider the hyperbolæ as representing unit pseudo-circles in our non-Euclidean plane and consider the rays as representing the radii of these pseudo-circles.

A non-Euclidean rotation of axes will then be represented by changing from the axes OX_1 and OX_4 to $OX_1{}'$ and $OX_4{}'$, and taking Oa' and Ob' as unit distances along the axes instead of Oa and Ob.

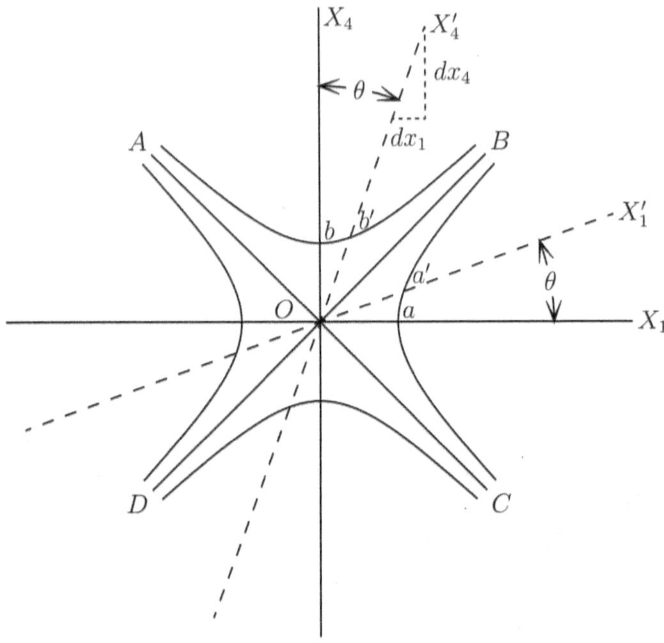

Fig. 18.

It is easy to show, as a matter of fact, that such a change of axes and units does correspond to the Lorentz transformation. Let x_1 and x_4 be the coördinates of any point with respect to the original axes OX_1 and OX_4, and x_1'' and x_4'' the coördinates of the same point referred to the oblique axes OX_1' and OX_4', no change having yet been made in the actual lengths of the units of measurement. Then, by familiar equations of analytical geometry, we shall have

$$x_1 = x_1'' \cos\theta + x_4'' \sin\theta,$$
$$x_4 = x_1'' \sin\theta + x_4'' \cos\theta, \tag{305}$$

where θ is the angle X_1OX_1'.

We have, moreover, from the properties of the hyperbola,

$$\frac{Oa'}{Oa} = \frac{Ob'}{Ob} = \frac{1}{\sqrt{\cos^2\theta - \sin^2\theta}},$$

and hence if we represent by x_1' and x_4' the coördinates of the point with respect to the oblique axes and use Oa' and Ob' as unit distances instead of Oa and Ob, we shall obtain

$$x_1 = x_1'\frac{\cos\theta}{\sqrt{\cos^2\theta - \sin^2\theta}} + x_4'\frac{\sin\theta}{\sqrt{\cos^2\theta - \sin^2\theta}},$$

$$x_4 = x_1'\frac{\sin\theta}{\sqrt{\cos^2\theta - \sin^2\theta}} + x_4'\frac{\cos\theta}{\sqrt{\cos^2\theta - \sin^2\theta}}.$$

It is evident, however, that we may write

$$\frac{\sin\theta}{\cos\theta} = \tan\theta = \frac{dx_1}{dx_4} = \frac{V}{c},$$

where V may be regarded as the relative velocity of our two sets of space axes. Introducing this into the above equations and also writing $x_1 = x$, $x_4 = ct$, $x_1' = x'$, $x_4' = ct'$, we may obtain the familiar equations

$$x = \frac{1}{\sqrt{1 - \dfrac{V^2}{c^2}}}(x' + Vt'),$$

$$t = \frac{1}{\sqrt{1 - \dfrac{V^2}{c^2}}}\left(t' + \frac{V}{c^2}x'\right).$$

We thus see that our diagrammatic representation of non-Euclidean rotation in the X_1OX_4 plane does as a matter of fact correspond to the Lorentz transformation.

Diagrams of this kind can now be used to study various kinematical events. δ-curves can be drawn in the quadrant AOB to represent the space-time trajectories of particles, their form can be investigated using different sets of rotated axes, and the equations for the transformation of velocities and accelerations thus studied. γ-lines perpendicular to the particular time axis used can be drawn to correspond to the instantaneous positions of actual lines in ordinary space and studies made of the Lorentz shortening. Singular vectors along the asymptote OB can be used to represent the trajectory of a ray of light and it can be shown that our rotation of axes is so devised as to leave unaltered, the angle between such singular vectors and the OX_4 axis, corresponding to the fact that the velocity of light must appear the same to all observers. Further development of the possibilities of graphical representation of the properties of our non-Euclidean space may be left to the reader.

PART II. APPLICATIONS OF THE FOUR-DIMENSIONAL ANALYSIS.

191. We may now apply our four-dimensional methods to a number of problems in the fields of kinematics, mechanics and electromagnetics. Our general plan will be to express the laws of the particular field in question in four-dimensional language, making use of four-dimensional vector quantities of a kinematical, mechanical, or electromagnetic nature. Since the components of these vectors along the three spatial axes and the temporal axis will be closely related to the ordinary quantities familiar in kinematical, mechanical, and electrical discussions, there will always be an easy transition from our four-dimensional language to that ordinarily used in such discussions, and necessarily used when actual numerical computations are to be made. We shall find, however, that our four-dimensional language introduces an extraordinary brevity into the statement of a number of important laws of physics.

Kinematics.

192. Extended Position. The position of a particle and the particular instant at which it occupies that position can both be indicated by a point in our four-dimensional space. We can call this the extended position of the particle and determine it by stating the value of a four-dimensional radius vector

$$\mathbf{r} = (x_1\mathbf{k}_1 + x_2\mathbf{k}_2 + x_3\mathbf{k}_3 + x_4\mathbf{k}_4). \tag{306}$$

193. Extended Velocity. Since the velocity of a real particle can never exceed that of light, its changing position in space and time will be represented by a δ-curve.

The equation for a unit vector tangent to this δ-curve will be

$$\mathbf{w} = \frac{d\mathbf{r}}{ds} = \left(\frac{dx_1}{ds}\,\mathbf{k}_1 + \frac{dx_2}{ds}\,\mathbf{k}_2 + \frac{dx_3}{ds}\,\mathbf{k}_3 + \frac{dx_4}{ds}\,\mathbf{k}_4 \right), \tag{307}$$

where ds indicates interval along the δ-curve; and this important vector $\mathbf{w}$ may be called the extended velocity of the particle.

Remembering that for a δ-curve

$$ds = \sqrt{dx_4{}^2 - dx_1{}^2 - dx_2{}^2 - dx_3{}^2} = c\,dt\sqrt{1 - \frac{u^2}{c^2}}, \tag{308}$$

we may rewrite our expression for extended velocity in the form

$$\mathbf{w} = \frac{1}{\sqrt{1 - \dfrac{u^2}{c^2}}} \left\{ \frac{\mathbf{u}}{c} + \mathbf{k}_4 \right\}, \tag{309}$$

where $\mathbf{u}$ is evidently the ordinary three-dimensional velocity of the particle.

Since $\mathbf{w}$ is a four-dimensional vector in our imaginary space, we may use our tables for transforming the components of $\mathbf{w}$ from one set of axes to another. We shall find that we may thus obtain transformation equations for velocity identical with those already familiar in Chapter IV.

The four components of $\mathbf{w}$ are

$$\frac{\dfrac{u_x}{c}}{\sqrt{1 - \dfrac{u^2}{c^2}}}\,\mathbf{k}_1, \qquad \frac{\dfrac{u_y}{c}}{\sqrt{1 - \dfrac{u^2}{c^2}}}\,\mathbf{k}_2, \qquad \frac{\dfrac{u_z}{c}}{\sqrt{1 - \dfrac{u^2}{c^2}}}\,\mathbf{k}_3, \qquad \frac{\mathbf{k}_4}{\sqrt{1 - \dfrac{u^2}{c^2}}},$$

and with the help of table (302) we may easily obtain, by making simple algebraic substitutions, the following familiar transformation equations:

$$u_x' = \frac{u_x - V}{1 - \dfrac{u_x V}{c^2}}, \qquad u_y' = \frac{u_y \sqrt{1 - \dfrac{V^2}{c^2}}}{1 - \dfrac{u_x V}{c^2}}, \qquad u_z' = \frac{u_z \sqrt{1 - \dfrac{V^2}{c^2}}}{1 - \dfrac{u_x V}{c^2}},$$

$$\frac{1}{\sqrt{1 - \dfrac{u'^2}{c^2}}} = \frac{1 - \dfrac{u_x V}{c^2}}{\sqrt{1 - \dfrac{u^2}{c^2}}\,\sqrt{1 - \dfrac{V^2}{c^2}}}.$$

This is a good example of the ease with which we can derive our familiar transformation equations with the help of the four-dimensional method.

194. Extended Acceleration. We may define the extended acceleration of a particle as the rate of curvature of the δ-line which determines its four-dimensional position. We have

$$c = \frac{d^2\mathbf{r}}{ds^2} = \frac{d\mathbf{w}}{ds} = \frac{d}{ds}\left[\frac{\dfrac{\mathbf{u}}{c} + \mathbf{k}_4}{\sqrt{1 - \dfrac{u^2}{c^2}}}\right]. \tag{310}$$

Or, introducing as before the relation $ds = c\,dt\sqrt{1 - \dfrac{u^2}{c^2}}$, we may write

$$c = \frac{1}{c^2}\left\{ \frac{1}{\left(1 - \frac{u^2}{c^2}\right)}\frac{d\mathbf{u}}{dt} + \frac{1}{\left(1 - \frac{u^2}{c^2}\right)^2}\frac{u}{c^2}\frac{du}{dt}\mathbf{u} \right.$$

$$\left. + \frac{1}{\left(1 - \frac{u^2}{c^2}\right)^2}\frac{u}{c}\frac{du}{dt}\mathbf{k}_4 \right\}, \quad (311)$$

where $\mathbf{u}$ is evidently the ordinary three-dimensional velocity, and $\dfrac{d\mathbf{u}}{dt}$ the three-dimensional acceleration; and we might now use our transformation table to determine the transformation equations for acceleration which we originally obtained in Chapter IV.

195. The Velocity of Light. As an interesting illustration of the application to kinematics of our four-dimensional methods, we may point out that the trajectory of a ray of light will be represented by a singular line. Since the magnitude of all singular vectors is zero by definition, we have for any singular line

$$dx_1^2 + dx_2^2 + dx_3^2 = dx_4^2,$$

or, since the magnitude will be independent of any particular choice of axes, we may also write

$$dx_1'^2 + dx_2'^2 + dx_3'^2 = dx_4'^2.$$

Transforming the first of these equations we may write

$$\frac{dx_1^2 + dx_2^2 + dx_3^2}{dx_4^2} = \frac{dx^2 + dy^2 + dz^2}{c^2\,dt^2} = 1$$

or

$$\frac{dl}{dt} = c.$$

Similarly we could obtain from the second equation

$$\frac{dl'}{dt'} = c.$$

We thus see that a singular line does as a matter of fact correspond to the four-dimensional trajectory of a ray of light having the velocity c, and that our four-dimensional analysis corresponds to the requirements of the second postulate of relativity that a ray of light shall have the same velocity for all reference systems.

The Dynamics of a Particle.

196. Extended Momentum. We may define the extended momentum of a material particle as equal to the product $m_0\mathbf{w}$ of its mass m_0, measured when at rest, and its extended velocity $\mathbf{w}$. In accordance with equation (309) for extended velocity, we may write then, for the extended momentum,

$$m_0\mathbf{w} = \frac{m_0}{\sqrt{1 - \dfrac{u^2}{c^2}}}\left(\frac{\mathbf{u}}{c} + \mathbf{k}_4\right). \tag{312}$$

Or, if in accordance with our considerations of Chapter VI we put for the mass of the particle at the velocity u

$$m = \frac{m_0}{\sqrt{1 - \dfrac{u^2}{c^2}}},$$

we may write

$$m_0\mathbf{w} = m\frac{\mathbf{u}}{c} + m\mathbf{k}_4. \tag{313}$$

We note that the space component of this vector is ordinary momentum and the time component has the magnitude of mass, and by applying our transformation table (302) we can derive very simply the transformation equations for mass and momentum already obtained in Chapter VI.

197. The Conservation Laws. We may now express the laws for the dynamics of a system of particles in a very simple form by stating the principle that the extended momentum of a system of particles is a quantity which remains constant in all interactions of the particles, we have then

$$\sum m_0\mathbf{w} = \sum \left(\frac{m\mathbf{u}}{c} + m\mathbf{k}_4\right) = \text{ a constant,} \tag{314}$$

where the summation $\sum$ extends over all the particles of the system.

It is evident that this one principle really includes the three principles of the conservation of momentum, mass, and energy. This is true because in order for the vector $\sum m_0\mathbf{w}$ to be a constant quantity, its components along each of the four axes must be constant, and as will be seen from the above equation this necessitates the constancy of the momentum $\sum m\mathbf{u}$, of the total mass $\sum m$, and of the total energy $\sum \dfrac{m}{c^2}$.

The Dynamics of an Elastic Body.

Our four-dimensional methods may also be used to present the results of our theory of elasticity in a very compact form.

198. The Tensor of Extended Stress. In order to do this we shall first need to define an expression which may be called the four-dimensional stress in the elastic medium. For this purpose we may take the symmetrical tensor T_m defined by the following table:

$$T_m = \begin{cases} p_{xx} & p_{xy} & p_{xz} & cg_x, \\[2mm] p_{yx} & p_{yy} & p_{yz} & cg_y, \\[2mm] p_{zx} & p_{zy} & p_{zz} & cg_z, \\[2mm] \dfrac{s_x}{c} & \dfrac{s_y}{c} & \dfrac{s_z}{c} & w, \end{cases} \tag{315}$$

where the spatial components of T_m are equal to the components of the symmetrical tensor $\mathbf{p}$ which we have already defined in Chapter X and the time components are related to the density of momentum $\mathbf{g}$, density of energy flow $\mathbf{s}$ and energy density w, as shown in the tabulation.

From the symmetry of this tensor we may infer at once the simple relation between density of momentum and density of energy flow:

$$\mathbf{g} = \frac{\mathbf{s}}{c^2}, \tag{316}$$

with which we have already become familiar in Section 132.

199. The Equation of Motion. We may, moreover, express the equation of motion for an elastic medium unacted on by external forces in the very simple form

$$\operatorname{div} T_m = 0. \tag{317}$$

It will be seen from our definition of the divergence of a four-dimensional tensor, Section 187, that this one equation is in reality equivalent to the two equations

$$\operatorname{div} \mathbf{p} + \frac{\partial \mathbf{g}}{\partial t} = 0 \tag{318}$$

and

$$\operatorname{div} \mathbf{s} + \frac{\partial w}{\partial t} = 0.$$

The first of these equations is identical with (184) of Chapter X, which we found to be the equation for the motion of an elastic medium in the absence of external forces, and the second of these equations expresses the principle of the conservation of energy.

The elegance and simplicity of this four-dimensional method of expressing the results of our laborious calculations in Chapter X cannot fail to be appreciated.

Electromagnetics.

We also find it possible to express the laws of the electromagnetic field very simply in our four-dimensional language.

200. Extended Current. We may first define the extended current, a simple but important one-vector, whose value at any point will depend on the density and velocity of charge at that point. We shall take as the equation of definition

$$\mathbf{q} = \rho_0 \mathbf{w} = \rho \left\{ \frac{\mathbf{u}}{c} + \mathbf{k}_4 \right\}, \tag{319}$$

where

$$\rho = \frac{\rho_0}{\sqrt{1 - \dfrac{u^2}{c^2}}}$$

is the density of charge at the point in question.

201. The Electromagnetic Vector M. We may further define a two-vector $\mathbf{M}$ which will be directly related to the familiar vectors strength of electric field $\mathbf{e}$ and strength of magnetic field $\mathbf{h}$ by the equation of definition

$$\mathbf{M} = (h_1 \mathbf{k}_{23} + h_2 \mathbf{k}_{31} + h_3 \mathbf{k}_{12} - e_1 \mathbf{k}_{14} - e_2 \mathbf{k}_{24} - e_3 \mathbf{k}_{34})$$

or $\tag{320}$

$$\mathbf{M}^* = (e_1 \mathbf{k}_{23} + e_2 \mathbf{k}_{31} + e_3 \mathbf{k}_{12} + h_1 \mathbf{k}_{14} + h_2 \mathbf{k}_{24} + h_3 \mathbf{k}_{34}),$$

where e_1, e_2, e_3, and h_1, h_2, h_3 are the components of $\mathbf{e}$ and $\mathbf{h}$.

202. The Field Equations. We may now state the laws of the electromagnetic field in the extremely simple form

$$\Diamond \cdot \mathbf{M} = \mathbf{q}, \tag{321}$$

$$\Diamond \times \mathbf{M} = 0. \tag{322}$$

These two simple equations are, as a matter of fact, completely equivalent to the four field equations which we made fundamental for our treatment of electromagnetic theory in Chapter XII. Indeed if we treat $\lozenge$ formally as a one-vector

$$\left(\mathbf{k}_1 \frac{\partial}{\partial x_1} + \mathbf{k}_2 \frac{\partial}{\partial x_2} + \mathbf{k}_3 \frac{\partial}{\partial x_3} - \mathbf{k}_4 \frac{\partial}{\partial x_4} \right)$$

and apply it to the electromagnetic vector $\mathbf{M}$ expressed in the extended form given in the equation of definition (320) we shall obtain from (321) the two equations

$$\operatorname{curl} \mathbf{h} - \frac{1}{c} \frac{\partial \mathbf{e}}{\partial t} = \rho \frac{\mathbf{u}}{c},$$
$$\operatorname{div} \mathbf{e} = \rho,$$

and from (322)

$$\operatorname{div} \mathbf{h} = 0,$$
$$\operatorname{curl} \mathbf{e} + \frac{1}{c} \frac{\partial \mathbf{h}}{\partial t} = 0,$$

where we have made the substitution $x_4 = ct$. These are of course the familiar field equations for the Maxwell-Lorentz theory of electromagnetism.

203. The Conservation of Electricity. We may also obtain very easily an equation for the conservation of electric charge. In accordance with equation (284) we may write as a necessary mathematical identity

$$\lozenge \cdot (\lozenge \cdot \mathbf{M}) = 0. \tag{323}$$

Noting that $\lozenge \cdot \mathbf{M} = \mathbf{q}$, this may be expanded to give us the equation of continuity.

$$\operatorname{div} \rho \mathbf{u} + \frac{\partial \rho}{\partial t} = 0. \tag{324}$$

204. The Product $\mathbf{M} \cdot \mathbf{q}$. We have thus shown the form taken by the four field equations when they are expressed in four dimensional language. Let us now consider with the help of our four-dimensional methods what can be said about the forces which determine the motion of electricity under the action of the electromagnetic field.

Consider the inner product of the electromagnetic vector and the extended current:

$$\mathbf{M} \cdot \mathbf{q} = (h_1 \mathbf{k}_{23} + h_2 \mathbf{k}_{31} + h_3 \mathbf{k}_{12} - e_1 \mathbf{k}_{14} - e_2 \mathbf{k}_{24} - e_3 \mathbf{k}_{34}) \cdot \rho \left\{ \frac{\mathbf{u}}{c} + \mathbf{k}_4 \right\}$$

$$= \rho \left\{ \mathbf{e} + \frac{[\mathbf{u} \times \mathbf{h}]^*}{c} \right\} + \rho \frac{\mathbf{e} \cdot \mathbf{h}}{c} \mathbf{k}_4. \quad (325)$$

We see that the space component of this vector is equal to the expression which we have already found in Chapter XII as the force acting on the charge contained in unit volume, and the time component is proportional to the work done by this force on the moving charge; hence we may write the equation

$$\mathbf{M} \cdot \mathbf{q} = \left\{ \mathbf{f} + \frac{\mathbf{f} \cdot \mathbf{u}}{c} \mathbf{k}_4 \right\}, \quad (326)$$

an expression which contains the same information as that given by the so-called fifth fundamental equation of electromagnetic theory, $\mathbf{f}$ being the force exerted by the electromagnetic field per unit volume of charged material.

205. The Extended Tensor of Electromagnetic Stress. We may now show the possibility of defining a four-dimensional tensor T_e, such that the important quantity $\mathbf{M} \cdot \mathbf{q}$ shall be equal to $-\operatorname{div} T_e$. This will be valuable since we shall then be able to express the equation of motion for a combined mechanical and electrical system in a very simple and beautiful form.

Consider the symmetrical tensor

$$T_e = \begin{cases} T_{11} & T_{12} & T_{13} & T_{14}, \\ T_{21} & T_{22} & T_{23} & T_{24}, \\ T_{31} & T_{32} & T_{33} & T_{34}, \\ T_{41} & T_{42} & T_{43} & T_{44}, \end{cases} \tag{327}$$

defined by the expression

$$\begin{aligned} T_{jk} = \tfrac{1}{2}\{ & M_{j1}M_{k1} + M_{j2}M_{k2} + M_{j3}M_{k3} - M_{j4}M_{k4} \\ & + M_{j1}{}^{*}M_{k1}{}^{*} + M_{j2}{}^{*}M_{k2}{}^{*} + M_{j3}{}^{*}M_{k3}{}^{*} - M_{j4}{}^{*}M_{k4}{}^{*}\}, \end{aligned} \tag{328}$$

where $j,\ k = 1,\ 2,\ 3,\ 4$.

It can then readily be shown by expansion that

$$- \operatorname{div} T_e = \mathbf{M} \cdot (\Diamond \cdot \mathbf{M}) + \mathbf{M}^{*} \cdot (\Diamond \cdot \mathbf{M}^{*}).$$

But, in accordance with equations (321), (326), (292) and (322), this is equivalent to

$$- \operatorname{div} T_e = \mathbf{M} \cdot \mathbf{q} = \left\{ \mathbf{f} + \frac{(\mathbf{f} \cdot \mathbf{u})}{c}\, \mathbf{k}_4 \right\}. \tag{329}$$

Since in free space the value of the force $\mathbf{f}$ is zero, we may write for free space the equation

$$\operatorname{div} T_e = 0. \tag{330}$$

This one equation is equivalent, as a matter of fact, to two important and well-known equations of electromagnetic theory. If we develop the components T_{11}, T_{12}, etc., of our tensor in accordance with equations

(328) and (320) we find that we can write

$$T_e = \begin{cases} \psi_{xx} & \psi_{xy} & \psi_{xz} & \dfrac{S_x}{c}, \\[2mm] \psi_{yx} & \psi_{yy} & \psi_{yz} & \dfrac{S_y}{c}, \\[2mm] \psi_{zx} & \psi_{zxy} & \psi_{zz} & \dfrac{S_z}{c}, \\[2mm] \dfrac{s_x}{c} & \dfrac{s_x}{c} & \dfrac{s_x}{c} & w, \end{cases} \tag{331}$$

where we shall have

$$\psi_{xx} = -\tfrac{1}{2}(e_x{}^2 - e_y{}^2 - e_z{}^2 + h_x{}^2 - h_y{}^2 - h_z{}^2),$$
$$\psi_{xy} = -(e_x h_y + h_x h_y),$$

etc.

$$s_x = c(e_y h_z - e_z h_y),$$

etc.

$$w = \tfrac{1}{2}(e^2 + h^2),$$

$$\tag{332}$$

ψ thus being equivalent to the well-known Maxwell three-dimensional stress tensor, s_x, s_y, etc., being the components of the Poynting vector $c\,[\mathbf{e} \times \mathbf{h}]^*$, and w being the familiar expression for density of electro-magnetic energy $\dfrac{e^2 + h^2}{s}$. We thus see that equation (330) is equivalent to the two equations

$$\operatorname{div} \psi + \frac{1}{c^2}\frac{\partial s}{\partial t} = 0,$$
$$\operatorname{div} \mathbf{s} + \frac{\partial w}{\partial t} = 0.$$

The first of these is the so-called equation of electromagnetic momentum, and the second, Poynting's equation for the flow of electromagnetic energy.

206. Combined Electrical and Mechanical Systems. For a point not in free space where mechanical and electrical systems are both involved, taking into account our previous considerations, we may now write the equation of motion for a combined electrical and mechanical system in the very simple form

$$\operatorname{div} T_m + \operatorname{div} T_e = 0.$$

And we may point out in closing that we may reasonably expect all forces to be of such a nature that our most general equation of motion for any continuous system can be written in the form

$$\operatorname{div} T_1 + \operatorname{div} T_2 + \cdots = 0.$$

APPENDIX I.—Symbols for Quantities.

Scalar Quantities. (Indicated by Italic type.)

c speed of light.

e electric charge.

E energy.

H kinetic potential.

K kinetic energy.

l, m, n direction cosines.

L Lagrangian function.

p pressure.

Q quantity of electricity.

S entropy.

t time.

T temperature, function $\sum m_0 c^2 \left(1 - \sqrt{1 - \dfrac{u^2}{c^2}} \right)$.

U potential energy.

v volume.

V relative speed of coördinate systems, volume.

w energy density.

W work.

ϵ dielectric constant.

$$\kappa \quad \frac{1}{\sqrt{1 - \dfrac{V^2}{c^2}}}.$$

μ index of refraction, magnetic permeability.

ν frequency.

ρ density of charge.

σ electrical conductivity.

ϕ non-Euclidean angle between time axes.

$\phi_1\phi_2\phi_3\cdots$ generalized coördinates.

ψ scalar potential.

$\psi_1\psi_2\psi_3\cdots$ generalized momenta.

Vector Quantities. (Indicated by Clarendon type.)

B   magnetic induction.

c   extended acceleration.

D   dielectric displacement.

e   electric field strength in free space.

E   electric field strength in a medium.

f   force per unit volume.

F   force acting on a particle.

g   density of momentum.

h   magnetic field strength in free space.

H   magnetic field strength in a medium.

i   density of electric current.

M   angular momentum, electromagnetic vector.

p   symmetrical elastic stress tensor.

q   extended current.

r   radius vector.

s   density of energy flow.

t   unsymmetrical elastic stress tensor.

u   velocity.

w   extended velocity.

ϕ vector potential.

APPENDIX II.—Vector Notation.

Three Dimensional Space.

Unit Vectors, $\mathbf{i}\,\mathbf{j}\,\mathbf{k}$

Radius Vector, $\mathbf{r} = x\mathbf{i} + y\mathbf{j} + z\mathbf{k}$

Velocity,

$$\mathbf{u} = \frac{d\mathbf{r}}{dt} = \dot{x}\mathbf{i} + \dot{y}\mathbf{j} + \dot{z}\mathbf{k}$$
$$= u_x\mathbf{i} + u_y\mathbf{j} + u_z\mathbf{k}$$

Acceleration,

$$\dot{\mathbf{u}} = \frac{d^2\mathbf{r}}{dt^2} = \ddot{x}\mathbf{i} + \ddot{y}\mathbf{j} + \ddot{z}\mathbf{k}$$
$$= \dot{u}_x\mathbf{i} + \dot{u}_y\mathbf{j} + \dot{u}_z\mathbf{k}$$

Inner Product,

$$\mathbf{a} \cdot \mathbf{b} = a_x b_x + a_y b_y + a_z b_z$$

Outer Product,

$$\mathbf{a} \times \mathbf{b} = (a_x b_y - a_y b_x)\mathbf{ij} + (a_y b_z - a_z b_y)\mathbf{jk} + (a_z b_x - a_x b_z)\mathbf{ki}$$

Complement of Outer Product,

$$[\mathbf{a} \times \mathbf{b}]^* = (a_y b_z - a_z b_y)\mathbf{i} + (a_z b_x - a_x b_z)\mathbf{j} + (a_x b_y - a_y b_x)\mathbf{k}$$

The Vector Operator Del or ∇,

$$\nabla = \mathbf{i}\,\frac{\partial}{\partial x} + \mathbf{j}\,\frac{\partial}{\partial y} + \mathbf{k}\,\frac{\partial}{\partial z}$$

$$\operatorname{grad} A = \nabla A = \mathbf{i}\,\frac{\partial A}{\partial x} + \mathbf{j}\,\frac{\partial A}{\partial y} + \mathbf{k}\,\frac{\partial A}{\partial z}$$

$$\operatorname{div} \mathbf{a} = \nabla \cdot \mathbf{a} = \frac{\partial a_x}{\partial x} + \frac{\partial a_y}{\partial y} + \frac{\partial a_z}{\partial z}$$

$$\operatorname{curl} \mathbf{a} = [\nabla \times \mathbf{a}]^*$$

$$= \left(\frac{\partial a_z}{\partial y} - \frac{\partial a_y}{\partial z}\right)\mathbf{i} + \left(\frac{\partial a_x}{\partial z} - \frac{\partial a_z}{\partial x}\right)\mathbf{j} + \left(\frac{\partial a_y}{\partial x} - \frac{\partial a_x}{\partial y}\right)\mathbf{k}$$

Non-Euclidean Four Dimensional Space.

Unit Vectors, $\mathbf{k}_1\ \mathbf{k}_2\ \mathbf{k}_3\ \mathbf{k}_4$
Radius Vector,

$$\mathbf{r} = x_1\mathbf{k}_1 + x_2\mathbf{k}_2 + x_3\mathbf{k}_3 + x_4\mathbf{k}_4$$
$$= x\mathbf{i} + y\mathbf{j} + z\mathbf{k} + ct\mathbf{k}_4$$

One Vector,

$$\mathbf{a} = a_1\mathbf{k}_1 + a_2\mathbf{k}_2 + a_3\mathbf{k}_3 + a_4\mathbf{k}_4$$

Two Vector,

$$\mathbf{A} = A_{12}\mathbf{k}_{12} + A_{13}\mathbf{k}_{13} + A_{14}\mathbf{k}_{14} + A_{23}\mathbf{k}_{23} + A_{24}\mathbf{k}_{24} + A_{34}\mathbf{k}_{34}$$

Three Vector,

$$\mathcal{A} = \mathfrak{A}_{123}\mathbf{k}_{123} + \mathfrak{A}_{124}\mathbf{k}_{124} + \mathfrak{A}_{134}\mathbf{k}_{134} + \mathfrak{A}_{234}\mathbf{k}_{234}$$

Pseudo Scalar,

$$\boldsymbol{\alpha} = \alpha\mathbf{k}_{1234}$$

Transposition of Subscripts,

$$\mathbf{k}_{abc\cdots} = -\mathbf{k}_{bac\cdots} = \mathbf{k}_{bca\cdots}$$

Inner Product of One Vectors,
(*See Section* 183).
Outer Product of One Vectors,

$$\mathbf{k}_{ab\cdots} \times \mathbf{k}_{nm\cdots} = \mathbf{k}_{ab\cdots nm\cdots}$$

Complement of a Vector,

$$\boldsymbol{\phi}^* = \phi \cdot \mathbf{k}_{1234}$$

The Vector Operator Quad or $\lozenge$,

$$\lozenge = \mathbf{k}_1 \frac{\partial}{\partial x_1} + \mathbf{k}_2 \frac{\partial}{\partial x_2} + \mathbf{k}_3 \frac{\partial}{\partial x_3} + \mathbf{k}_4 \frac{\partial}{\partial x_4}$$